# Interactive Media

Shaleph O'Neill

# Interactive Media

## The Semiotics of Embodied Interaction

 Springer

Shaleph O'Neill, PhD, BA
University of Dundee
Scotland

ISBN 978-1-84800-035-3          e-ISBN 978-1-84800-036-0
DOI: 10.1007/978-1-84800-036-0

British Library Cataloguing in Publication Data

Library of Congress Control Number: 2008928135

Printed on acid-free paper

9 8 7 6 5 4 3 2 1

Springer Science + Business Media
springer.com

# Acknowledgements

I sincerely thank Professor David Benyon for his continued support of this project and for his crucial feedback in the early stages of writing this book. I also thank my brother Dr. Nathan O'Neill for his penetrating critique of early drafts of some chapters and his keen editorial eye. Thanks also to the staff at Springer who have supported this project and helped make it happen. A further thanks extends to all my colleagues at the University of Dundee who are involved in running the Interactive Media Design program. Last but not least, a special thanks to my wife Linda for her continued support over the long months it has taken to see this project come to fruition.

# Contents

# Chapter 1
# Introduction

## 1.1 Brave New Media World

Everywhere you look, numerous manifestations of new interactive mediating technologies surround us. We pay our bills automatically; we purchase fuel and food without having to engage with sales people, we pass barriers and open doors with electronic identity keys. We are never lost thanks to our GPS systems that keep track of our whereabouts and help us navigate; we are constantly tracked via hour upon hour of digital CCTV footage and electronically recorded transactions. Our pockets are filled with data, and our cameras, phones and other appliances are merging into one multipurpose device. We have a vast array of information at our fingertips as we search the Internet; communicate through electronic mail or on the move with mobile telecommunications devices.

Everyday we are bombarded by hundreds of digitized images transmitted through computer display screens and television sets. We are kept up to date with constant news bulletins from mainstream broadcasts, digital radio and downloadable podcasts.

We are plugged into our music collections in cars, on trains or on foot. We are invited to take our place in online communities and share files and photographs with friends and strangers alike. We are even able to inhabit purely digital worlds, acting out roles and fantasies from the comfort of our living rooms. We are always on, anytime, anywhere, anyplace. We are the technological 'Martini' generation, intoxicated by a technological cocktail of various media devices.

Our lives from labor to leisure are deeply entwined with these new interactive technologies and as time passes the number of devices we own only seems to increase. As these technologies become increasingly more sophisticated and embedded in our surroundings, we come to rely on them more and more. As this process continues, we gradually become inured to the way in which our surroundings are being re-structured and we take this technologically enhanced environment for granted.

S.O'Neill, *Interactive Media: The Semiotics of Embodied Interaction*, doi: 10.1007/978-1-84800-036-0, © Springer Science + Business Media, LLC 2008

## 1.2   McLuhan and the Environmental Thesis

Forty years ago, Marshall McLuhan theorized at great length about the impact of electronic media, such as television and radio, on our immediate environment and our culture. Back then, he described us metaphorically as 'fish' that are unaware of the mediating water that surrounds us (McLuhan 1994). Fish of course, having evolved to be perfectly adapted to life in the medium of water, are not aware of its existence; water is the ecological niche into which they are born. In the same way, so McLuhan argues, we are born into our own ecological niche. But rather than being surrounded by water, we are immersed in the medium, or media (plural), of our technologically enhanced society. For instance, the everyday world of streets and houses, cars and trucks, computers and telecommunications that we encounter is as much our 'natural habitat' as are the trees and shrubs that seem to fill in the gaps. Like the fish in the water we are rarely aware of how much we rely on it.

This is McLuhan's 'environmental thesis' (Lister et al 2003), whereby he proposes a largely deterministic outlook on the way in which the technologies that surround us have a direct yet almost imperceptible effect on our culture. McLuhan argues that if we really want to understand what is going on in our technologically enhanced society, we have to look beyond the content of the media that we consume to the imperceptible effects that environmentally embedded media have on our actions, interactions and perceptions.

McLuhan's two famous edicts "The medium is the message" and "the medium is the massage" (McLuhan and Fiore, 1967) are attempts to make us aware of the effects of media on our perceptions and interactions with the world around us. The word "massage" (originally a printing error on the cover of the book), in particular denotes the way in which the sensory organs of our bodies are subliminally affected by the media that surround us.

At the core of McLuhan's ideas is the central theme of media as extensions of the human body. Much as a tool, such as a hammer, can be seen as an extension of the arm, McLuhan sees electricity as an extension outwards of the central nervous system into the environment. For example, the ability of television and radio to bring us images and sounds from far off lands are extensions of the eye and of the ear.

Making no distinction between the idea of tool and medium, McLuhan argues that it is this extension of the human body into the world, through media, that affects the way in which we sense the world around us. When we become adapted to using media in such a way, they become natural to us. We only see what they allow us to see, or touch what they allow us to touch. The mediating technologies themselves seem to disappear as the content is delivered and yet continually affect our perceptual capacities, shaping the way in which we relate to the world, without us being aware of it. Bandwidth and digitization, for instance, restrict the quality of images delivered through media as compared to seeing with the naked eye.

## 1.3   The Anti-Determinist View

McLuhan's deterministic view of the technological effect on culture and society has long been disputed. Indeed, Raymond Williams' counter-thesis has been so successful in mainstream media studies that McLuhan's view has been largely abandoned as seemingly absurd (Lister et al. 2003; Williams 1974).

Where McLuhan proposes that technology has a determining effect on our culture, Williams argues the exact opposite. For Williams it is human agency and the activities of societies and cultures that affect the nature of technology, not the other way around. Importantly for Williams, technology is always developed with some human need or intention in mind. It is always aimed at solving some problem or improving some pre-existing social situation. People are always in control of its development.

Williams promotes an extension of this idea of intentionality whereby, due to the nature of social dynamics and cultural diversity, not all the outcomes of some technological development project can be foreseen. Indeed different groups of people use different technologies for different ends. People can appropriate, adapt and subvert technologies beyond their initial purposes.

In this sense, technology comes hand in hand with the knowledge that is necessary to use it. Any theory of technology or indeed mediation must include the knowledge of skillful practices as an integral part of its make up. Williams holds that McLuhan ignores this aspect of mediation, wrongly giving a medium the status of an autonomous object that stands between two or more other entities. That is, McLuhan would view the medium of the photograph as something separate from the photographer who took it and the viewer looking at it. This excludes the skill of the photographer, his intentions to make a picture and the social situations in which a viewer might see the image such as a gallery or a newspaper article.

Thus, our environment and behavior, according to Williams, is determined not by technology itself but by the intentions of those with the power and money to develop such technology. This moves the site of determinism back to people and the power struggles within society, where technology is simply a tool to be used by those with access to it. These notions expressly reject McLuhan's thesis and return control to human agency over technology.

These two contrasting views of media remain interesting today because it is not clear that the argument was ever settled. Furthermore, as mediating technologies continue to advance into every facet of our lives, the issues of who controls the media and whether or not the media itself has an effect on us, remain important. As technologies are developed that track our every move, physically, financially and personally (in terms of identity), it remains difficult to establish whether these technologies themselves contribute to the Orwellian sense of control or if they are just the tools of an increasingly 'nanny' state. Arguably, it is not even clear if the state is in control of these technologies either. Increasingly, large global corporations seem to be holding the reins of the media, where big business is the driver of technological development rather than ideological intention. Furthermore, it is also possible that this new media technology is in fact having a democratizing effect, by putting the people themselves in control of how they establish their identities and represent themselves.

## 1.4   On-line Social Networks

Thanks to Williams, it is now a widely held belief, in the domain of cultural and media studies, that communities, societies and culture as a whole are fashioned by the variety of individuals who contribute to the intellectual climate and technological infrastructure of society, rather than the effects of media itself.

For example, virtual communities and on-line social networks are predominantly collections of people, who use the communicative infrastructure (media environment) of the Internet to communicate or interact with each other around shared interests. More recently, websites that offer online media tools, which make it simpler to post text, photos, music and homemade videos, have turned social networking into a rapidly developing phenomenon (numerous online communities now have between hundreds and millions of members). Amateur authors, musicians and film-makers are now using such sites to publish their material, which give them the opportunity to gain an instant response from their burgeoning audiences. Coupled with low cost media production software (in the case of open-source communities, sometimes free software), we are arguably witnessing a further revolution in the way in which people are producing and consuming digital media. Sites such as MySpace, Bebo and YouTube have fuelled this social networking trend.

However, given both Williams' and McLuhan's theories on media, it is not entirely clear how to explain these phenomena. For instance, Williams's views certainly explain the social aspects of these communities and squarely place human agency as the source of control over these media. For example, initially started by small groups of people, these sites are now attracting the money of big business with media corporations starting to buy them up and changing the way they operate. But this is only one part of the picture.

From a McLuhanite perspective, we can see something interesting about the kinds of media that are being produced. Cheap production facilities are limited in functionality; only certain features are enabled and only certain tasks can be performed. Amateurs, having little skill, and perhaps only coming to the technology for the first time without any training, use only what features are available. As Bardzell point out, these limited features result in a kind of homogeneous look and structure to the media that is produced by these amateur artists (Bardzell 2006). The restrictive features of the media are affecting the output on two levels. Firstly, the simplicity is offering a greater number of users the potential to exercise their creativity and secondly, the same simplicity is restricting what can be produced in the media format. And yet this limited format is proving to be a phenomenal success for millions of users who accept it as the nature of the medium.

For example, MySpace is a social networking service that allows its members to create unique personal profiles online in order to find and communicate with old and new friends. The current network involves over 94 million members (and counting) across the globe. Through various mediating and communication facilities, members are able to form bonds with each other. Thus, they develop individual and group identities through associations that unite them within real world communities. However, the identity formed in MySpace is only really a place-holder that signifies an existence within the digital realm. In McLuhan's terms, it is only an extension of a personality, not the whole personality. It is an identity projected into a digital community that is shaped and facilitated by digital mediating technology.

Similarly, the virtual world of Second Life is a highly sophisticated online social network where around 400,000 users play out their virtual lives in thousands of acres of digital space. Just like real life, Second Life offers rich and engaging interactions between its users. For example, it offers musicians features to play live concerts on virtual stages, as well as offering entrepreneurs the opportunity to make real world money through virtual businesses, which may include designing virtual clothes or owning a casino. Even newspapers and big commercial enterprises are interested in capitalizing on Second Life, as if one wasn't enough.

But what are we to make of this second life? Are we really having a rich and engaging authentic experience within this digital communal space? Or are we forgetting that our bodies are in fact physically excluded from this world as we are stripped, extruded, reinvented and projected into this world via the code and graphics of the media conduit?

## 1.5  The Need for New Theory

What we are seeing now is that changes in the availability, usability and distribution of technology is vastly altering the way in which we interact with the world around us and with each other. The whole of our cultural life and environment is now entwined with mediating computerized technologies. Culture is being transformed by technology and technology is being transformed by culture. But how can we theorize about what is really going on?

A look at on-line social networks and amateur media use raises some fascinating questions about how our theories need to evolve in order to keep up with these changes. Both McLuhan and Williams were writing over thirty-to-forty years ago. The changing landscape of new media, described at the start of this chapter, may yet show Williams' rebuttal of McLuhan's ideas to have been too hasty a dismissal. Neither author could have foreseen the extent to which computerized technologies have colonized our environment. Nor could they have seen the ways in which we have adapted them for our own purposes. It would appear that the determinist/anti-determinist debate about technology has not yet been fully resolved. In order to understand new media, this is something that we should bear in mind as we get to grips with the different approaches that attempt to theorize how we interact with it. While McLuhan and Williams provide an excellent starting point for theories of new media, we need to explore other existing theories and find new ways in which to understand what is going on around us as these new interactive media evolve.

Arguably, the central problem in understanding the effects of these new mediating technologies relates to how our notions of media in general have been altered. For instance, what do we mean when we use the term 'media' these days? Are we talking about mass media, media news, artistic and creative media or communications media? What are the distinctions, if there are any, and how might we be able to use them to theorize more clearly about how we interact with them?

## 1.6   The Aim of this Book

In this book I will attempt to address as many of these questions as I can, by looking first at what the term 'media', as used today, really means to us. I will explore this issue from the point of view of what it means to exist physically within the mediating world that surrounds us and I will develop a picture of interacting with that world, and the technology embedded in it that foregrounds the role of the body as the root of all our mediating activities.

In chapter two, I will look more closely at the existing theories that attempt to explain how we interact with interactive media. In particular, I will explore several strands of Human Computer Interaction (HCI) theory as a way of getting to grips with how we understand what it means to interact with new types of technology. These include the traditional cognitive approach to HCI as well as the phenomenological and the semiotic approaches. I will also consider how these different strands of thought affect our understanding of our relationship with interactive media and I will uncover how each one only gives us a particular perspective on the issue rather than the complete picture.

In chapter three, I will explore how these particular theories can become entangled and confused if care is not taken in how I develop our description of our relationship with our media-rich environment. In particular, I will focus on the issue of affordance in HCI theory, and I will attempt to clarify how this term should be used in relation to interactive media from an embodied perspective rather than a cognitive one.

In chapter four I move on from the issue of affordance to explore the issue of mediation in relation to semiotic theory. Here I encounter important semiotic concepts and explore their explanatory power as appropriate concepts for understanding interactive media.

In the following chapters (five and six) I explore further elements of semiotic theory as applied in the domains of graphic design, film studies, architecture and product design. The aim of this is to establish how semiotic theory might be applied to interactive media in a useful and appropriate way. We will also encounter the limits of semiotic theory and re-establish the importance of the role of the body in interaction.

Example case studies are outlined, which aim to punctuate the theorizing with real world examples of a semiotically informed understanding of interactive media.

In chapters seven and eight, I recap the various theories encountered so far and attempt to further clarify the relationships between semiotics, phenomenology, ecological psychology and embodied cognition, being careful to ensure that the resulting explanation retains compatibility. On the basis of this, we move toward a place where a more complementary integrated approach gives us a better picture of how we interact with new mediating technologies. The resulting theory provides a way to approach interactive media through establishing a spectrum of interaction possibilities that can be understood in terms of an embodied semiotic perspective.

Finally, in chapter nine, I consider a number of examples of interaction design from this new integrated perspective in order to show how this kind of integrated thinking results in richer descriptions of our relationship with interactive media. This is particularly important as these examples of interactive media are at the cutting edge of media design and point toward the kinds of media experiences we are likely to have in the future.

# References

McLuhan, M. (1994) *Understanding Media: The extensions of Man.* Routledge, London.

Lister, M., Dovey, J., Giddings, S., Grant, I. and Kelly, K. (2003) New Media: A Critical Introduction. Routledge, London.

McLuhan, M. and Fiore, Q. (1967) The Medium is the Massage: An Inventory of Effects. Bantham Books, New York.

Williams, R. (1974) Television: Technology and Cultural form Collins, London.

Bardzell, J. (2006). Creativity in Amateur Multimedia: Popular Culture, Critical Theory and HCI. Human Technology, 3(1), 12–33.

# Chapter 2
# Media, Mediation and Interactive Media

## 2.1 The Root of Media?

If interactive media is changing the way in which we relate to our surroundings by changing the nature of the media that we are already familiar with, then how do we establish what those changes are, and what the characteristics of the resulting new interactive media are going to be? This is a fundamental question that we must attempt to answer before we can theorize any further on interactive media. In order to do so, we must start from first principles and explore what the meaning of the term 'medium' means in a linguistic sense and then move on to establish how this meaning has evolved, as it has been used in different domains. By surveying the theory that surrounds media in general, we can hopefully uncover the roots of interactive media and shed some light on what this term means, as well as the characteristics that define it.

Starting simply by limiting ourselves to an analysis of the meaning of the word 'medium', we encounter several other terms such as 'intermediary', 'go-between', 'middle', 'channel', 'conduit' and 'vehicle'. Each one expands our understanding of what a medium might be. For example, if we think of a medium as an 'intermediary' or 'go-between', then we think of it as something that is in-between (in the 'middle' of, as in its original Latin meaning) two other things, perhaps doing something, performing a task or relaying a message. If we think of a medium as a 'channel' or a 'conduit', then this expands on this intermediary idea by making us think that a medium is something that can somehow be traveled 'through' or 'on', e.g., a 'vehicle'. If we press further on with this conduit idea, we hit upon a deeper meaning of what we should consider a medium to be, that is, a means of expression or a mouthpiece. It is with these notions that we finally arrive at what our general understanding of a medium is, namely, a means of expressing ourselves or communicating with others.

So far so good, we have now established that a medium is something we use to communicate with. It is something we use that sits in-between us and those we are communicating with. It acts on our behalf by relaying messages that we send to one another. It is something we use to put our thoughts, ideas and feelings into. It is something that holds them for us, so we can see them ourselves or pass them on to others.

S.O'Neill, *Interactive Media: The Semiotics of Embodied Interaction*,
doi: 10.1007/978-1-84800-036-0, © Springer Science + Business Media, LLC 2008

Thinking on this further reveals that a medium must have some tangible physical component to it that allows it to exist in-between us. Were it not the case, how could we be sure that a medium makes its content available for others to witness? How could we know that we had expressed ourselves? Indeed, if we now think about all the different manifestations of media that there are in the world and all the different opportunities and 'vehicles' there are for expressing ourselves we realize that, of course, a medium has to be some kind of physical entity.

In its most straightforward form, the physical act of opening a mouthpiece and uttering a few words gives us the medium of speech, where sounds are formed and carried through the physical medium of air. Similarly, the flick of a wrist and the wink of an eye give us gestures by which we can also express ourselves, where our bodily movements in space and time are our medium of expression. Should we extend that flick of the wrist to include a pen and a piece of paper, we have at our finger tips a written language, a diagram or a drawing. We have now, yet more ways of expressing our thoughts and our ideas, where the physical qualities of the pen mediate our act of placing our thoughts on the paper, which in turn mediates our thoughts to others who might look at those pen marks.

Thinking in such a way reveals to us that the primary element of every medium at work in every act of mediation is in our bodies, acting in someway upon some material of the world that surrounds us. The very nature of being physically embodied in the world is at the root of all mediation, for without a body, even if we had minds the size of planets, with ideas to match, we would have nothing by which to render them observable in our surroundings. In short, without bodies there would be nothing to mediate our thoughts. All media and acts of mediation are at least in part, as McLuhan has said, 'extensions of man', extensions of ourselves into the world (McLuhan 1994). Media then, are the physical elements and attributes of our relationship to the world that allow us to embed our thoughts and ideas in them in order to make them manifest.

## 2.2   Two Different Ways to Think about Media

When we think of 'The Media' we unfortunately think only of the mainstream, centralized notion of global television news and the tabloid press (Lister et al. 2003). Indeed the term has become so synonymous with this form of media that other ways of thinking about media tend to get marginalized or excluded from our theories. News reporting, the tabloid press and global telecommunications companies are certainly powerful players that shape the way in which we consume certain kinds of information. Equally though, media can be thought of on a smaller, more local, scale, where people make and consume media under their own volition according to rules that are negotiated on a daily basis by all those involved.

For Instance, what sort of relationship do artists have with media as they express themselves giving form to some kind of vision or idea? Poets, painters and musicians all have intimate relationships with their chosen medium (sometimes range of media) with which they personally connect.

Likewise, media can be used to describe the material that someone might work with in other creative ways. Traditional examples of craft based practices might include textiles, glassware and pottery, whereas newer materials might include the plastics and electronics of mass production which have given rise to things like televisions and computers. Like art, all of these things are media in the sense that they require physical materials to give some kind of expression or form to an idea. But more than that, they have a functional purpose built into them. Media materials carry ideas for us, they give us a place to express our thoughts but they also give us something to think about, reflect on and use.

The characteristics, affordances and constraints of certain materials mean that we can never successfully make a working motorcar out of a piece of string or make strong chairs out of balsawood. Certain ideas and certain functions require certain qualities of material to become manifest in the world. In order to understand how they work we must study and work closely with them, experimenting and prototyping our ideas as we go. Even writing usually takes this form. How many attempts do you think it took me to get this sentence right?

Media have many different forms and the materials of the world provide many of the characteristics that allow us to engage in mediation. New interactive media challenge the way we think about media but in what sense is this kind of media any different from older types of media? Before engaging with this question, it is worth exploring some of the different ways in which we think about media and mediation in general in order to grasp some fundamental concepts that influence our understanding.

## 2.2.1  Artistic and Creative Media

Artists, artisans and trades people have an uncanny tacit knowledge of the medium they work with. Painters understand not only the colors that they apply to their canvases, but also the consistency of their paints, how to mix them and how long they will take to dry. Sculptors have a vast amount of knowledge about how to manipulate raw materials such as clay, wood, steel and marble. This knowledge is developed through a particular understanding of the characteristics of such materials, even down to different types of wood or different types of paint for example.

Artistry, in a traditional sense, is very much about working with your hands and traditional artistic media reflect this creative process of manipulation and reflection involved in making an artwork. Consider the array of brushes, tools, pots and paints in a painter's studio. Each one of these elements is readily at hand and in combination they are used to manipulate the fluid material of paint over the rough surface of a canvas to form some kind of image.

The characteristics of the medium provide the artist with useful knowledge about the kinds of things a material can be used to express. For example, clay is a particularly good medium for modeling the human figure. It is malleable, with just enough resistance to hold the shape it has been formed into. It can be squashed, torn, formed, built up and shaved away as desired. It is this malleability or 'plasticity' that gives artistic materials some of their most important qualities.

The 'plastic process' as described by Mark Rothko (Rothko 2004) is an eloquent and fascinating insight into the relationship between an artist and the forming of his ideas through the medium of paint. Indeed, Rothko's notion of the plastic process covers the materials of stone and clay as well as paint, but it is in painting in particular the he is an expert. For Rothko, the plastic process is about manipulating paint in such a way as to produce a sense of form or movement in space like that of manipulating clay or stone. The painter, restricted by the two dimensions of the medium, must employ the malleable characteristics of paint such as tone and color in order to produce the required sensation of form. The skill of the artist then is in understanding the affordances and constraints of this particular medium that allows the creative process to manifest a work of art.

The concept of 'affordance' (Norman 1998) is something that has often been expounded in interaction design literature, where everyday things, to paraphrase Norman, are designed, with the user in mind, to afford a particular kind of use. For example, chairs afford sitting, stairs afford climbing and hammers afford hitting. The problem with thinking about interactive media from the perspective of affordance is that computers have very few physical properties that behave in the same way as traditional materials. Computers are supposedly representations of minds rather than bodies or materials, minds that behave in a very particular and abstract way. Computers do not behave like clay or wood, nor do they afford sitting or climbing on. If form follows function, what computers do afford is computing, i.e. crunching numbers very quickly. However, the rapid development of interactive media appears to be changing this view of the computer. McCullough, for example, advocates the abstraction of craft to the point where computational power is used to develop interactive media that compute things like the consistency of paint or resistance of materials to simulate the specific feel of certain creative activities (McCullough 1996, 2001). This can be viewed as an attempt to imbue interactive media with some kind of 'plasticity', in Rothko's sense of the word. It is an important step away from the streamlining and automation of creative practices and towards a clearer understanding of the relationship between creative practitioners and their media.

In general then, artistic and creative media are essentially understood in the age old tradition of an individual artist working very closely with some group of material elements and tools in order to produce some kind of finished artwork. Granted, this has not always been the case, and many artists over the years have challenged this view of both the creative process and the nature of the artwork. Indeed, Cubist, Dadaist and conceptual artists' ideas have focused on the characteristics of various media for making art by experimenting with new materials and technologies that have changed the way in which artist can conceptualize and manifest their work (Genesko 1999). As we will see later a great deal of this exploration of the qualities of materials in late modernism and notions of mediation and 'inter-media' explored by the conceptual artists and American avant-garde have had a palpable yet indirect affect on the development of new forms of media (Packer and Jordan 2001).

For now, it is enough to understand that creative and artistic new media are still emerging and evolving as technology develops, but the main driving force behind understanding these remains the artistic desire to create and express ideas through a medium. Attempting to understand the characteristics of interactive media from this perspective is essential if we want to understand our attempts to interact with them and what they might afford.

## 2.2.2   Communications Media

In "Understanding Media" (McLuhan 1994) among other things, Marshall McLuhan shows a fundamental concern with the way in which communication media, in the form of Global TV networks, have been made possible through the electrification of industrialized societies. His statement "The Medium is the Message", (McLuhan 1994 p12) is an attempt to address the way in which the electrification of media affected the way in which we communicate. As McLuhan saw it, the very nature of a medium has an affect on the way in which the content of ideas expressed in that medium are represented. It is this affect of a medium that McLuhan was most concerned with. He pointed out that while the content of the representation is usually immediately obvious, the nature of the medium itself often goes unnoticed.

Examples of this exist in abundance in the arts. Consider the number of paintings of Jesus there must be in the churches of Venice. Granted, many of them are by different artists, and therefore exemplify their own expressions, but many of them look the same and indeed the content is immediately identifiable. Now consider a statue and a painting of the same subject by the same artist side by side. The content is still the same and still obvious but one occupies three-dimensional space and the other only pictorial space. Clearly the nature of the statue has a different affect on the viewer from the painting but this might actually not be at the forefront of the viewers mind.

For McLuhan the way in which the electronic mass distribution of TV differed in affect from media such as newspapers and films was one of his main concerns. He pointed out that the very characteristics of electricity and light, inherent in the medium of television are what afford the extension from localized communication to global communications and reshaped the way in which we construct, transmit and receive our messages. His intention in claiming the medium as the message highlights the way in which these sometimes-unnoticed characteristics of media change the way in which we apprehend and comprehend the content on display. Increasingly for McLuhan the content mattered less and less as he focused on the affects of mediation in various forms.

This kind of understanding of media begins to address some key themes that are central to a much critical media theory, such as the social and political repercussions of a move towards a larger passive receiving population, coupled with a monopolization of the powerful message making elite. In this view, mass media is essentially one-way traffic, from producers to consumers, or authors to readers. As we have already seen, Raymond William's theories of media problematise this even further to the point that our experience of media is not just determined by the form of the material representing an idea but also by the social situations and context of use, as well as the power struggles between political/commercial interests that want to control the media conduits.

New communications media are already distributed everywhere and we seem to be increasingly dependent on them as we, not only interact with, receive and transmit through, but also wear and live inside computer-supported media rich environments. Interactive media are rapidly becoming part of the fabric of our day-to-day lives and understanding the characteristics of this media is becoming an essential aspect of 21st century living.

Like McLuhan's television, some of the constituent components of the Smartphone for example, are still light and electricity, which are central to understanding their capacity for screen-based input/output of communication elements over vast area networks. However, McLuhan's notion of mass media becomes problematic in relation to trying to understand them because of the shift away from the broadcast and passive reception of media to the interactive qualities that are now inherent in all mobile communications devices.

The problem here is with understanding the changes in the characteristics of an older medium that has undergone a transformation through the convergence and computerization of various media forms. The reception of messages is no longer passive and one-way but interactive and multidirectional. Smart-phone users can send and receive media rich texts of their own making as well as download film clips and music from the Internet.

An interesting aspect of this in relation to understanding new media in general, is the blur between the role of the author and the reader. Interactive media allow users to be much more in control of how they interact with and interpret the material they receive, as well as the construction and transmission of their own media rich messages. The centralized view of mass media communication technologies still persists and is in the hands of the giant global corporations that produce the technology. The move to using interactive technology has put the users in control of the content that the medium transmits, but the corporations still control the medium itself. As a result we are increasingly becoming more creative and media savvy in our personal communications with one another, but we may not always be aware of the restrictions that come hand in hand with adopting this technology.

## 2.3   The Rise of Interactive Media

Of course, computers consist of many different elements and materials that make them what they are. The metal and plastic of in-put/output devices (e.g. keyboards, mice and screens) are just one element along with others such as; the electricity that provides the power to make them run, the ROM and RAM memories that store data as well as the actual data and software that manipulate them. All of these elements combine together to form a unique device or tool that accommodates different situations of use, from word processing to exploring virtual environments.

This fairly traditional view has long been established in HCI circles, but thinking of the computer as a medium in its own right (Andersen, Holmqvist and Jensen 1993), with each of these elements contributing different qualities to it, asks a different set of questions. For example, we never see or touch the 1s and 0s of the data in the same way that people manipulate other more traditional media. So how can we understand the qualities of a medium that seems so far removed from its basic characteristics? What are the qualities that make something a medium and what exactly do we hope to gain from thinking about computers in this way?

In terms of trying to understand the computer as a medium, it is important to highlight that there is a big difference between the qualities of interactive media supported by computers these days and the qualities that computers were originally designed with. Early computers were calculating machines, where programmers spent their time writing software and inputting data commands laboriously, either to calculate something or to control some other machine.

Computers these days are complex convergent multimedia machines that employ sophisticated computer graphics, video imaging techniques and high-fidelity sound reproduction equipment.

Users no longer directly manipulate the binary code. They manipulate higher-level abstracted signs and representations of the data in order to perform tasks. While binary code still remains at the centre of the computational process, graphical and lexical sign systems that represent concepts and familiar activities have been introduced as the front end, or interface, that allow us to understand and operate them in our own terms.

As technology has developed, more and more sign systems from older media have been assimilated, through abstraction and remediation, into the language of the computer interface. Furthermore, the remediation of these sign systems has lead to transformations within their own internal structures, forcing us to re-evaluate how we interpret and make sense of the evolving media that surrounds us.

For example, the interactive media used to manipulate digital images, such as Photoshop, are new versions of the old sign systems of photographers, painters and artistic practitioners. The computerization of this medium has transformed not only the way in which we produce images, but also the way in which we interpret them and consume them.

Digital cameras employ photosensitive cells to capture images stored as bits of information in a computer memory, as opposed to the light reactive chemicals of traditional photography. While the mechanics of capturing an image are essentially similar i.e. light falls into the camera onto a sensitive surface, the results are quite different. Digital images are not fixed in the same way that traditional photographs are. This allows for a radical transformation in the way that images are manipulated after they have been captured.

Traditional photography uses equipment such as enlargers, various chemical developing baths and varying exposure times in order to manipulate the tone and color saturation of images. Essentially the image, once captured, retains its initial composition as it has been fixed by the chemical reaction caused by the light hitting the film or paper.

However, the retouching and compositing techniques of digital photography radically alters this fixed nature of the photographic image and as a result alters the way in which we interpret digitally produced or altered images.

Once, we used to believe that the camera never lied because through the fixing nature of the chemical reactions to light photographic film and photographic paper were directly linked to the objects of the image by the reflection of light from the real object into the camera. Photographs were by and large considered to be direct representations of reality.

Digital photography techniques challenge this very relationship with reality by allowing us to manipulate and alter images that look real enough but which might be radically different in origin. The cult of the 'Photoshopped' image where details can be altered and collages of images can be seamlessly woven together to produce composites, removes the photographic image from its duty as a record of reality. The color and tone of pixels is never fixed and software allows us to alter faces or reposition elements in pictorial space as we please.

Digital images now offer us a whole range of possible imaginary visual worlds as opposed to a record of just one. There is no longer the same immediate contact with reality, although as we will see shortly many new technologies attempt to reclaim and improve upon this situation.

## 2.4  Remediation

Bolter and Grusin propose the idea that one way to understand new media is through understanding the way in which it evolves within a tradition of what they identify as "remediation" (Bolter and Grusin 1999). In remediation, new technologies assimilate ideas from older technologies and present them as new and better versions of the previous media form. For example, consider the relationships between photography and painting, television and film or, more pertinently, computer games and film.

Each one of these new technologies is informed by and benefits from the wealth of knowledge and cultural appreciation of the older form that it remediates. For instance, the language and composition of photography is undoubtedly greatly indebted to the tradition of painting - a claim most obviously exemplified in the fact that portraiture and landscape pictures make up the mainstay of both art forms.

In attempting to put the argument across that new media are simply extensions of this idea of remediation, Bolter and Grusin identify two archetypal forms of remediation: Technologies that attempt to address our desire for the "immediacy" of content and technologies that promote the "hypermediacy" of the medium itself.

## 2.4.1 Immediacy

Immediacy is best understood in terms of media that offer windows onto represented content while hiding the nature of the medium itself form our perceptions (Bolter and Grusin 1999 pp 21–30). If one thinks of looking through a window at a scene outside, one is largely concerned with the scene rather than the window itself (Bolter and Gromala 2003). The window has disappeared from our attention and has become a seemingly natural aspect of the medium that we no longer notice. Many technologies attempt to create this feeling of 'non-mediation (Lombard and Ditton 1997). Painting, television and virtual reality technologies all play with the immediacy trick at some level.

A good example of this type of media would be a flight simulator that offers a virtual first person perspective of flying a plane. Obviously the ultimate experience of flying a plane is actually flying a plane, but for those of us who can't afford it or would rather watch than do, other media provide a window into this world. Of course there are films we can watch, television programs that have been made, even drawings and photographs that show in detail what might be involved. Each one provides insight into what it might actually be like to fly a plane without having to do it. Indeed, pilots learn a lot about how to fly by reading books as well as practicing in simulators and real planes.

Bolter and Grusins arguments suggest that the flight simulator is not simply a simulation of the real experience but also a 'remediation' of the televisual experience, which in turn, is a remediation of cinema or photography that portrays the same scenario. Each successive remediation is considered as an upgrade, a step closer to reality for the viewer. The medium, by which the experience is conveyed, is either hidden or systematically removed from the experience, resulting in a unified space of reality and the illusion of non-mediation. What appears on the screen gets closer and closer to representing a real experience of flying, providing a sense of actually being there when in fact you are not. The notion of 'telepresence', see for example (Lombard, et al. 1997; Riva, Davide and Ijsselsteijn 2003; Schuemie, VanDerStraaten, Krijn and Mast 2001; Slater 2003; Waterworth and Waterworth 2003), is the feeling of being immersed in a mediated virtual environment, while physically being located somewhere else (Witmer and Singer 1998) without necessarily being aware of mediation taking place, thus the experience of the flight simulator is experiencing the virtual environment as your 'immediate' surroundings. That is to say, that the media presented to you is done in such a way as to make you believe that you are actually flying a plane.

Interestingly, Oliver Grau's book "Virtual art" (Grau 2003), traces the development of this type of immersive technology back through the renaissance to the frescoes of ancient Rome, where the interiors of some houses were painted with representations of outdoor scenes in order to make the viewer feel that they were outside when in fact they were inside. Grau's path from Roman frescoes to panoramic painting, immersive cinema and virtual reality echoes Bolter and Grusins argument about remediation. In particular Grau highlights the debt that modern technologies owe to artistic pursuits and older forms of media.

Particular aspects of new media that follow this trend are digitally rendered 3D graphics, digitally composite photo-realistic images and photo-realistic virtual environments.

## 2.4.2   Hypermedia

Hypermedia or media that promote hypermediacy are in effect the exact opposite of those that promote immediacy. Unlike immediacy the aim of hypermedia is to bring the medium itself into focus rather than the content, which remains secondary.

These types of media are perhaps best understood as the combination or recombination of various older media types that overtly display the nature of the mediating technology (Bolter et al. 1999 pp 31–44). They are heterogeneous and multifaceted groupings of multiple media elements, where the manipulation of the medium itself is the most important factor.

The difference between immediacy and hyper media can best be exemplified in its simplest form by comparing representational painting with abstract painting. Representational painting generally attempts to create an image of something, be it a person or landscape, through the careful manipulation of paint, by giving maximum attention to the content of the image rather than the nature of the brush strokes and marks that make the image possible. Abstract painting, in its broadest sense, is almost the reverse of this. It is not about the content but about the consistency of the paint, the quality of the brush strokes, the drips and daubs that cover the canvas. Abstract painting draws attention to the medium of paint itself rather than attempting to represent an image through paint. Abstract painting is essentially hypermedia whereas representational painting is immediate.

In relation to new media, Microsoft 'Word' is an excellent example of hyper media technology at work. While 'Word' effectively remediates the activity of writing by hand, it also remediates the world of typesetters and printers of a previous age. It is profuse with discrete elements (signs and symbols) that constitute the make up of the medium. When manipulated these symbols allow you to write, organize and rearrange a text as you see fit. Moreover, other signs and symbols from other software can be integrated into the mediated workspace. For example, Endnote and Acrobat can be used in conjunction with Word, producing a combined 'hypermedium' with which to manipulate entire documents. Indeed, documents might be linked to one another, both on or offline, extending the hyper connections. All of these connections are made explicit within the medium by having some symbol or sign present to identify them. As you write, your awareness flips back and forth from focusing on what you want to say to how you manipulate the technology that allows you to say it.

Essentially, hypermedia is the combination of fragmented disparate media elements through connection rather than the seamless integration of elements into one presented reality or space. Bolter and Grusin again identify that while this is promoted in new media as a particularly new phenomenon, it is in fact evident throughout the history of media, from medieval illuminated manuscripts right through to the collages of modern art and on to the present day graphical interfaces of computer systems.

Packer and Jordan also define hypermedia as the connections between different discrete media elements that provide a personal trail of association among them (Packer and Jordan 2001, pxxxi). Paul also discusses this fragmentary, yet integrated, multiplicity in relation to new media art installations that combine numerous physical and new media elements in the space of a gallery. These installations constitute information spaces, offering interactive and participatory roles to the viewer in making the artwork (Paul 2003). Examples of new media that follow this trend are graphical user interfaces, the World Wide Web, augmented reality and ubiquitous computing.

## 2.5   The Essential Characteristics of Interactive Media

Computers have become highly complex devices that consist not only of simple computational forms but also of complex cultural forms (sign systems) derived from the older media that they have now assimilated (Manovich 2001). The parameters and qualities of the computer as a medium have increased dramatically as they have taken these new forms on board. Interactive media retains some of the qualities of both artistic media and mass media. However, the very nature of these older media forms has been subject to change by the qualities of the computer and must now be understood within new contexts. With the relationship between old and interactive media in mind, it is important to establish the fundamental characteristics of which aspects of old media still apply to interactive media and more importantly, what is 'new' about interactive media?

A number of different theorists have attempted to identify the characteristics of interactive media. Many of their ideas are similar, but few of them offer clear definitions of what the fundamental features of interactive media are. Largely, this is because there is a wide range of interactive media types that do not always combine the same characteristics. Therefore, it is only through scrutinizing a wide range of media that recurrent characteristics can be identified.

Martin Lister and his colleagues (Lister et al. 2003) define new media in relation to the characteristics of: *digitality, interactivity, hypertextuality, dispersal* and *virtuality*. Christiane Paul classifies the artistic aspects of the new media features as: *recombinant, interactive, participatory, dynamic and customizable* (Paul 2003). Randall Packer and Ken Jordan also provide a categorisation of the characteristics of multimedia in their book "Multimedia from Wagner to Virtual Reality" (Packer, et al. 2001). They include *integration, interactivity, hypermedia, immersion* and *narrative* in their definitions. Similarly, Lev Manovich provides another list of characteristics in his book "The Language of Interactive media" (Manovich 2001). Essentially, Manovich's interactive media characteristics are: *Numerical representation, Modularity, Automation, Variability* and *Transcoding*.

While there are many different kinds of terminology used to describe interactive media, it is clear that many of them have overlapping descriptions. For example, much of what Paul terms as *recombinant*, i.e. the discrete yet re-usable features of interactive media, is the same as Packer and Jordan's *integration* or Manovich's term *modularity*. Similarly, much of what Lister et al. discuss in relation to *virtuality* and features of simulation is essentially the same as that which Packer and Jordan describe as *immersion* i.e. the capacity for what Bolter and Grusin term as the quality of *immediacy*.

In considering all of these descriptions together, it is important to identify the essential characteristics of interactive media that set it apart from older media and other technology, while being derived from the combination of the two. These are the technological convergence of multiple media forms, the digitization, abstraction and simulation of old media and the interactive authoring and interpretation of meaning.

## 2.5.1  The Technological Convergence of Multiple Media Forms

An essential aspect of interactive media is the convergence of media forms that has come about through multimedia practices in the arts and the development of the personal computer. The "intermedia", so sought after by the avant-garde artists of the early 20th Century, has become a reality in interactive media technology, where multiple images, multiple film clips and multiple sound sources become integrated in interfaces and artifacts.

The invention of 'Hypertext' by Ted Nelson, although traced back to Vannevar Bush's Memex machine, really originates in trends within the avant-garde and conceptual art movements of the 1950's and 60's. The likes of John Cage, Robert Rauschenburg, William Burroughs and their associates were all interested in pushing the boundaries of their chosen medium, exploring notions of randomness and chance as a tool for making art (Osborne 2002; Packer, et al. 2001; Pritchett 1993). Several of these artists employed the idea of the 'cut-up'. Literally cutting up sections of text, musical scores, sound recordings or images and rearranging them with other elements to produce a kind of collage effect, resulting in the first attempts at new types of narrative and media exploration. Indeed, Ted Nelson saw the ideas behind the Memex as a potential way to write non-linear narratives or texts that were inspired by the novels of William Burroughs (Burroughs 1968; 1971)

Similarly, a number of these artists were also exploring the notion of rule-based systems to create artworks. John Cage, for example, wrote many scores that were simple instructions for the performer, without writing a single note of music. Allan Kaprow formulated a set of rules as a medium through which anyone could take part in one of his 'happenings'. The Fluxus movement, in general, contributed to ideas of 'intermedia', where multiple media (music, dance, painting, sculpture etc.) converged in performances that finally resulted in 'scores' and 'instructions' becoming artworks in themselves (Osborne 2002).

These notions challenged the accepted understanding of the artwork and indeed the artists' medium, often attempting to combine different media together into collages made from various physical objects, sound and light, performance or indeed all of these elements at once. This convergent impetus, along with a desire within the avant-garde to challenge the relationship of the artist and the viewer (beginning with audience participation), exist as part of a tradition of the subversion of traditional art forms, artistic expression and the use of creative media, which is directly related to the climate of exploration and invention in the late '50s and early '60s America, that spawned today's personal computer.

Indeed, Artists and engineers collaborated on numerous projects at this time, e.g. Robert Rauschenberg's collaborations with Billy Klüver from Bell Laboratories in Experiments in Art and Technology (E.A.T.), (Mattison 2003), and the important exhibition "Cybernetic Serendipity" at London's ICA in 1968 had a marked effect on the way in which artists engaged with technology in the pursuit of creative expression.

While it may be too much to suggest that the avant-garde had a direct part to play in the invention of the personal computer, it is possible to say that the spirit of exploration and the desire to push the boundaries of multiple media, championed by these artists, finally found its ultimate expression in the form of today's convergent new media.

Alan Kay and Adele Goldberg in their 1977 proposal for the 'Dynabook' put forward a compelling argument for considering the computer as a medium in its own right. Their vision for the Dynabook was one that saw the potential of a device that could not only store, retrieve and manipulate messages, like many other media, but which also could act as a meta-medium i.e. it had the potential to encompass many forms of media in one place. (Packer et al. 2001 pp 169–170)

. The notion of the database as a source material that is queried/manipulated by users/artists via algorithms and rules (or coded messages) that formally describe their intentions is an enduring description of the new media that has its roots in this fertile territory (Manovich 2001).

Indeed, the artistic aspects of convergent media forms go further still, when artists start to use interactive devices such as smart phones and mobile phone networks, as elements of their live interactive installations, capable of transmitting and receiving video messages to members of their audience/users. Convergent mobile interactive media promise the possibility of 'anytime anywhere' communication facilities where we can create, send and receive multi-media messages allowing for the further production and interpretation of participatory cultural elements. This again is different from traditional technology, where the extent of convergence was once the 'calculator digital watch' or even the 'tea's made'. The convergent functionality of interactive media is now about the production, communication and interpretation of messages on a global scale. This is perhaps one of the clearest insights into the nature of interactive media and the role of artistic and scientific exploration that has pushed forward the development of modern computer systems.

## 2.5.2   The Digitization, Abstraction and Simulation of Old Media

The digitization and abstraction of older media forms into the domain of interactive technologies is another aspect of what sets interactive media apart from old media. Interactive media are "remediated" (Bolter et al. 1999) and "abstracted" (McCullough 1996) digital versions of older media that retain some of their initial characteristics. For example, new creative software tools such as Photoshop or illustrator contain elements that represent the colors of paint, mixing palettes and brushes. However, these are transformed by taking on digital qualities e.g. storage as binary data, multiple versioning, transcoding and digital manipulation via algorithms.

Interactive media include digitally abstracted versions of drawing, painting, film-making, music production and writing. They are essentially different from traditional technologies and machinery, in that there is an important focus on the manipulation of materials that attempts to retain the feel of older media, while capitalizing on the storage, versioning and networking possibilities offered by digitization.

These remediated media attempt to present themselves as newer and better versions of older media. The desire for mediated representations that promote immediacy and reality traditionally drives the process of remediation. Advances in mediating technology are generally measured in terms of increases in fidelity and quality of representation, e.g. Virtual Reality and High Definition television are arguably the latest version of this trend.

As this type of technology becomes more complex, the qualities of hypermedia often take over; particularly when the illusion of non-mediation becomes apparent or it needs to be altered in some way. Hypermedia ultimately reveals the nature of the mediating technology itself by allowing us to manipulate its content and explore multiple versions of the representation. The technologies of immediacy, on the other hand, attempt to hide the act of mediation by presenting their content as if it were the only natural reality available.

Bolter and Grusin point out that interactive media show a propensity to oscillate between these two mediating forms, highlighting the interdependency of one upon the other. Similarly, they also point out that remediation is a reciprocal process where it is not always easy to identify which media is being remediated and which is doing the remediating (Bolter et al., 1999 p 106). Ultimately what we see with remediation and the computerization of new media is an explosion in the types of images and representations that are available to us in multiple formats and versions.

However, Christiane Paul contends that the opposite trend may also be in effect. While the heterogeneity of images seems undeniable with the advent of image manipulation software such as Photoshop, it is possible that the functionality of these new media only offer us limited choices of manipulation. The popular explosion in the use of cheap image and video production software has put millions of images and short films online. But as Bardzell points out, it is interesting to find that so many of them look so similar in style and content (Bardzell 2006). Perhaps this new technology is ultimately delivering a new kind of homogenous media experience in the guise of a heterogeneous one.

Whatever the answer to this conundrum turns out to be, one thing seems to ring true. What seems like the relatively new phenomenon of 'Interactive media', in fact stems from what is actually a long and continuing development of older media. The fundamentally important thing in all of this is the way that computing technology has revolutionized all of our existing media activities, from paper to film, becoming integral in the production and reception of its various forms and sign systems. Moreover, as technology develops, the integration and networking capabilities that computers have brought to older media continue to affect these sign systems and ultimately the very fabric of our surroundings.

## *2.5.3   The Interactive Authoring and Interpretation of Meaning*

The concept of interactivity itself deserves some special consideration in relation to the nature of media transformed by computerization. Both Paul and Manovich claim that the over use of this term has in some way rendered it at best confusing and at worst meaningless as a way to describe new media technologies.

From a traditional HCI perspective, Heath and Luff (Heath and Luff 1996), in their studies of the London underground control room, contend that computerized technologies offer the potential of interaction 'with' and interaction 'through' them. Interaction 'with' involves the manipulation of the interface to perform certain tasks, whereas interacting 'through' is the resultant goal achieved by interacting 'with'; such as sending a message to someone at another computer over a network or perhaps printing a finished document after a spell of word processing.

While Heath and Luff's interaction 'with' and 'through', still hold true for interactive media, clearly new types of interaction with the convergent multiple sign systems of interactive media require better understanding. Bolter and Gromala's analysis of interactive art installations from the perspective of 'Windows and Mirrors' (Bolter et al. 2003) offers a similar exploration of these ideas. Tied into the notions of immediacy and hypermedia, the idea of technology acting as windows and mirrors is simply used to show how many new mediating technologies offer windows onto new forms of content or act as mirrors reflecting the mediating experience itself. Windows allow you to act through the technology where as mirrors allow you to interact directly with the technology itself. Bolter and Gromala highlight the way in which new media technology allow us to constantly shift from one type of interaction to the other.

However, interaction with interactive media is not just about 'with' and 'through'. Interaction with interactive media is about the relationship between the production and interpretation of interactive media sign systems. For example, traditional media, such as film, TV and even painting, were largely focused, by an elite, on the production of messages for consumption by the masses. While this is still very much the case, interactive media brings the relationships between the designer/user, author/reader and producer/consumer into question. There is a blurring between what were once sharply defined roles.

For example, the availability of high quality video editing software has had a major impact on the way in which film is produced and consumed within our culture today. No longer do films have to be made in vast studios with equally vast budgets, although they frequently are. Alternatively, light and agile teams of just a few people can make them. The material can be edited on location, rather than having to book out expensive edit suites, and the finished article can be streamed over the Internet rather than having to be distributed to film houses and other such outlets.

The way in which we produce and consume films has also been changed by the nature of computerization. Interactive films allow you to watch scenes in a different order or make decisions about the piece of film that is being shown. The narrative structures of these films now must have multiple threads and a number of possible endings in order to provide a suitable route through the material that is engaging in an interactive way.

As users take up this kind of technology they can edit their own version of a popular film or create their own film for friends and family. As this happens it is no longer clear who the author is and who the reader is. There are new ways of interacting with this technology that challenges these assumptions.

Older media have always been interactive for those that have attempted to use them to express themselves, but they have not always been interactive in the same sense for the interpreters of those expressions. Traditional painting is about an artist interacting with the medium of paint to produce visual messages that are interpreted by a viewer. The interactive media equivalent sees an artist having to interpret a complex software interface in order to interact with and customize digitized paint.

At the same time, this artist is using that system to produce artwork to be interpreted by other viewers. If this artist's goal is to produce interactive art, the role of the viewer is no longer about the passive interpretation of art but about the active manipulation of interactive media in order to make sense of it. The boundaries between author and reader have been eroded to the point where the production and consumption of meaning, in once static forms, is now constantly in flux through the dynamic activities of both parties.

The traditional HCI view of the designer/user maintains the separation of the two with designers designing interfaces to be 'used' by users. The convergent nature of interactive media brings this sharply into focus, by highlighting that it is no longer adequate to think of designers and users in this way. Designers and users both interactively produce and interpret interfaces at different times and in different ways.

Manovich states that:

"Once an object is represented in a computer, it automatically becomes interactive. Therefore, to call computer media 'interactive' is meaningless- it simply means stating the most basic fact about computers."(Manovich 2001, p. 55)

Of course, this is absolutely correct. However, by adopting a traditional HCI approach, Manovich fails to understand the key aspect of interaction with interactive media, which highlights the change in relationships between major stakeholders such as designers and users. Where Manovich terms everything rendered by computers as interactive, Paul makes a distinction that helps to clarify a difficulty with the term in relation to the production and interpretation of interactive media:

"Ultimately, any experience of an artwork is interactive, relying on a complex interplay between contexts and productions of meaning at the recipient's end. Yet, this interaction remains a mental event in the viewer's mind when it comes to experiencing traditional art forms: the physicality of the painting or the sculpture does not change in front of his or her eyes. With regard to digital art, however, interactivity allows different forms of navigating, assembling, or contributing to an artwork that go beyond this purely mental event." (Paul 2003 p 67).

The interpretation and interaction with interactive media then, relies on the oscillation between two types of interactive quality. On one level there is the sense making interaction of the reader with the content presented by an author through the medium and at the other there is the physical interaction of the reader with the manipulation and transformation of the content structure. Each type of interaction is deeply entwined with the other as the process of interpretation takes place. In interacting with new media a reader takes on some of the role of the author by having to organize the material into a structure that makes sense to him as part of the process of interpretation. This is radically different from watching a film from start to finish, where the structure has already been set by the author.

## 2.6  Summary

Clearly new technologies are altering the way in which we relate to previous forms of media. As a result of these kinds of transformations in our experience of mediation, our assumptions about how to understand them are forced to change. We need new theories that throw light on these problems offering us new ways to understand and criticize the changes that are happening around us.

In this chapter we have attempted to survey some of the existing theories about the characteristics of media in general and interactive media in particular. In doing so we have cast some light on a complex situation where a cultural collision has occurred between the domain of computer science, which wants to store, retrieve and manipulate symbolic information about the world, and the creative practices that represent ideas and imaginations in numerous interesting and creative ways. As a result we are now better equipped with an understanding of the origins of interactive media, as well as an understanding of its fundamental characteristics.

In the next chapter we will consider three important ways of understanding interactive media that are derived from the development of HCI theory. In doing so we will see how different theoretical positions give rise to different understandings of how we interact with technology and how these theories relate to one another. Not only will we find that different theories give us very different views of technology but also of who we are as human beings. This of course gives rise to problems in deciding which theory provides the best description of our relationship with interactive technology. Rather than choose one over all the others we will attempt to find where the common ground lies, and in later chapters we will explore how several elements of these descriptions can come togerether to provide a more holistic view of how we understand interactive media.

# References

Andersen, P. B., Holmqvist, B. and Jensen, J. F. (Eds.) (1993) *The Computer as Medium.* Cambridge University Press, Cambridge.

Bardzell, J. (2006) Creativity in Amateur Multimedia: Popular Culture, Critical Theory and HCI. *Human Technology*, 3(1), 12–33.

Bolter, J. and Gromala, D. (2003) *Windows and Mirrors: Interaction Design, Digital Art and the Myth of Transparency.* The MIT Press, Cambridge, MA.

Bolter, J. D. and Grusin, R. (1999) *Remediation: Understanding New Media.* The MIT Press, Cambridge, MA.

Burroughs, W. (1968) *The Soft Machine.* Flamingo, London.

Burroughs, W. (1971) *The Wild Boys.* Grove Press, New York.

Genesko, G. (1999) *McLuhan and Baudrillard: The Masters of Implosion.* Routledge, London.

Grau, O. (2003) *Virtual Art: from Illusion to Immersion.* The MIT Press, Cambridge, MA.

Heath, C. and Luff, P. (1996) Convergent Activities: Line Control and Passenger Information on London Underground. In: Y. Engestrom and D. Middleton (Eds.), *Cognition and Communication at Work.* Cambridge University Press, Cambridge, pp. 96–129.

Lister, M., Dovey, J., Giddings, S., Grant, I. and Kelly, K. (2003) *New Media: A Critical Introduction.* Routledge, London.

Lombard, M. and Ditton, T. (1997) At the Heart of it All: The Concept of Presence. *Journal of Computer-Mediated Communication*, 3(2).

Manovich, L. (2001) *The Language of New Media.* The MIT Press, Cambridge, MA.

Mattison, R. S. (2003) *Robert Rauschenberg: Breaking Boundaries.* Yale University Press, New Haven.

McCullough, M. (1996) *Abstracting Craft: The Practiced Digital Hand.* The MIT Press, Cambridge, MA.

McCullough, M. (2001) On Typologies of Situated Interaction. *Human Computer Interaction. Special Issue on Context Aware Computing*, 16(2–4).

McLuhan, M. (1994) *Understanding Media: The Extensions of Man.* Routledge, London.

Norman, D. (1998) *The Psychology of Everyday Things.* The MIT Press, London.

Osborne, P. (Ed.) (2002) *Conceptual Art.* Phaidon, London.

Packer, R. and Jordan, K. (Eds.) (2001) *Multimedia: from Wagner to Virtual Reality.* Norton, New York.

Paul, C. (2003) *Digital Art.* Thames and Hudson, London.

Pritchett, J. (1993) *The Music of John Cage.* Cambridge University Press, Cambridge.

Riva, G., Davide, F. and Ijsselsteijn, W. (Eds.) (2003) *Being There: Concepts, Effects and Measurement of User Presence in Sythetic Environments.* Ios Press, Amsterdam.

Rothko, M. (2004) *The Artist's Reality: Philosophies of Art.* Yale University Press, New Haven.

Schuemie, M. J., VanDerStraaten, P., Krijn, M. and Mast, C. A. P. G. V. D. (2001) Research on Presence in Virtual Reality: A Survey. *CyberPsychology & Behaviour*, 4(2).

Slater, M. (2003) A Note on Presence Terminology. *Presence-Connect*, 3(3).

Waterworth, J. and Waterworth, E. (2003) The Meaning of Presence. *Presence-Connect*, 3(3).

Witmer, B. G. and Singer, M. J. (1998) Measuring Presence in Virtual Environments: A Presence Questionnaire. *Presence: Teleoperators and Virtual Environments*, 7(3), 225–240.

# Chapter 3
# Approaching Interaction

## 3.1 Interactive Media Today

As we have seen, changes in technology have brought computers into the realms of already established media, resulting in new types of interaction. The convergence of digital technologies has brought TV, video, audio, multimedia and computers closer together in the form of new interactive media.

For example, the environments we live in today are becoming increasingly computerized through the placement of embedded media devices such as sensor controlled micro-controllers and 'push' enabled information technologies that are networked together, sometimes locally and sometimes globally. In such cases, interaction takes a leap from the desktop model of personal computers (PC), to a far more complex and contextually defined type of interaction. Here different convergent layers of media are simultaneously engaged with, in three-dimensional space.

In this respect, there is something fundamentally different about understanding interactions with the new interactive media compared to our traditional understanding of interactions with computers. Interactive media are now much more complex and subtle in manifestation than simple desktop delivery through a PC. Interactive media range from websites and interactive DVDs to delivery through sensor controlled interactive spaces and sophisticated networked mobile communications devices e.g., Nintendo Wii. The design of media content has to be considered in relation to the design of platforms and devices, not to mention the contexts of use, and meaning-making circumstances.

Clearly, there is much more going on in the interpretation of an interactive movie than in a traditional movie. Likewise, there must also be more happening in the interaction with such a movie than compared to watching a traditional movie. Interacting with an interactive movie involves some form of continued interpretation, manipulation and formulation of numerous sign systems in relation to the personal, social and cultural backgrounds, which are not always easily articulated from a traditional Human Computer Interaction (HCI) perspective. As we saw in the previous chapter, interactive media require a special contribution in the form of a physical engagement that goes beyond the purely mental event of interpretation.

S.O'Neill, *Interactive Media: The Semiotics of Embodied Interaction*,
doi: 10.1007/978-1-84800-036-0, © Springer Science + Business Media, LLC 2008

What we once understood as distinct entities such as platforms, interfaces and content are now becoming blurred in interactive media design. Interaction designers move seamlessly from the physical prototyping of electronic devices to complex coding and to the creation of interactive video content as well. A range of new skills are now at the fingertips of the next generation of designers and users, whereas once they were the domain of singular specialists such as 'the programmer' or 'the artist'. This is no longer the case. Artists are learning electronics, programmers are learning how to make meaningful images and designers are learning to code. All of them are becoming creative practitioners versed in each other's skills, and all of them are the audience for each other's work. It is those people with this combination of skills that are determining what interactive media is today.

## 3.2   Human Computer Interaction

Traditionally, it is HCI that offers theories in terms of understanding how people interact with computer systems and new technology. Originally conceived as a conjunction between psychology and computer science, over the last 30–40 years, HCI has emerged as its own scientific research domain, which continues to expand its understanding. In this respect, it would be fair to say that the main goal of HCI is to improve the interaction between users and computers by making computer systems more user- friendly, usually by improving the usability of the systems' interface. Specifically, HCI research is concerned with:

- Methods and approaches for designing computer system interfaces.
- Methods and approaches for building and programming computer system interfaces.
- Methods for evaluating and comparing the usability of interfaces.
- Exploring new interaction paradigms as technology evolves.
- Developing predictive models of user interaction.
- Developing descriptive theories of user interactions.

This traditional approach to HCI considers interaction from a largely cognitive psychological, or cognitive science perspective (Card et al. 1983; Dix et al., 1998). For example, cognitive ergonomics views HCI, according to de Hann (2000), as 'a matter of knowledge representation and information processing'. The development of user-centered design methodologies such as ETAG (Extended Task-Action Grammar) based design (de Haan 1994, 1997) and Display-Based HCI (Katajima and Polson 1992, 1995) as formal methods, focus largely on the use of the knowledge to operate computers based on the execution of tasks to achieve goals in an action/ evaluation cycle (Norman 1998). Other standard approaches to HCI evaluation include user observation studies, GOMS (Goals, Operations, Methods, Selection) models and cognitive architectures (Katajima and Polson 1995; Byrne 2003; Kieras 2003).

### 3.2.1 The Conventional View of Perception and Cognition

One logical place to start in terms of understanding the influence of psychology on HCI is to look at how theories of perception and cognition have informed HCI theory from its very beginning.

In general terms, perception is described as the process by which features of our external world are detected by our senses e.g., seeing and hearing, encoded by the brain and integrated into representational information, whether abstract, symbolic or iconic images, and then presented to individual awareness as conscious experience (Rakova 2006). The conventional view of visual perception, for example, is that it involves a forward progression of sense-data from the retina, through the optic nerve and onto various stages of feature detecting brain activity. At each stage the information becomes more abstract and compressed, resulting in an increasingly symbolic representation of the perceived object, which allows us to think about it. See for example Marr (1982).

When we have perceptual experiences e.g., seeing a dog or hearing it bark, we feel as though we are immediately aware of an external reality, which is independent from ourselves e.g., it has spatial extent, it exists beyond our minds and is comprised of many different seemingly individual material aspects. However, our perceptual experiences are not always accurate. Often we can be confused or even tricked into seeing things that are not really there e.g., when a stick looks bent when it is partially submerged in water. Moreover various substances ingested or otherwise, such as drugs or toxins, can alter the way we perceive the world, resulting in hallucinations. These experiences force us to question whether the immediate objects of our perceptions are actually outside or inside our minds.

The leading theory of perception, which is at the root of the cognitive psychological approach to HCI, is Representationalism, which holds that perceptual processes (particularly vision) are computational-inferential processes that deliver representations of distal objects and properties on the basis of proximal (retinal) stimulations. This is essentially based on a Cartesian view of how the mind works. Accordingly, perception is viewed as a process whereby the mind receives sense-data that is then manipulated in our minds to form particular ideas of things in order to think about them. These are thought to be picture-like mental copies of external objects or abstract information about these objects that are separate from the objects themselves. This view renders perception as indirect; i.e., access to the world is access only to one's own representations of it.

In HCI this manifests itself as the principle that all activity engaged in by human beings, whether it is mental or physical activity, is characterized by their cognitive ability to process raw perceptual data in a computational or representational way inside the brain. This information is considered to be the result of stimulation across all five senses (touch, taste, smell, sight and hearing). This is seen as the input to the human information processing system that is manipulated in the brain by a number of discrete stages, resulting in an output, often manifested by some sort of action (Dix et al. 1998).

Essentially then, the cognitive approach to HCI views humans as information processing systems much like computers. They have input and output units (the senses and the limbs), they have a central processing unit (the brain), and they have a memory for storing abstracted pieces of information that can be manipulated inside the central processing unit. This is essentially a 'Representational Theory of Mind' (RTM) which holds that intentional states in the mind (e.g., thoughts, beliefs, etc.) represent the world and can be semantically evaluated, i.e., it is the view that the language of thought (LOT) is the medium of mental representation (Rakova 2006, p. 161). The LOT hypothesis states that mental representation is symbolic and thus discrete or digital because each symbol has specific contents. Interestingly, this is best demonstrated in digital computers where binary data is stored as information that is manipulated by the central processing unit. Thus, the representational success of computers has re-shaped our understanding of the brain.

## 3.2.2 Mental Modeling

A great deal of HCI theory is based on versions of these postulates of how the mind works. Don Norman, for one, has been a great exponent of these ideas and his description of concepts, such as mental modeling, the gulf of evaluation, execution and affordance, are widely accepted within HCI and interaction design in general.

In short, Norman follows the conventional view of perception, which is that cognition, i.e., information processing of a representational nature, has to be involved in perception in order to make sense of things. For Norman, we only fully understand our perceptions of the world by drawing on our memories of previous experiences and the other knowledge (e.g., from family members, teachers, culture, etc.) that we have stored in our minds, as representations. Norman sees this as an integral part of how we continually process 'sense-data' from the real world, placing his theoretical models firmly in the representational camp of how the mind works.

This approach to HCI has helped to derive the notion of conceptual (or mental) modeling as a way of understanding and predicting how users might interact with computer interfaces. Conceptual modeling is essentially about understanding a person's ability to interpret the visible structure and functionality of a device based on previously developed models that have been derived from prior experiences with similar devices (Norman 1998); i.e., the mind builds representational models (mental models) of the world inside the mind and manipulates them accordingly in order to act on the world. These models are stored as knowledge in memory and are called upon whenever a user interacts with a particular device. The idea that people develop a mental model of how to use a particular device, and furthermore, adapt existing conceptual models to similar devices, has provided a basis within HCI to predict human behavior at the interface.

### 3.2.3  The Model Human Processor

The Model Human Processor (Fig. 3.1) is a detailed model of how computer users process information that is intended to help designers predict how users will behave (Card et al. 1983). It is an attempt at modeling the activities in the user's brain and consists of specialized processing units and memories that are characterized by speed, decay time, capacity, and encoding. The principles of the model human processor rely on the idea that users act rationally, most of the time, and that the goals and tasks that they attempt to execute are constrained by their processing limitations.

Perceiving the system and processing the information takes time, depending on the intensity of the stimulus, the information load and how well practiced the user might be. The model human processor, then, identifies where these limitations are and attempts to address them in the design of computer systems, hopefully making them easier to use.

The Model Human Processor and the related GOMS (Goals, Operations, Methods and Selection) were among some of the first models to be used in HCI as methods conceptualizing human computer interaction simply as an extension of human information processing. That is to say, all aspects of computer operation, from the information displayed on a screen to the sensitivity of a keyboard, are considered to be sensory input for humans to process. The clearest manifestation of these ideas on how the mind works have manifested in computer science as explanations of how to build artificially intelligent (AI) machines.

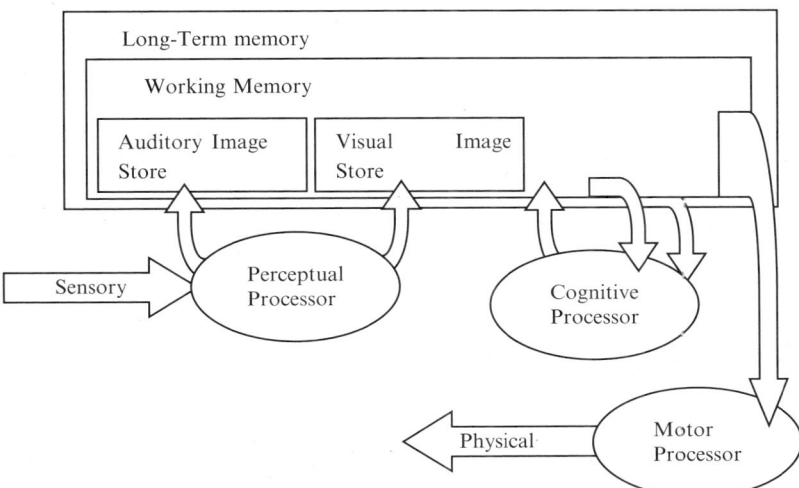

**Fig. 3.1**  The Model Human Processor (After Card et al., 1983, p.24)

### 3.2.4   Execution and Evaluation

Norman's view of interaction also involves what he terms an 'execution/evaluation cycle' (Fig. 3.2), which is an extension of the cognitive model of information processing. Here one step follows another in terms of perceiving a system state, processing the information that represents that state in the mind and then acting accordingly on that information. The sequence of stages continues over and over throughout an interaction until the established goal has been achieved.

While this cycle of events can start from anywhere in the loop, the two most important parts of it are carrying out actions on the world (execution) and comparing what happened with what was expected to happen (evaluation). These give rise to Norman's gulfs of execution and evaluation, where the user has to establish how to translate his/her intentions (in the mind) into actions and then how to understand the effects of those actions on his/her goals. Norman attempts to bridge this gulf by promoting the idea of providing clearer mappings between the user's intentions and the system interface through high visibility and feedback that allow the user to determine whether his/her goals have been satisfied by those actions on the system.

### 3.2.5   The Changing Face of HCI

Until recently, the traditional cognitive approach to HCI has been very successful at improving interface design and system usability. However, a number of criticisms have emerged within the discipline as it evolves to face new challenges. Firstly, approaches based on user observations and on cognitive psychology, while scientifically sound, can take a very long time to develop in relation to system design and evaluation; this is not always cost effective. Secondly, standard approaches, particularly cognitive models, by their very nature require to be constrained to specific aspects of interaction. This limits the re-usability of such

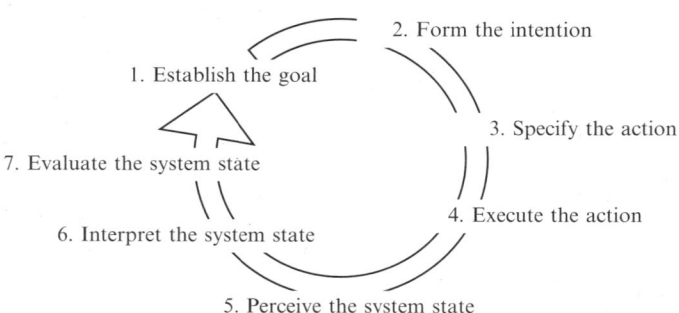

**Fig. 3.2**  Norman's execution/evaluation cycle

methods, where cognitive models have to be built for each interactive situation, before the system can be thoroughly evaluated (Byrne 2003). Thirdly, as technology moves out of the laboratory and further into our homes and everyday lives, HCI models must either become more descriptively detailed or quicker at concentrating on the broad aspects of these new types of interaction (Karat 2003; van der Veer and del Carmen Puerta Melguizo 2003).

To deal with these problems, some researchers have moved to characterize HCI in terms of interactive systems design (Preece et al. 1994, 2002) while others look for alternative positions from which to understand interaction with computers, such as the embodied approach of Dourish (Dourish 2001a, 2001b) or the experiential approach of McCarthy and Wright (McCarthy and Wright 2004).

Indeed, the field of HCI has undergone something of a transformation over the last ten years, in that it has embraced new ideas from an increasingly diverse range of disciplines, such as phenomenology, ethnomethodology, semiotics and social science, in the search for new theories and descriptions of interaction.

Computer supported co-operative work (CSCW), for example, involves social theories of distributed cognition that explore groups of people interacting socially, often across great distances through interactive technology (Dourish 2001). Similarly, ubiquitous computing explores theories that try to understand the convergence of communication and computational technology, which has extended from the work place into our everyday lives (Dourish 2001a, 2001b; Moran and Dourish 2001). Thus, HCI is continually exploring its theoretical position, as highlighted officially in the Association for Computing Machinery (ACM) documents that consider the development of an HCI curriculum (Grover 2001; Hewett et al. 1992).

As advances in technology change the way in which we interact, the demands on the theories that HCI uses to understand interaction increase dramatically. While the traditional HCI approach remains concerned with the discussion of usability issues and system design methodologies, the more critically framed approaches, such as semiotics and media studies, offer broader insights into the transformation that interactive media is having on our production, reception and interpretation activities at a cultural level. However, the cognitive psychology approach to improving usable interfaces remains the mainstay of the HCI theory and while it is perhaps no longer enough in terms of understanding the bigger picture of our relationship with the new media landscape, it continues to have a dominant influence over any other emerging approach. Arguably, this continues to force a compartmentalization of cognitive structures and a distinction between the world of the mind and the world around us.

## 3.3   Phenomenology and HCI

In recent years the phenomenological approach to HCI has emerged as a powerful challenger to the dominance of compartmentalization in cognitive approaches. The philosopher Edmund Husserl developed the concept of phenomenology to describe the contents of consciousness in a manner that did not reduce them to mere scientific data (Moran 2000). For Husserl, an individual's experience is the experience of 'something'. By focusing on the act of 'experiencing' rather than an objective concern about the thing being experienced or the subjective experience of the person who was having the experience, Husserl developed a way of understanding consciousness that is based on theorising the emergence of phenomena that arise from our experience of the world. Essentially, Husserl became interested in a form of idealism, whereby he argued that we can never truly know the world as it is, but only as it appears to us, and that the contents of our mind are in some way related to our experience of the external world. As it developed, Husserl's study moved towards concerns with establishing the 'essential' aspects of consciousness, resulting in what he termed idealistic transcendental phenomenology. While this was a move away from Cartesian dualism it still retained an element of separation of mind and world that was unacceptable to the phenomenologists who came after Husserl.

Both Martin Heidegger and Maurice Merleau-Ponty rejected Husserl's view of the transcendental, favoring an approach that focused on understanding the role of the body and 'being-in-the-world' prior to understanding how the mind worked. For Merleau-Ponty in particular, the role of perception and the relationship between the body and the world was central to his account of how we are able to move around and do things in the world, as well as how we think about the world around us (Dreyfus 1990; Heidegger 1962; Merleau-Ponty 1998; Moran 2000).

### 3.3.1 Being-In-The-World

For Heidegger, consciousness or 'being' is always embedded in our surroundings. That is to say, his fundamental conception of what it is to 'Be' is that human beings exist as 'Being-in-the-world' (the hyphenation represents the closeness of being and world, there are no gaps between the two) (Dreyfus 1990; Mulhall 1996). This is very different from the cognitive view of how we perceive and engage with the world, where the things in our minds and the things in the world are essentially split, following Cartesian dualism.

For Heidegger, the very nature of our being is directly related to the world, that is to say, that our particular type of being would not exist without the world, it would be some other type of being. Moreover, Heidegger makes explicit the idea that the nature of our being-in-the-world is not only related to the world we inhabit, but to the fact that we are aware that we exist in that world. In short, a fundamental aspect of our being-in-the-world is that we are concerned about (aware of) ourselves being-in-the-world.

Furthermore, another aspect of Heidegger's conception of 'Being' is that our being-in-the-world is a being-with-other-beings (beings as people, things or other entities that exist in the world around us). These other beings may or may not have a concern for being with us, but we most definitely have a concern for being-with them as they have an effect on how we exist. Our consciousness and our knowledge of the world are deeply entwined with our phenomenological relationship to it.

For Merlau-Ponty, the thing that entwines our consciousness with the world is having a body that allows us to perceive it. Moreover, the very nature of perceiving is a natural activity that often gets overlooked when we concentrate on trying to understand how the mind works. For Merleau-Ponty, there is no mind without the body, because it is the body that first brings us into contact with the world and allows us to experience the things of the world, without the need for categories or concepts to understand them. The body gives us a prior understanding of the world, through our direct perception of it. This in turn, lets us interact with the stuff of the world without thinking about what we are doing, or calling upon any form of explicit knowledge that we may or may not have stored in our heads. Merleau-Ponty called this tight coupling between the body and the world 'the intentional arc', which tends towards a 'maximum grip' on a situation by maintaining embodied tacit knowledge that is developed in practiced engagement with the world (Dreyfus 1998, 2004).

## 3.3.2   Ready-To-Hand Vs Present-At-Hand

Interestingly, Heidegger essentially posits two different ways of being-in-the-world in relation to the stuff or *equipment*, to use Heidegger's term, that one finds there (physical entities, such as tools and technologies that for our purposes, we shall identify as media); these are ready-to-hand and present-at-hand (Dreyfus 1990; Heidegger 1962).

Heidegger's conception of things as ready-to-hand is based on his fundamental concern with being-in-the-world as an everyday experience. Heidegger claims that our everyday encounters with the phenomena of our world are the 'first' way in which we come to understand them. That is to say, our being-in-the-world and our concern for being-in-the-world are first and foremost 'disclosed' to us through our bodily use of the things that we encounter everyday. In other words, the primary and most revealing way of encountering the equipment of the world around us is through our embodied interaction with the physical matter that constitutes it. Through this process of interaction we develop skillful use of the material of the world and we in turn develop tacit, embodied knowledge or 'know-how' that allows us to cope smoothly with the world around us, enabling our immediate survival.

In addition to this, Heidegger explains the concept of present-at-hand as our ability to reflect upon the phenomena that we encounter and upon our encounters with them. Present-at-hand is an essentially different 'disclosure' of being, whereby we are no longer engaged in using the equipment of the world, but we instead are thinking about it. Our activities are internal and mental rather than physical and active. This type of being-in-the-world provides us with a second kind of knowledge, 'know-that' rather than 'know-how'. The things disclosed to us through thinking about the world around us are experientially different in character from those disclosed to us through acting upon the world directly. Heidegger's famous example of the hammer is best used to explain these ideas.

Heidegger states that a hammer is experienced as ready-to-hand in our everyday experiences when we use it. What is disclosed about it, through our using it, is different from our thinking about it. He explains that while we are using it we are not reflecting on its use, we are doing something different, we are being-with the hammer, doing hammering. Conversely, when the hammer breaks, or no longer functions as we expect it to, our being-with the hammer in 'hammering' changes. We start reflecting on the nature of the hammer and our concern is why it is no longer ready-to-hand. We have moved to a different mode of being, that of the hammer being present-at-hand.

Of course these two modes of being are not mutually exclusive; they are complementary. As Michael Wheeler points out, most expertly, there are not just simply two ways of interacting with the world that surrounds us. These two poles provided by Heidegger, represent the extreme ends of a spectrum of interaction opportunities that blend into one another (Dreyfus 1990; Wheeler 2005). Much of how we really encounter the world around us is experienced to a greater or lesser degree between these to poles, as different degrees of 'smooth (or not so smooth) coping', where we are often shifting quickly from one mode to the other in a very inexpert 'unready-to-hand' way. For a full and thoroughgoing explication of these ideas see Wheeler (2005).

What is perhaps most important about this approach to understanding our relationship to things in the world and interactive technologies in particular is that, while it does not deny that we might have some forms of representational knowledge about the world, it focuses on our connection to the world through our bodies in the first instance, promoting the idea that we are so connected to our surroundings that we need not build mental models of the world around us in order to act, but that we might simply act through a 'direct' relationship to them. This is very different from the original cognitive approach to HCI.

### 3.3.3   Computers and Cognition

In their book "Understanding Computers and Cognition, a New Foundation for Design" (Winograd and Flores 1986) Winograd and Flores put a case together that intricately points out the underlying assumptions of the 'rationalist tradition' in computer science and the effects it has on so-called scientific endeavour as a whole. They then take on a pro-Heideggerian position that is rooted in phenomenology and hermeneutics as the basis of a new computer design paradigm aimed mostly at the AI community. Winograd and Flores claim that the cognitive scientific approach to understanding computers is based on a rational scientific approach that uses experiments to judge between competing hypotheses about cognitive mechanisms (Winograd and Flores 1986, p. 24).

They go on to say, that this approach is based on restrictive, laboratory- controlled empirical data gathering/generating laws that can supposedly be applied to more general cases, but with little reference to real world cases. From this position, they argue that cognitive scientific approaches based on the rationalistic tradition are fundamentally flawed because they are essentially reductionist in character, i.e., they define 'reality' too narrowly, in order to cope with complexity.

Offering an alternative to this situation, they outline four main ideas that are based on Heidegger's 'Being and Time' as a contribution to HCI:

- The assumption of an interpretive or 'hermeneutic' position makes us aware of the impossibility of finding a neutral standpoint from which we can see the world objectively, because we always operate within the framework of our beliefs.
- "Practical understanding is more fundamental than detached theoretical understanding" (Winograd and Flores 1986, p. 32). Our primary understanding of the world is derived from experiencing the world as ready-to-hand. Our ability to reflect on the world that surrounds us comes after our ability to act in it.
- The rejection of the idea that we relate to things, primarily, through having representations of them in our minds. It is possible that our ability to act in the world does not rely on any prior knowledge of the world but simply in our familiarity of being-in-the-world.
- Social activity is the foundation of meaning. There is no individual point of view that can have an interpretation of something that is not linked in someway to social structures. (Winograd and Flores 1986, pp. 32–33)

This type of phenomenological thinking has contributed to what we shall call here "the embodied turn" in the fields of both HCI and cognitive science. Indeed, the embodied turn in cognitive science is having an additional impact on theories of HCI, which we will turn to later (Imaz and Benyon 2007). Suffice to say that this embodied turn in HCI takes the focus away from trying to model complex cognitive processes as the basis of understanding interaction and moves towards reinstating the body as the central site where interaction takes place.

## 3.3.4  Embodiment

The work of Paul Dourish is particularly relevant in relation to the embodied turn in HCI. For instance, Dourish notes that for the phenomenologists, embodiment does not just mean a manifestation of the physical. More importantly, he points out that it means "being grounded in everyday, mundane experience" (Dourish 2001b p. 125), i.e., the being-in-the-world of Heidegger. Secondly, Dourish notes that the phenomenologists tend to focus on the practice of everyday engagement with the world, i.e., on the accomplishment of tasks that shape and are shaped by our existence in the world. Finally, Dourish points out that this situated practical activity in the world is the source of our meaning-making. In other words, our ability to act and be acted upon in our environment is what gives our lives mean-ing. His definition of embodied interaction is then given as "the creation, manipula-tion and sharing of meaning through engaged interaction with artifacts" Dourish 2001b, p. 126).

Taking these ideas further, Dourish goes on to discuss the important aspects of meaning that are central to embodied interaction, i.e., ontology, inter-subjectivity and intentionality.

Dourish explains that ontology (the branch of metaphysics that deals with the nature of being) is about the separation, identification and relation of entities based on the differences and similarities that are disclosed as we experience them. "Ontology deals with how we can describe the furniture of the world" (Dourish 2001b, p. 129). It is essentially about the categorization of phenomena and how we are able to classify our experiences of things in the world.

Inter-subjectivity is about sharing our understanding of the world, which is derived from our ontological relationship to it. The problem of inter-subjectivity is that, while we can each experience the world in an ontological sense, how can we know that each of us is experiencing the same things, given that we do not have direct access to each other's thoughts and experiences? Inter-subjectivity, for Dourish, is about establishing the common ground between people interacting in a shared world, which allows us to align our attempts at categorization of experiences and sense-making in relation to one another.

The third aspect of meaning that Dourish focuses on is 'intentionality'. He suggests that the directedness of intentionality is derived from the relationship between our thoughts, memories and utterances and their meanings. Dourish points out that this is a very tricky subject to understand, which is still at the centre of continuing debates in philosophy and cognitive science. For instance, it is not always clear exactly how words come to have meaning. Do they carry meaning with them because they are causally related to the things they represent, or does their meaning come from the context in which they are used and the cultural situation in which they are interpreted?

Bringing these ideas together, Dourish introduces the notion of coupling. Essentially, Dourish posits that intentionality sets up the relationship between embodied action and meaning (Dourish 2001b, p. 138). Coupling is how this rela-tionship is managed to become effective, i.e., it is the connection between a directed intention, its effect in the world and the people that witness that effect. To para-phrase Heidegger, coupling is the relationship between the intention to hammer a nail into a wall (perhaps to hang a picture on it), the physical entities in the environ-ment (such as the nails and the picture), the mechanisms of knowledge that allow the hammering activity to take place and the cultural significance of hanging pictures for others to see.

All of this offers a great deal in terms of establishing a strong philosophical position in relation to understanding the user and the user's body in terms of interacting with the world. Indeed, as can be seen from Dourish's work and from Winograd and Flores, the embodied perspective is very useful in helping to develop HCI theory that focuses on the physical aspects of interaction. This type of understanding has been particularly effective in helping to understand tangible and ubiquitous computing, where we use our bodies to interact with specially designed physical interfaces that couple together computational power and representational output that responds in a more 'fluid' way to physical input, rather than concentrating on a cognitive approach.

This type of approach also offers a great deal in relation to understanding the same kind of physical aspects of new media and media-rich environments. However, to make this kind of theorization really effective, one would have to develop a phenomenological position that considers a whole range of different media, such as graphics, visual display, film and narrative, in relation to the notions of embodiment and embodied cognition, as well as theories about mediation and communication. Indeed, as we will see in later chapters, understanding the relationship of all of these theories is crucial to the ideas presented here about understanding new media.

## 3.4 Semiotics and HCI

So far we have looked at two different approaches to understanding interaction with computerized media: The cognitive theories from psychology, which tend to understand human beings as information processing units and phenomenological approaches, which turn towards the importance of the body and action without thought. An alternative strand of theory that is particularly relevant to our concerns with new media is that of semiotics, which tries to understand interaction from the perspective of signification and communication.

As the study of sign systems, semiotics has had a major impact on the way we approach the critical theory of most of the major media forms. Derived initially from the structural linguistics of Saussure and the phenomenological pragmatics of Peirce, semiotics has evolved to theorize literature, painting, photography, film, and architecture. Given that new media seems also to encompass many aspects of these art and design forms, it seems entirely appropriate that semiotics should be employed at some level to help in understanding them. Semiotics is such a vast area of study that it is almost impossible to cover all the necessary ground here. Chapter 4 deals with semiotic theory in much greater detail. Suffice to say that here, we will attempt an overview of some important semiotic theory and highlight its place within HCI.

### 3.4.1 Computer Semiotics

Particularly interesting to us is that over the past decade or so, Semiotics has begun to emerge as an interesting area of research in relation to HCI issues. However, only a handful of experts have really made any headway in bringing semiotics to HCI. Among them are Peter Bøgh Andersen's Danish group of semioticians (Andersen

1990, 1993, 1999, 2001) and Clarisse Sickenius de Souza's Semiotic engineering Group (SERG) in Brazil (Barbosa et al. 1999; de Souza 2004; de Souza et al. 2000, 2001; Prates et al. 2000a, b)

Andersen's development of a semiotic approach in "A Theory of Computer Semiotics" (Andersen 1990) comes from a concern within HCI to design systems that successfully support tasks in work environments. As he sees it, the context of the work environment has a direct affect on the language that people use to talk about the tasks that they are performing in that environment. This he sees as an excellent place for semiotics and linguistics to enter the field of HCI, where words/signs are the vehicles that express related concepts, similar to the use of words in language. With this in mind, he develops a tentative method for interface design based on a semiotic analysis of observing language in the work place. This attention to the work environment remains the focus of most of Andersen's work where he concentrates on semiotics as a method of gathering user requirements for building computer systems.

Perhaps the most interesting contribution Andersen has to offer HCI is his taxonomy of computer-based signs and concepts surrounding the process of interaction itself. For example, having established a set of requirements from a work domain, Andersen's idea is to transform the meaning of words into meaningful signs within an interface. What Andersen does that is unique, is to classify these interface signs in terms of their functional features. The resulting taxonomy of computer-based sign types looks something like this:

- **Interactive signs**: Interactive signs are unique to computers. They are distinguished from other signs by permanent features such as shape and size, but the unique features that make them interactive are the handling features that allow for the transformation of other signs within the interface. To this end interactive signs are generally representative of our manipulating activities.
- **Actor Signs**: In effect actor signs are signs that are set in motion by users. They often begin at the start of a program, e.g., when game play is activated, or they sit dormant waiting to be activated by a user. They tend to have an activity or function, which they perform either autonomously or through user interaction. Buttons are a good example of this. They tend to denote a function, performed by the computer, which is related to the task in hand. This is engaged with through the use of an interactive sign as controlled by a user. Actor signs then are generally representative of computer functions and contain permanent and transient characteristics.
- **Controller signs**: Controller signs only change the properties of other signs, not of themselves. They are often invisible in themselves, only making their presence known through the effect they have on other signs, e.g., when the cursor changes, depending on what it is positioned over.
- **Object signs**: Object signs are predominantly the signs which interactive signs are used to alter. They have permanent and transient features but they cannot be handled like interactive signs, e.g., the paper in a drawing program.
- **Layout signs**: Layout signs are signs that set the scene or, as Andersen puts it, 'mere decoration'. They are blessed only with permanent features (Andersen 1990, pp. 199–213).

This taxonomy is generally based on the analysis of computer interfaces that were being devised towards the end of the 1980s and early 1990s. While everything that Andersen outlines in this taxonomy is still relevant today, it is important to point out that new media sign systems are much more complex than they were in the early 90s. Many new sign systems are being assimilated into computerized technology and new media is changing the way in which we use our sign systems in general. Relying on Andersen's taxonomy alone runs the risk of essentially restricting our semiotics of new media to describing the relationships between signs that are specific to an older generation of computer systems. It is essential then, to reconsider the limitations as well as the strengths of Andersen's work in relation to exploring the wider scope of semiotics from numerous other media forms.

Andersen's later work has concentrated on developing his ideas in relation to the computer interfaces used for navigating and maneuvering ships in the maritime domain (Andersen 1999, 2001; Andersen and May 2001). Particularly, May and Andersen focus on the analysis and identification of the necessary constituent parts of tailorable interfaces that can be modified by users as their information requirements alter. This work continues Andersen's interest in using the semiotic analysis of language in work domain situations as the basis for developing signs for computer-based support. Andersen's most recent work has seen him move these interests into the mobile and ubiquitous computing domains. Here he has begun to develop a formal notation for developing 'digital habitats' and complex mediation across multiple systems, which can be used to describe complex activities involving multiple users and information artifacts within digitally enhanced spaces (Andersen 2004; Brynskov and Andersen 2004; Bødker and Andersen 2005).

## 3.4.2   Semiotic Engineering Research Group (Serg)

Like Andersen, SERG have been researching the relationship between semiotics and HCI for a number of years now. Based in Brazil and directed by Clarrise Sieckenius de Souza, they are concerned with the application of semiotic theory to the process of interface design (de Souza et al. 2000, 2001). For the most part, their input seems to be strongly related to usability in terms of the ability of an interface to communicate its functionality by itself.

The main thrust of the SERG approach is the viewpoint that a user interface can be seen as a "One shot message" (Prates et al. 2000a, b) sent from a designer to a user, which can be seen as a representation of the user's needs as defined by the designer. Furthermore, this message contains a number of smaller messages that constitute the functional aspects of the interface, which are delivered and articulated by the signs as the "designer's deputies". These ideas have been developed into what SERG call a "Communicability Evaluation Method" (Barbosa et al. 1999; Prates et al. 2000a, b), which is comprised of three stages.

During the first stage, a set of predefined words or 'Tags' (e.g., error, lost, confused, success) that might describe the situations that they will find themselves in are given to the users, during monitored interaction. Interactions are recorded verbally and through video screen grab techniques, so that actual interface activities can be correlated to the use of the tags. In the second stage the tags are interpreted by mapping them against a set of established evaluation criteria, much as would occur in many usability evaluation techniques. The final stage is where 'semiotic profiling' is completed by comparing the evaluated tags to the signs that exist in the interface. This stage is completed by a semiotics 'expert'.

What SERG have done in developing this approach is to devise a usability evaluation method in line with field observation techniques from HCI, which uses ideas from semiotic theory as a basis. Their notion of the one shot message and their ideas about the relationship between the designer and the user, as mediated by the interface, are all clearly derived from semiotic concepts and echo Barthes' concern with the author and the reader, e.g., the relative opacity of texts. By concentrating on the details of developing a semiotically informed design methodology they have managed to frame the use of semiotics in relation to breakdowns in usability within HCI. This is a useful contribution to the HCI debate as it brings semiotics and HCI closer together, throwing the semiotic spotlight on some crucial HCI issues such as the relationship between the designer, the interface and the user.

### 3.4.3   Current Semiotic Approaches in HCI

Andersen and SERG are not the only experts who look to semiotics as a method for encompassing the diversity of HCI issues. Individuals, such as David Benyon, Mihai Nadin, Frieder Nake and Susanne Grabowski, among others, offer further perspectives on the use of semiotics in HCI. A special edition of the Knowledge Based Systems journal (2001) highlights these approaches, which are summarised below.

Benyon is of the opinion that semiotics has something to say about concepts of navigation in what he terms 'information spaces' (Benyon 1994, 1998, 2000, 2001). Through an understanding of how signs function in environmental contexts, Benyon is able to bring to computing notions of navigation in virtual environments. Indeed, through the common understanding of semiotics, Benyon shows how real environments and virtual environments are fundamentally similar. The notion of the information space is then extended to encompass all human activities that require an understanding of environmental signs.

Nadin is another believer in semiotics' ability to deliver useful concepts to HCI from the multitude of disciplines it touches on (Nadin 1997a, b; 2001). As Nadin says, "One cannot not interact and because interaction is based on signs, one cannot not semiotize." (Nadin 1997a, 2001b). Nadin calls for a radical re-evaluation of HCI in semiotic terms. He points out that semiotics can be used as a unifying foundation in HCI from system design to the usability testing concerns of SERG. He also calls for a fundamental change in academic programs of HCI, which should include semiotics as part of the curriculum in interaction design.

Nake and Grabowski have a fairly technical view of semiotics in relation to HCI. They are concerned with the differences between how humans and computers interpret signs. They point out that human interpretation of signs is based on knowledge and social codes, whereas computer interpretation has to be seen as an act of signal processing dependent on the commands of a computer program. Although similar, these two things are fundamentally different. With this in mind, they argue that a semiotic approach is useful in engaging with this dichotomy because it can take into account the transformation process from sign to signal and back again. Through its notion of sign systems as codes, semiotics levels the field enabling HCI to look at software and its commands in relation to human activities of sign processing (Nake and Grabowski 2001).

The advantage that the inclusion of semiotics in HCI research has brought, is new possibilities of criticism through an overarching discipline already equipped to analyse convergent media, such as TV, cinema, theatre, etc., that HCI has to account for as it addresses interactive media. Andersen describes semiotics as 'the mathematics of the humanities', which provides a language of sign use that allows us to bring insight from older media to descriptions of computerized media (Andersen 2001).

In other words, the semiotics of older media can be employed here to uncover the related concepts that are pertinent to a semiotics of interactive media, in order to cross-fertilize terminology from field to field. This firmly places the study of interactive media within the historical tradition of the arts and media studies, rather than the limited parameters of usability in HCI.

## 3.5  Summary

This chapter has demonstrated that the cognitive, embodied phenomenological and semiotic approaches to understanding H C I offer different things in terms of understanding interactive media.

The cognitive approach offers us a great deal in terms of trying to understand what is going on inside the heads of human users. It gives us tools by which to understand human thought processes and how we might perceive the world. However, it is restricted to treating humans and computers as the same thing in terms of viewing thought as a representational computation process that is at the centre of our interaction with the world. To some extent this is problematic because it tends to exclude the role of the body and the embodied nature of our existence in a world full of mediating things, that we must engage with, often without thinking about them. Moreover, thinking about minds in this way leads to all sorts of impossible situations, such as the problem of computational explosion in performing simple tasks, which have dogged the development of artificial intelligence.

The embodied phenomenological approach does much better at describing the way in which we inhabit our media-saturated environments. The description of using the 'equipment' of our world in a ready-to-hand way gives us a way into theorizing about how we can manipulate the stuff of the world and make it mediate our thoughts, concepts, and ideas for us. The strength of this approach is in ensuring we start with the body and the body's relationship with the stuff of the world as the basis for how we might think. Its weakness is that it does little to explain how we make the transition from acting and doing in the world to thinking, reflecting and imagining about things that may or may not yet exist in the world. The movement from doing to thinking and thinking back to doing is not entirely clear. The one piece missing here is a theory that concentrates on the role of the stuff of the world itself in terms of how it can signify what we mean when we manipulate it.

This of course is the strength of semiotics. Understanding semiotics is about understanding how the material of the world supports and structures the sounds we make, the pictures we draw and the words we write. It is about understanding how we manifest our minds by inscribing them on the world in order to help us think and communicate, as well as how this act of signification can convey meaning for us to interpret.

As old media forms converge and combine with technology to produce interactive media, it is clear that the traditional, cognitively focused HCI approach does not deliver the whole picture of interaction that is needed to fully articulate the transformation in media that is currently taking place.

From the psychological approach, the traditional user/computer or designer/user models are still useful for explaining interactions within clearly defined system parameters, as well as giving us a way to build usable interfaces. However, they do little to explain the growing complexity of simultaneous interactions with convergent media forms, nor do they offer adequate explanations of the changing relationship between author/reader in relation to the production and interpretation of meaning in interactive sign systems and their wider cultural implications.

The phenomenological approach at the centre of the embodied turn within HCI offers far more potential for understanding new media in relation to the body and the body within mediated environments. Of course, there is still a great deal of work to be done here in terms of understanding the body's role in mediation and the relationship between the body, the mind and interactive media. However, it is quite possible that in combination with various other theories, an approach that draws on an understanding of embodiment could help draw together the numerous ideas that surround emerging interactive media.

Semiotics, while having already had a relatively long association with HCI, has not yet been fully explored in relation to the nature of evolving interactive media. Neither has there been a wide ranging survey of semiotic theory in relation to this evolution. Previous semiotic theories of computing (Andersen 1990) are specific to the technology of that decade and draw very little from the broad spectrum of semiotic theories and approaches that are available from other media in various domains. Indeed, it is perhaps the theoretical richness of both phenomenology and semiotics, with regard to 'old media', that could now offer insight into the problem areas of understanding interaction with new media.

As we have seen, interactive media are essentially older forms of media that have been transformed by convergent computerized technologies, blurring the boundaries between designer/user, author/reader and producer/consumer relationships. Interaction with interactive media relies on the interpretation of complex interface/content sign systems as well as the embodied participative manipulation or 'use' of those sign systems that produce transformations in the content in order to complete the experience.

The relationship of the body, media and its interpretation has to be understood if we are to get a handle on interacting with these new types of media. Arguably, a new form of integrated embodied-semiotic theory that is unique to the characteristics of interactive media is required. Thus, the approach that is developed here is derived from phenomenology and semiotics in relation to the particular problem of interpretive interaction and meaning-making with interactive media. However, before this can be explored more deeply, we have to revisit an old problem in HCI to try and prevent us from falling into a familiar trap, the problem of Affordance.

In the next chapter I will explore how arguments in cognitive psychology in particular, coupled with the misunderstanding of complex theories of mind, have led to a very confused picture of what affordance is and how it works. This has had a knock on effect in understanding HCI. In exploring this issue I will attempt to shed new light on this issue and clarify what might be a fruitful way to think about affordance and how that may lead us to a richer explanation of interactive media.

# References

Andersen, P. B. (1990). *A Theory of Computer Semiotics*. Cambridge University Press, Cambridge.

Andersen, P. B. (1993). A Semiotic Approach to Programming. In: P. B. Andersen, B. Holmqvist and J. F. Jensen (Eds.), *The Computer as Medium*. Cambridge University Press, Cambridge, pp. 16–67.

Andersen, P. B. (1999). Dynamic Semiotics and Hydrodynamics. An exercise in applied semiotics. Paper presented at the 7th International congress of the International Association for Semiotic Studies, Dresden.

Andersen, P. B. (2001). What Semiotics Can and Cannot Do for HCI. *Knowledge-Based Systems*, 14 (8), 419–424.

Andersen, P. B. and May, M. (2001). Tearing Up Interfaces. In: K. Liu, R. J. Clarke, P. B. Andersen and R. K. Stamper (Eds.), *Information, Organisation and Technology. Studies in Organisational Semiotics*. Kluwer, Boston, pp. 299–338.

Andersen, P. B. (2004) Habitats: Staging life and art, COSIGN 2004: Computational Semiotics, University of Split, Croatia, 14–16th September. Addenda to A. Clarke (ed): Cosign 2004 Proceedings, Art Academy University of Split: Split.

Barbosa, S. D. J., Prates, R. and deSouza, C. S. (1999). Direct and Indirect User-to-Developer Messages through Communicability Evaluation. Paper presented at the Representational Support for User Developer Communication workshop, INTERACT'99.

Benyon, D. (1994). A Functional Model of Interacting Systems: A Semiotic Approach. In: J. H. Connelly and E. A. Edmonds (Eds.), *CSCW and Artificial Intelligence*. Springer Verlag, London, pp. 105–125.

Benyon, D. (1998). Cognitive Ergonomics as Navigation in Information Space. *Ergonomics*, 41 (2), 153–156.

Benyon, D. (2000). Beyond the Metaphor of Navigation in Information Space. Paper presented at the CHI2000, The Hague.

Benyon, D. (2001). The New HCI? Navigation of Information Space. *Knowledge-Based Systems*, 14 (8), 425–430.

Bødker, S. and Andersen, P.B., (2005) Complex mediation. In Human-Computer Interaction (20)(4), 353–402.

Brynskov, M. and Andersen P.B., (2004) Habitats, Activities and Signs, The 7th International Workshop on organizational Semiotics, OS 2004 19–20th July 2004, Setubal, Portugal.

Byrne, M. D. (2003). Cognitive Architecture. In: J. A. Jacko and A. Sears (Eds.), *The Human-Computer Interaction Handbook, Fundamentals, Evolving Technologies and Emerging Applications.* Erlbaum, Hillside New Jersey, pp. 97–117.

Card, S. K., Moran, P. T. and Newell, A. (1983). *The Psychology of Human Computer Interaction.* Erlbaum, Hillside New Jersey.

de Haan, G. (1994). An ETAG-based Approach to the Design of User-interfaces. Paper presented at Interdisciplinary approaches to System Analysis and Design, Scharding, Austria.

de Haan, G. (1997). How to Cook ETAG and other Related Dishes: Uses of Notational Language for User-Iterface Design. Paper presented at First Interdisciplinary Workshop on Cognitive Modeling and User Interface Development. Vienna, Austria.

de Souza, C. S. (2004). *The Semiotic Engineering of Human-Computer Interaction.* The MIT Press, Cambridge, MA.

de Souza, C. S., Barbosa, S. D. J. and Prates, R. O. (2001). A Semiotic Engineering Approach to User Interface Design. *Knowledge-Based Systems*, 14 (8), 461–465.

de Souza, C. S., Prates, R. and Carey, T. (2000). Missing and Declining Affordances: Are these Appropriate Concepts? *Journal of the Brazilian Computer Society*, 7 (1), 26–34.

Dix, A., Finlay, J. E., Abowed, G. D. and Beale, R. (1998). *Human-Computer Interaction.* Prentice Hall, Harlow.

Dourish, P. (2001a). Seeking a Foundation for Context-Aware Computing. *Human Computer Interaction. Special Issue on Context Aware Computing*, 16 (2–4).

Dourish, P. (2001b). *Where the Action Is: The Foundations of Embodied Interaction.* The MIT Press, Cambridge, MA.

Dreyfus, H. L. (1990). *Being-in-the-world: A commentary on Heidegger's Being and Time, Division 1.* The MIT Press, Cambridge MA.

Dreyfus, H. L. (1998). Intelligence Without Respresentation, from http://www.hfac.uh.edu/cogsci/dreyfus.html

Dreyfus, H. L. (2004). A Phenomenology of Skill Acquisition as the Basis for a Merleau-Pontian Nonrepresentationalist Cognitive Science, from http://ist-socrates.berkeley.edu/~hdreyfus/pdf/MerleauPontySkillCogSci.pdf

Grover, J. (2001, No longer available). Human Computer Interaction (HCI) Report N501. Retrieved 09/12/02, 2002, from http://www.kiva.net/~jgrover/hci/HCIReport4N501.html

Haan, G. de (2000). ETAG: A Formal Model of Competence Knowledge for User Interface Design. PhD thesis, Free University of Amsterdam, The Netherlands.

Heidegger, M. (1962). *Being and Time.* SCM Press, London.

Hewett, Baeker, Card, Carey, Gasen, Mantei, Perlman, Strong and Verplank. (1992, 2002-05-30). ACM SIGCHI Curricula for Human-Computer Interaction. Retrieved 30/05/02, 2002, from http://sigchi.org/cdg/cdg2.html

Imaz, M. and Benyon, D. (2007). *Designing with Blends: Conceptual Foundations of Human-Computer Interaction and Software Engineering.* The MIT Press, Cambridge, MA.

Karat, J. (2003). Beyond Task Completion: Evaluation of Affective Components of Use. In: J. A. Jacko and A. Sears (Eds.), *The Human-Computer Interaction Handbook, Fundamentals, Evolving Technologies and Emerging Applications.* Erlbaum , Hillside New Jersey, pp. 1152–1164.

Kitajima, M. and Polson, P. G. (1992). A Process Model of Display-Based Human Computer Interaction. Paper presented at CHI 1992 Research Symposium.

Kitajima, M. and Polson, P. G. (1995). Measuring the Gulf of Evaluation in Display-Based HCI. Paper presented at CHI 1995.

Kieras, D. (2003) Mental Models, in The Human-Computer Interaction Handbook: Evolving Technologies and Emerging Applications, J.A. Jacko and A Sears (Eds), Lawrence Earlbaum Associates, New Jersey, pp. 1139–1151.

Marr, D. (1982). *Vision*. W. H. Freeman, San Fransisco.

McCarthy, J. and Wright, P. (2004). *Technology as Experience*. The MIT Press, Cambridge, MA.

Merleau-Ponty, M. (1998). *Phenomenology of Perception*. Routledge, London.

Moran, D. (2000). *Introduction to Phenomenology*. Routledge, London.

Moran, T. and Dourish, P. (2001). Introduction. Human Computer Interaction. special issue on Context Aware Computing, 16 (2–4).

Mulhall, S. (1996). *Heidegger and Being and Time*. Routledge, London.

Nadin, M. (1997a). Signs and Systems. In: *Signs and Systems, A semiotic Introduction to systems Design*. Cambridge University Press, Cambridge.

Nadin, M. (1997b). Visible Signs – The language of Multimedia. *In: Signs and Systems, A semiotic Introduction to systems Design*. Cambridge University Press, Cambridge.

Nadin, M. (2001). One Cannot Not Interact. *Knowledge-Based Systems*, 14 ( 8), 437–440.

Nake, F. and Grabowski, S. (2001). Human-Computer Interaction Viewed as Pseudo-Communication. *Knowledge-Based Systems*, 14 (8), 441–447.

Norman, D. (1998). *The Psychology of Everyday Things*. The MIT Press, London.

Prates, R. O., de Souza, C. S. and Barbosa, S. (2000a). A Case Study for Evaluating Interface Design through Communicability. Paper presented at the ACM Designing Interactive Systems, DIS'2000., Brooklyn, NY.

Prates, R. O., de Souza, C. S. and Barbosa, S. (2000b). A Method for Evaluating the Communicability of User Interfaces. *Interactions* (Jan/Feb), 31–38.

Preece, J., Rogers, Y., Sharp, H., Benyon, D., Holland, S. and Carey, T. (1994). *Human-Computer Interaction*. Addison-Wesley, Wokingham.

Preece, J., Rogers, Y. and Sharp, H. (2002). *Interaction Design*. Wiley, New York.

Rakova, M. (2006). *Philosophy of Mind A-Z*. Edinburgh University Press, Edinburgh.

van der Veer, G. C. and del Carmen Puerta Melguizo, M. (2003). Mental Models. In: J. A. Jacko and A. Sears (Eds.), *The Human-Computer Interaction Handbook, Fundamentals, Evolving Technologies and Emerging Applications*. Erlbaum, Hillside New Jersey, pp. 52–80.

Wheeler, M. (2005). *Reconstructing the Cognitive World: The Next Step*. The MIT Press, Cambridge, MA.

Winograd, T. and Flores, F. (1986). *Understanding Computers and Cognition: A New Foundation for Design*. Addison-Wesley Professional,Boston, USA.

# Chapter 4
# Affordance: A Case of Confusion

## 4.1 The Many Faces of Affordance

The concept of Affordance appears a great deal in HCI literature. In general terms it is used to explain aspects of people's relationships with technologies where common sense ergonomic designs and usability are paramount. Technologies that exhibit affordances are generally considered to be more attuned to the everyday concerns of people and therefore easier to use.

However, there is a great deal of debate about the true nature of affordance and throughout its history as a design concept it has been so overused and misappropriated that it is difficult to tell if the term still has any currency in helping us to understand how we relate to interactive media.

Arguably, much of this confusion is derived from Don Norman's appropriation of Gibson's original term. In The Psychology of Everyday Things (Norman 1988, 1998), Norman adopts it to describe how users can easily apprehend what an object is used for by perceiving the properties it exhibits.

"Affordances provide strong clues to the operations of things. Plates are for pushing, knobs are for turning, slots are for inserting things into, balls are for throwing or bouncing. When affordances are taken advantage of, the user knows what to do just by looking, no picture, label or instruction is required." (Norman 1988, p.9).

In a sense these ideas are similar to those outlined by Gibson. However, a significant confusion resides in how each psychologist explained the process of affordance in relation to the process of perception. The best way to understand this problem is to return to Gibson himself.

### 4.1.1 Gibson's Original Concept of Affordance

Gibson's book "The Ecological Approach to Visual Perception" (Gibson 1979) evolved from studies into the perceptual workings of fighter pilots during WWII. Unsatisfied with the conventional theories of perception and studies that failed to predict flight performance, Gibson was forced to consider developing an alternative theory of perception (Oliver 2005).

S.O'Neill, *Interactive Media: The Semiotics of Embodied Interaction*, doi: 10.1007/978-1-84800-036-0, © Springer Science + Business Media, LLC 2003

His "Theory of Ecological Perception" begins by considering the relationship between living entities that perceive things in the world and the environment that surrounds them. For Gibson, this perceptual relationship is irreducible to smaller component parts, "animal and environment make an inseparable pair" (Gibson 1979, p 8). It is for this reason that Gibson proposes the idea that animals can sense things in their environments because their perceptual capacities are directly related to the causal aspects of the physical properties of nature. Some elements of the environment reflect light, while others vibrate and produce sound. Animals have evolved to be sensitive to these physical properties of the environment because they too are physical elements in such environments, embodied entities that are driven by a fundamental need to survive and reproduce. For Gibson, information is simply present in the world around us as the qualities that manifest when certain things act on other things in causally related physicality. This information is apparent in reflected light, vibrations, textures etc. and is readily available to us through perception.

Gibson states that this concept of information is not the same as our usual understanding of it i.e., "[it] is not transmitted, does not consist of signals, and does not entail a sender or receiver" (Gibson 1979, p 63). This differs greatly from other influential and traditionally linear theories of information and communication e.g., Shannon and Weavers model from the 1940s (Shannon and Weaver 1949). Instead, Gibson's idea is that our perceptual capacities are naturally attuned to the surrounding ambient energy that we are continually picking up.

Invariant information picked up in the ambient array of the eye, for example, specifies the persistence of the environment and of oneself, e.g., distant hills and the shape of your own nose as seen looking out from your face. Variant information or disturbances in the array specify the changing properties of the environment and oneself e.g., passing ones hand over ones face. The perceiver is then aware of her own existence in a persistent environment relative to her own and others' movements within that environment. This awareness provides us with information about the possibilities for action that the world around us directly affords.

Affordances, as Gibson originally conceived them are a direct result of the relationship between the objective physical properties of the environment and the subjective experience of the perceiving actor within that environment. They are not just simply the properties of the environment nor are they representations of the environment inside the head of a viewer (Gibson 1971). In a bid to escape the objective/subjective dichotomy, Gibson characterizes affordances as being both objective and subjective at the same time. This is a novel approach to understanding how we relate to the world in a perceptual sense.

As he expounds this notion of affordance, Gibson repeatedly attacks the idea that mental activity is a necessary aspect of perception. He whole-heartedly rejects the idea of abstract representational information processing in the mind as too complex to be a satisfactory explanation of perception. Instead he proposes a more direct perception of the world, through information pick-up in our perceptual arrays.

Affordances then, as Gibson originally envisaged them, have nothing to do with cognitive modeling or thinking. They are an emergent property of the physical relationship between environments and the direct perceptual acts of embodied beings. For example, babies respond to face-like stimuli within hours post-birth and are aware of the 'danger' in visual cliff experiments (Johnson 2001; Le Grand et al. 2001).

### 4.1.2 Norman's Concept of Affordance

Norman, an ex-student of Gibson's, disagreed with him quite strongly about how we perceive the world around us. Following the conventional view of perception, Norman could not accept Gibson's adherence to 'direct perception' and concluded that Gibson's view must, at least in part, be flawed.

As a result Norman's views about affordances are radically different from Gibson's. Rather than trying to elucidate Gibson's ideas of how an affordance can be both objective and subjective at the same time, Norman shifts the emphasis towards the perceptual acts of the individual and thus the subjective side of the problem. Norman separates 'real' affordances (the physical properties of the world) from 'perceived' affordances (subjective representations in the mind), and is more concerned with the perceptual properties of affordances rather than the actual properties of the objects themselves (Norman 2004a,b). This change is completely at odds with Gibson's original idea. When followed to its logical conclusion this position results in the exclusion of the actual properties of real objects from perception leaving us only with sense data and representations of things in our minds, rather than direct perception.

"The notion of affordance and the insight it provides originated with J. J. Gibson, A psychologist interested in how people see the world. I believe that affordances result from the mental interpretation of things, based on our past knowledge and experience applied to our perception of things about us. My view is somewhat in conflict with the views of many Gibsonian psychologists." (Norman 1988, p. 219).

The strength of Norman's version of how perception and affordance work is that it attempts to solve the problem of how to explain the role of knowledge in understanding the world around us. However, the problem with Norman's version of affordance is that it abandons the unique contribution of Gibson's ideas in bridging the gap between the object and the subject.

Rex Hartson, a champion of Norman's position, also approaches affordance within the context of HCI (Hartson 2003). Aiming to clarify the concept, Hartson outlines the difference between Gibson and Norman on the basis of a distinction between real affordances and perceived affordances. This is a distinction introduced by Norman in order to differentiate Gibson's concerns with describing the ecological environment from the perception of the physical properties of that environment. The problem with this of course is that this distinction is made on the basis of a misunderstanding of Gibson's theory of affordance. For Gibson there is no separation from the environment and the perceiving animal. Both Norman and Hartson make the mistake of equating real affordances with the physical properties of the world and fail to engage with Gibson's notion of affordance that includes the perception of those physical properties in order to disclose them. This misunderstanding is the result of Norman's disagreement with Gibson on how perception works; i.e., it is the direct result of Norman favoring a cognitive representational model of perception over the direct perception theory proposed by Gibson.

In an attempt to clarify how affordance could be used in HCI Hartson outlines 4 different types of affordance: perceptual affordance (a term he introduces himself) real affordance (meaning the physical properties of the world) cognitive affordance (Norman's perceived affordance) and functional affordance. While this is a well developed idea, the problem still remains that what is being described ignores a great deal of the context in which the theory of affordances originated i.e., as part of Gibson's radically new ecological theory of perception that opposed cognitive/representational models of perceptual processes.

### 4.1.3  Affordance in Technology Design

Bill Gaver (a former student of Norman) returns to Gibson's ideas and attempts to extend them in relation to designing technological affordances (Gaver 1991). He starts by describing the traditional cognitive representational approach to understanding perception and then distances himself from it by re-examining Gibson's ecological approach. For Gaver, the conventional approach can 'often seem baroque and overly complicated', whereas Gibson's ideas about affordance can be best used to explain simpler physical interactions. Arguably however, Gaver's view of affordances doesn't go far enough in terms of drawing a line between Norman's cognitive view and that of Gibson's.

Like Norman, Gaver takes Gibson's notion of affordances to be something 'independent of perception'. He gives, among others, the example of a glass of water, which for him, affords drinking whether he is thirsty or not. Similarly he discusses the notion of a pit affording 'falling' whether or not it is visible (Gaver 1991, p80). In such a way Gaver outlines the properties of certain physical objects in the world that contribute to the possibilities of affordance, which is in keeping with his claim that affordances are independent of perceptions.

However, it can be argued that a description of the properties alone is not enough to make them an affordance. A description of properties is an objective description of the world of things and unfortunately, as we have already seen, this goes against Gibson's original idea that an affordance cuts across the subjective/objective divide.

Gaver goes on to clarify his version of affordance by distinguishing between affordances themselves (i.e., the properties of things) and information about them (i.e., what we perceive). Gaver does this in order to show how we can be mistaken about affordances, claiming that if there is no information available for an affordance then it is hidden and that if information suggests a nonexistent affordance, a false affordance exists.

This is an interesting strategy that aims to solve the problem of how we can mistakenly interact with things or get things wrong when doing things in the world.

Arguably however, in separating perceptual information from the properties of things Gaver has already abandoned Gibson's original conception of affordance entirely. In doing so, what Gaver describes is not an affordance at all. It is something quite different.

In the first instance, where there is no information available for an existing affordance, Gaver attempts to describe a situation where a perceiver has not been able to pick-up information about the existing properties of an object. However, in such a case an affordance simply has not occurred because affordances are dependent on information pick-up. If there is no information about the properties of the environment, then there is no possibility of experiencing an affordance. Gibson states quite clearly that in this respect affordances either exist or do not exist; they are in effect binary. Gaver's description is not of a hidden affordance but of objects that have the potential to afford, which have not yet been perceived. To use his own example, a glass of water does not afford drinking until I am thirsty. It also does not afford putting out a fire until such time as there is a fire needing to be put out. These qualities will only be revealed to perception within a particular situation and should not be confused with having knowledge about the thirst quenching or fire extinguishing properties of water, which, according to Gibson, is not a matter for perception.

In the second instance Gaver describes how it is possible to pick–up information from the environment that makes us believe that something is there when it is not i.e., have a false affordance. Arguably, in such a case what Gaver is describing is again not an affordance as such, it is a particular form of perceptual anomaly such as an illusion or hallucination. Likewise, Gibson's original concept of affordance is open to criticism on this count, as direct perception comes under pressure if we agree that we can misperceive things. This opens the door to theories that rely on sense data and representationalism but as we shall see later, it is possible to counter this criticism. Suffice to say here that Gaver again misconstrues Gibson's original conception of what actually constitutes true affordance and leads us into confusion over the role of perception in making affordances possible.

This situation undoubtedly arises not from Gaver's lack of understanding Gibson, but from the confusion that Gibson creates in his own writing. On the one hand, Gibson clearly states that an affordance is a special kind of phenomenon encountered in perception that is both objective and subjective, but on the other, at various points in his work, he attempts to categorize different types of affordance. Unfortunately, this act of categorization takes the form of descriptions of environmental features and properties over descriptions of subjective experiences. As a result, they can be viewed as descriptions that are independent of perception. However, it is important to state that it was not Gibson's intention to describe only these features. One must bear in mind that Gibson is breaking new ground here and that his descriptions are a first attempt (albeit not a very clear one) at trying to explain how affordances are both objective and subjective.

It becomes important then, when drawing a clear distinction between Norman and Gibson, to be extra careful about how we conceive of affordances. It is particularly important to understand that Gibson is attempting to describe an affordance as an emergent property of the perceptual process consisting of the properties of the object itself and the perceptual capacities of the perceiver.

Gaver's paper provides some good insights into how affordance works and how the concept should be taken into consideration when designing technological elements such as computer interfaces. However, his particular reading of Gibson leads us to a situation where certain kinds of perceptual experiences and acts of signification or mediation are treated as affordances when, strictly speaking, they are not. Moreover, by claiming that affordances are independent of perception he moves closer to Norman's view rather than to that of Gibson's. This unfortunately contributes to a further confusion over the use of the term.

### 4.1.4   Clarification Or Further Confusion?

Similarly bewildered by the range of explanations of affordance and their use in HCI, McGrenere and Ho also produced a paper that attempts to clarify the concept and develop it in relation to software design (McGrenere and Ho 2000). However, in their attempts to elucidate the concept, they fail to appreciate the radical nature of Gibson's ecological theory, springing the same traps as Norman and Gaver. They start, as many others have done, by separating affordance from perception:

"Gibson intended an affordance to mean an action possibility available in the environment to an individual, independent of the individual's ability to perceive it" (McGrenere and Ho 2000 p. 179).

Let us consider this statement in relation to Gibson's original notions of direct perception and affordance. According to McGrenere and Ho, if affordances exist independently of a person's ability to perceive them then, regardless of an individual's perceptual abilities, they should somehow be available to everyone. But how can this be so?

Take my study for example, the room where I work, write and keep books. Of course you, the reader, are not here and the affordances present to me in my study are not perceptually available to you, but we can agree that the study still exists. This is a simple realist law that states that the world exists beyond our ability to perceive it. However, this is not the same as saying that affordances exist independently from our ability to perceive them.

For instance, a sightless person has no perceptual capacity to pick up information from the light present in the environment. If I were suddenly blinded momentarily, navigation and locomotion within my study would become difficult for me. What my study affords me in terms of positive action possibilities become negative action possibilities that might cause injury. Without being able to see, I would have to resort to sensing the environment through touching it. What the environment affords to these two versions of me is totally different depending on my perceptual ability.

If I should suddenly have no perceptual capacity at all, I wouldn't know that there was a world out there, even although it might still act upon me. Not being able to perceive it means that it is effectively not available. The information normally picked up through direct perception is not there to specify an affordance thus the affordance does not exist, even if we agree that a world does exist beyond our ability to perceive it. McGrenere and Ho miss the subtlety of Gibson's ideas by failing to realize that it is perception alone that makes anything in a given environment available to be acted upon in the first place. Perception is central to affordance.

From a realist perspective the properties of the environment exist independent of the perceiver but Gibson is quite clear that an affordance is both objective and subjective. An affordance must be considered as the relationship between the information available to the ambient array of a perceiver that specifies the properties of the environment and the self-awareness of that perceiver which contributes to the perceptual process. It is therefore quite a similar idea to Heidegger's 'being-in-the world' but couched in the language of perception. We shall return to this idea in later chapters.

Further confusion arises in McGrenere and Ho's attempt at clarification when they insist that:

"An affordance does not change as the needs and goals of the actor change" (McGrenere and Ho 2000, p. 179)

Given Gibson's insistence on the central relationship between an environment and a perceiver, this statement cannot be correct. An affordance must change as the needs and goals of a perceiver change because these changes in the perceiver affect how they perceive the environment. For example, a man foraging in a forest carrying a stick uses his stick to steady his steps as he walks. The stick affords support to the man as he is walking. However, if the man, driven by hunger, comes across some tasty looking apples high in a tree above him, the stick might be used to perform a different task i.e., to knock the apples out of the tree. The stick affords knocking, hitting and reaching rather than supporting. The properties of the stick have not changed but what the stick affords to the wielder has changed dramatically due to the goals and needs of the perceiver. The perceptual process is frequently evolving and changing, while the properties of an object e.g., a stick might exhibit invariant repertoires of behavior, this only means that it appears to the perceiver in a consistent and unchanging fashion. The invariant information provided by the persistent object thus provides the possibility of affording something to the perceiver. What that affordance is only emerges, as the object is perceived in relation to the goals and needs of a perceiver at any given time.

McGrenere and Ho do acknowledge that Gibson's notion of affordance cuts across the subjective/objective divide and they do understand that this is possible because we perceive things directly rather than interpret them. However, they also state that:

"Direct perception is possible when there is an affordance and there is information in the environment that uniquely specifies that affordance." (McGrenere and Ho, 2000, p.180).

Unfortunately, this statement seems to be the wrong way round. For Gibson, direct perception does not depend on the existence of affordances. Direct perception is what perceiving beings do naturally all the time. It is the process by which they encounter the mediums, surfaces and objects of the world. Through the process of direct perception information is constantly being picked up, sometimes that information is variant i.e., it keeps changing and at other times it is invariant. Invariant information provides a persistent source of unchanging information about the world to the perceiver. It is when this kind of information is present during perception that the affordance provided by the environment can be perceived by the perceiver in relation to its own current state of being. This is a very important distinction to get right.

Furthermore, McGrenere and Ho contradict themselves when attending to the differences between Gibson's and Norman's ideas. McGrenere and Ho state that the problem with Gibson's notion of perception is that it may be culturally and experientially dependant; i.e., to some degree learned or culturally determined. Logically this would mean that we would not be able to see until we were taught to see or unless we had some a priori knowledge about 'how to see' given to us, before we are able to engage our perceptual capacities. While it is possible to argue that we might be taught culturally to interpret our perceptions or how to see in different ways from a cultural perspective, it does not follow that culture affects the mechanics of the perceptual process at the level of information pick-up. Indeed this idea would go directly against Gibson's original ideas, because it would require the inclusion of some level of information processing to take place during pick-up. Healthy babies see the moment they open their eyes, they may not be able to clearly distinguish shapes or identify objects but they are not blind. More likely McGrenere and Ho mean that our perceptions are interpreted in relation to our past experiences and cultural knowledge, which unfortunately is exactly what Norman claims but Gibson denies. Thus they do not clearly differentiate between the two opposing theories of affordance.

### 4.1.5  Affordance in Information Systems

Ron Stamper is a founding member of the organizational semiotics community that works towards trying to understand how organizations use information, how they communicate and where automation can occur. Stamper has also drawn heavily on Gibson's notion of affordance to develop his theories (Stamper 2007, Forthcoming). As Stamper understands it, affordance occurs when animals construct their own models of reality by encountering the invariant repertoires of behavior in the environment in relation to their own perceptual capacities.

While Stamper does grasp exactly what Gibson means by affordance in relation to the combination of animal and environment, unfortunately he jumps too quickly to the idea of constructing mental models of reality. Gibson never denied that cognition might involve mental modeling of some representational kind. However, he did explicitly state that this form of mental modeling does not take place in the activity of perceiving the world. For Gibson the world is perceived directly and affordance is what is derived through this direct information pick-up from the environment. There is no processing of the data at the time of pick up or at the time of acting on the affordance. There might be processing and modeling afterwards, in order to consciously think about some aspect of the world, or to store and retrieve knowledge about the world but that is after the act of perception and not a part of it.

Stamper then moves from this modeling assumption of affordance to the cultural and social norms that determine what behavior the social world affords us claiming that the concept of affordance can be unified with his own concept of 'norms' (Stamper 2007, p. 4).

Attempting to understand how groups of individuals manage to inter-subjectively organize themselves, Stamper's concept of 'norms' is derived from the idea that, an organization is dependent on people sharing certain rules or conventions (norms) that govern their beliefs, values, perceptions and behaviors. These norms then are unconditional attitudes that people adopt as part of their cultural environment allowing them to agree with, disagree with, consent to, decent, support or subvert the laws of their social conventions. Stamper is also careful not to confuse the social norms that exist in people's heads with the rules or laws that exist in written form, which are the signs that represent those norms in a manifest physical sense.

Stamper's description of 'norms', not withstanding, his explanation of how these social norms can be considered to be the same as Gibson's notion of affordance is not fully explained. Indeed, it appears that norms are given a kind of special status as a social affordance, but this does not ring true with Gibson's original conception of affordance.

Stamper seems to agree that an affordance is derived from something in our environment exhibiting an 'invariant repertoire of behavior', that is, it is something which is perceptually available to us. The key pay off in Gibson's terms is that, this allows us to engage with (be aware of) our environment without having to consciously attend to it; i.e., we do not have to think about it in order to perceive it or act in it. It doesn't have to be modeled representationally in the mind, because as Gibson frequently states, information does not have to be stored in memory because it is always available in the environment (Gibson 1979, p. 250).

Confusion arises in Stamper's claim that norms and conventionally accepted rules, which are essentially social constructs regardless of whether they are written down or are in people's heads, provide affordances in the same way i.e., allow us access to our surrounding environment without recourse to mental modeling. This claim is undoubtedly unfounded. Indeed, norms, rules, conventions or whatever you want to call them may exhibit some form of 'invariant repertoire of behavior', but not in the same sense, as Gibson's understanding of directly perceiving reality. Any rule written down or otherwise must be interpreted to establish its meaning, and any rule is derived from a social process of argument and debate where agreement on its operation has to be negotiated. Therefore mental representation and computation has to be performed on the information in the mind in order to understand it. This is essentially representational cognition or thinking, which is in stark contrast to Gibson's ideas about directly perceiving the affordances of an environment.

Stamper has subsumed the affordance idea in a metaphorical sense to show how rules and regulations are instantiated and maintained within in organized groups of individuals. The idea that they exhibit invariant repertoires of behavior is true only in a conceptual sense, in that, once they are agreed upon, they tend to be maintained to ensure that order and organization can occur. However, this is not the same sense that Gibson attributed to the phrase, where he clearly differentiates between perception and conception, affordance being part of perception and not conception. Unfortunately Stamper does not make a clear case for social norms as affordances and in attempting to equate the two he misses the complexity of the situation.

## 4.2   Re-Evaluating Gibson's Original Concept of Affordance

Clearly affordance is an incredibly contested idea, one that has proved to be very influential in design and HCI circles. However, the great problem with the theory of affordance is that it is not an exportable commodity that can be recontextualised within design frameworks or theories of perception that do not include Gibson's ecological approach and his defense of direct perception. The theory of affordances, invariants and information pick up are all carefully interlinked in Gibson's original theory to give us an understanding of how we interact with the world around us through our perceptual capacities and movement capabilities. This is a very powerful and important theory that should be considered in its entirety rather than plundered for useful bits to be employed in other explanations that are not theoretically compatible. As the analysis of the various versions of affordance elucidates, none of them really manage to clearly identify Gibson's original formulation of the idea or to understand the implications of the philosophical underpinnings of Gibson's ideas. They all attempt, as Norman did, to appropriate the term for their own uses, which only adds to the confusion. This results in what appears to be, at best, a meaningless term and, at worst, a collection of incompatible ideas and flawed understanding.

The only true version of affordance that really matters is that proposed by Gibson. All other versions, appropriations or evolutions of this concept must keep his version intact, including his theory of information pick-up and direct perception. None of the theories critiqued manage to do that. However, many of the theories outlined above are genuine attempts to improve on Gibson's ideas, which in themselves are lacking in many quarters. Indeed, while Gibson's theory of affordance is the true original it does have some very specific problems and weaknesses of its own, which do need to be addressed in order to make it robust. But the fact remains that in order to improve on Gibson's ideas one needs to retain the essence of his theory and improve on it in such a way as to make the theory stronger and clearer, and not more confusing.

In terms of helping us understand interactive media, Gibson's theories still promise us a certain amount of leverage, particularly in relation to understanding how we physically interact with our environment. Therefore, adopting his theory as part of our understanding of interactive media would require some improvements that retain his initial concepts and help to combat his detractors.

As Martin Oliver points out (Oliver 2005), while this is straightforward in most cases, a number of problems arise from further exploration of Gibson's views.

The first weakness in Gibson's theory is that of misperception (e.g., hallucinations), which are the fault of the perceiver, and not a direct result of the physical properties of the world. The argument against Gibson's theory of direct perception is that it does not explain how mistakes or false perceptions can occur. The second weakness in Gibson's theory is that he maintains that directly perceived experiental information is different from mediated information. While this is entirely plausible Gibson unfortunately gives an inadequate account of what part affordance plays in providing for this difference. In relation to our understanding of interactive media, it is of key importance to clarify this point. Finally the third weakness in Gibson's theories is related to issues of learning and knowledge acquisition. While attempting to show how his idea of 'information' is different from traditional ideas about knowledge he continually returns to the idea of learning. If affordances have to be learnt, as he continually states, how is this possible without recourse to the mind? Again Gibson unfortunately fails to explain how this is possible without recourse to mental information processing. In order to save Gibson's theory of affordance and strengthen his ecological approach to perception, these three problem areas need to be addressed. While there is little room here to develop a full blown defense of Gibson's ideas, it is still possible to outline a preliminary defense and rally support from other theories that are compatible with his ideas. In such a way, Gibson's original ideas are maintained and his theory becomes more useful for our own purposes of understanding interactive media.

## 4.2.1 Saving Gibson from 'The Argument from Illusion'

Essentially, the criticism of a lack of explanation regarding misperception can be countered at a philosophical level because the argument leveled at Gibson is essentially a version of 'the argument from illusion' that appears regularly in the philosophy of mind. Gibson's adherence to the view that we perceive things directly is for all intents and purposes a version of direct realism. Direct Realists hold that perception is an immediate or direct awareness of mind-independent physical objects or events in the external world. This should not be confused with Naïve Realism, which holds that perceived objects or events always appear exactly as they are. In Direct Realism objects or events do not have to appear exactly as they are, they can appear to be different from what they are and still be apprehended in a direct and immediate manner. As a result they deny the existence of any form of representationalism during perception (Le Morvan 2004).

The argument from illusion runs something like this: Suppose we perceive a straight stick half submerged in water. As we perceive the stick, we are immediately aware that it appears bent where it enters the water. The bent stick cannot be identical to the straight stick because it appears to be different. Therefore Direct Realism must be false.

However, Direct Realists can explain why the stick may appear bent by appealing to physical considerations, e.g., a straight stick submerged in water may look bent because an intervening medium for one part of the stick (water) interacts with light photons differently than an intervening medium for the other part of the stick (air).

Indeed, Gibson himself was very aware of this argument and countered it with his own theory (Gibson 1966). Given the same premises for the argument, Gibson's way round this problem was to identify an experimental solution to the problem of illusion by examining the optical information available for the same stick as it is rotated in water:

"When a straight stick–in-water is rotated around its longitudinal axis the *perspectives of its edges remain unaltered.* The lines corresponding to its edges are bent to be sure, but they are unaltered by rotation and this invariant independently specifies a straight stick as against a bent stick" (Gibson 1966).

In other words a genuinely bent stick would appear to move quite differently as it was rotated around its longitudinal axis compared to a straight stick, e.g., the end of the bent section of the stick would cut a greater arc than the straight section. As this does not occur although the water appears to make it look bent, the stick must in fact be straight. Thus, the charge leveled at direct perception, that it cannot explain optical illusions, is easily countered.

More difficult though, is the related problem of countering the "argument from hallucination", which Le Morvan outlines as something like this (Le Morvan 2004): Consider the proverbial drunk who "sees' pink rats. Surely the drunk is immediately aware of something. However, no physical pink rats are present. Since the drunk is immediately aware of something but nothing physical is present then the thing that he is aware of must be something other than an external physical object. However, there is no significant, qualitative difference between the objects of awareness in cases of hallucination and in cases of accurate perception; for instance the pink rat appearing to the drunk may be phenomenally indistinguishable from a real rat painted pink. Then we have reason to suppose that, the objects of immediate awareness in accurate perception are also not external objects. Thus, Direct Realism is shown to be false. The objects of immediate awareness in hallucination and in accurate perception are something other than external physical objects i.e., representational in character.

However, this argument can be countered by conceding that (1) the drunk is immediately aware of something, and that (2) no physical pink rats appear to the drunk. But from (1) and (2), we need not conclude that (3) sense-data are the objects of immediate awareness in the case of hallucinations. For (3) neither follows deductively from (1) and (2), nor is it the only viable explanation of (1) and (2). For example, we can account for (1) and (2) in at least three other ways. One account takes the objects of awareness in cases of hallucination to be mental images (possibly representational and weak). A second account takes 'states of the brain' to be the objects of immediate awareness in cases of hallucination (chemical imbalances may affect how we perceive things). And a third account takes physical space occupants to be the objects of immediate awareness. For example, when air, clouds, light etc. appear to the percipient to be radically different from how they normally are (appearing to have properties they do not have) in the form of extreme illusions. Thus the argument can be moved from one of hallucination to one of illusion, which has already been countered, resulting in a more satisfying outcome in terms of defending direct realism, and Gibson's theory of direct perception.

### 4.2.2 Distinguishing between Direct and Mediated Perception

Strengthening this aspect of Gibson's theory is not simply a matter of establishing a direct defense on a philosophical level. It is more a matter of elaborating his ideas and establishing the role that affordance plays in both forms of perception. To this end we must recap that affordances occur in terms of the relationship between the properties of elements of the environment and the active perceiver of those environmental elements. In Gibson's view of perception, an active perceiver picks up and distinguishes between variant and invariant information. Either of these may be information about the perceiver or the environment but the distinction between the variant and invariant builds to create an awareness of the perceiver's place within that environment.

One key aspect of how the difference between what Gibson calls direct perception and mediated perception emerges in his description of the transformational capacities of individuals to inscribe the environment they inhabit. Gibson calls this 'The fundamental graphic act' [i.e., the act] of making marks on a surface that record the progression of the mark making movement (Gibson 1979, p 275). Gibson explains that seeing a progressive record of movement is lasting but he gives no real indication of how this is so. In fact, Gibson simply overlooks the need for such an explanation, as it seems to be obvious in that it follows from his theory of direct perception that this would be so. Here we shall elucidate this more clearly.

Let's say that when someone is scribbling, doodling or drawing in sand, earth clay or even on paper, that person is engaged in directly perceiving the properties of the environment that surrounds them, in this case the surface being inscribed. The properties of this surface are such that they afford inscribing, i.e., they are touchable, malleable or transformable. This is evident because once touched, the substance (or medium) retains the marks that are left in it. In other words the surface being inscribed exhibits an invariant repertoire of behavior that responds to being touched. Marks made on such a surface become persistent and available to direct perception. Through doodling and so on, the doodler, a child or prehistoric cave dweller as Gibson describes (Gibson 1965; 1969), establishes that certain materials afford certain kinds of transformation for mark holding. It is this fundamental property of direct perception of materials that is the beginning of mediation. Gibson provides the example of a clay surface that may be molded or shaped into various representations of a cow. e.g., it might take on the three dimensional form of a cow, it might be used as a surface for painting the likeness of a cow or it might equally be used as a surface in which to engrave symbols, such as letters of cuneiforms, that represent a cow. In each case what Gibson describes is the process of mediation, where knowledge of some form or another (in this case cows) is embedded into a medium in the form of signs that represent that knowledge, allowing us to experience something about cows in an indirect or second hand way (Gibson, 1979, p. 42).

For Gibson, first hand perception is that which comes from environmental sources, whereas second hand perception is that which comes indirectly through mediation. The clay is perceived naturally as clay but when a cow is perceived, the form taken by the clay is representing a cow. It hasn't become a cow, it has simply taken on the form of what looks like a cow and thus signifies a cow. This is essentially semiotic in character.

What is not clear here is how Gibson resolves this switch from one mode of seeing to another. He elucidates by suggesting that there are two different attitudes at work, the 'naïve' attitude and the 'pictorial' attitude (Gibson 1969). From the naïve attitude a perceiver is more concerned with paying attention to the medium itself i.e., the techniques and qualities that have been applied to the surface or clay in terms of its inscription. From the pictorial attitude the perceiver's focus of attention is on the information presented as content in the medium not on the medium itself. Unfortunately 'content' implies some form of cognition but we shall turn to this in the next session. Suffice to say here that for Gibson, these two modes of seeing are not to be thought of as mutually exclusive. Indeed, Gibson insists that we switch between the two constantly as we perceive our environment.

The key thing to establish here is that, for Gibson, mediated perception is not in any way different from direct perception in kind. In fact, mediated perception is entirely dependant on direct perception because without being able to directly perceive the affordances of mediating materials in the first place, surfaces would not be inscribed and mediation would not take place. The role of direct perception is in specifying information that conveys the invariants of mutable substances as affordances for manipulation and trace making. Thus we are able to mark our environment by drawing, painting or writing with various materials. Aspects of cognition may yet play a role in determining what it is that we are attempting to convey as we intentionally give form to our words or scribbles. As a result, the materials transformed by our inscriptions signify our intended expressions, thoughts and ideas by holding them as invariants that are perceptually persistent to others. Thus materials that mediate, allow us to communicate with one another. In the next chapter I will go on to argue that the study of this kind of communication is best understood by revisiting semiotic theory, some of which we have already encountered.

### 4.2.3   Providing an Adequate Theory of Knowledge as Skill Acquisition

Gibson identifies a problematic situation in the conventional view that perceptual and conceptual knowledge are generally considered as two entirely different types of knowledge. In developing his theory of perception, Gibson holds that this situation must be reconsidered as his new theory of perception has a knock on effect on that of conception. More importantly Gibson rejects this idea of perception and conception being 'different in kind' and states that they are both related to the perceptual process but occur in slightly different ways. However he offers little in terms of outlining what these differences are (Gibson 1974).

In developing his ecological theory of perception he returns to this problem and outlines how a child learns about the world through direct experiences of perception such as looking around, listening, touching and tasting. He moves on to explain how a child is then presented with mediated knowledge that facilitates learning; e.g., books, pictures, models etc. that provide learning at second hand. Encountering this kind of represented knowledge provides the child with valuable information about things without having to experience them directly. Gibson is careful to outline that this makes learning easier for the child but that these mediating elements are not knowledge in themselves, only aids to facilitate knowing. This then begs the question: how do these mediating elements facilitate knowing? The answer seems to lie in that they provide elements by which to practice perceiving.

Mediating elements such as books or pictures allow us to communicate knowledge to one another without having to extract information directly from the stimulus flux itself. We learn from the experience of others, who have formed representations of perceptual invariants as signs that we can perceive in a more controlled and clearer fashion.

Gibson intimates that as a child develops, exposure to these forms of mediated knowledge help both their verbal and visual systems to develop, honing and tuning their perceptual capacities. Eventually the perceptual systems begin to internalize their processes e.g., the verbal systems begins to verbalize silently, presumably inside the mind, and the visual system begins to visualize without the need for activity or stimulation but "within the limits of the invariants to which the system is attuned" (Gibson, 1979, p. 260–261)

Here, Gibson hints at the idea of perceptual stimulation and auto-sensory stimulation where memory is not a stored representation in the mind but the capacity for the mind to recreate stimulations similar to real perceptual ones; i.e., the process is relived by generating similar sensations as would occur during an 'online' perception in an 'offline' situation. Image information is thus not stored in memory, recalled and then displayed in the theatre of the mind. It is, in a sense, re-enacted over and over again. The question of learning then, is a question of honing and tuning the skills of perception and auto-stimulation that can be improved through practice. In turn knowledge becomes internalized auto-stimulation of the perceptual system that recreates the necessary information in relation to a particular situation.

Taking this idea one step further and coupling it to the notion of manipulating the material of the environment allows us to understand how we transform our environment in order to re-stimulate our perception in a given form. Out in the world the resulting mediated information is available to all, and anyone that can perceive, so long as they have tuned their perceptual and auto-perceptual capacities through practice, can pick up and interpret that information.

Support for this view of learning and knowledge as skill acquisition can be garnered with an appeal to the theories of the non-representational phenomenologist

Maurice Mearlau-Ponty and his ideas of the 'intentional arc' and 'maximum' grip, (Dreyfus 1998, 2004; Merleau-Ponty 1998).

"It is crucial that the agent does not merely receive input passively and then process it. Rather the agent is already set to respond to the solicitation of things. The agent sees things from some perspective [the perspective of its own being] and sees them as affording certain actions. What the affordances are depends on past experience with that sort of thing in that sort of situation." (Dreyfus 1998, p. 5)

In this explanation from Dreyfus, we see not only how the perceptual capacities of a being, determined by its body as part of its species, provide a perspective from which to encounter the world but also how past experience i.e., knowledge, as practiced perception which has tuned a given being's perceptual capacities, are brought into play to make sense of the environment that the being inhabits.

It is therefore important to understand more clearly how past experience is brought to bear on the perceptual process of the now. Past experience is not to be thought of as a form of representational knowledge stored in memory. Past experience is the capacity of a living being to perceive or auto-stimulate its system in a refined way, which has been developed through practice. The capacity of a mind-body system to do this is directly affected by how often it has done it in the past. Thus the past experience is inherent in the current state of the system, because the system has been trained over time to perceive or visualize in a more efficient and precise manner.

Giving the example of an expert tennis player, Dreyfus explains that the involved performer tends towards a maximum grip on the world, one that maintains equilibrium in as many situations as possible as a state of optimum survival. This is achieved by discriminating more and more refined situations and pairing them with more and more appropriate actions. This is not a goal oriented activity [it is simply a state of being]. All one can say is that in order to improve one's skill one must be involved, and get a lot of practice (Dreyfus 1998).

## 4.3  Summary

The aim of this chapter has not been to develop a watertight defense of Gibson's ecological theory of perception. Rather it has been to highlight the different ways in which the central idea from this theory i.e., affordance, has been confused and accidentally misappropriated by many theorists, particularly in the field of HCI. On the way we have had to clarify what Gibson's original ideas were and mount a preliminary defense for his ideas, in order to avoid the traditional cognitive reading of his work. In so doing, we have established more clearly how affordance works, what the difference is between direct perception and mediated perception and how they are intertwined. We have also now cleared the way for a re-evaluation of Gibson's ideas in relation to the embodied phenomenological perspective. Seen in this way, a strengthened version of Gibson's theory of affordances provides a powerful way to understand how we engage with the world around us in general and with media as a special case of perception. It also identifies mediated knowledge as a perennial feature of our environment that we have to engage with, at a fundamental level, from the day we are brought into this world.

In the next part of this book, I will look more closely at this idea of mediated knowledge, through the lens of semiotic theory. The purpose of this is to deepen our understanding of how we manipulate media to form signs that represent our ideas, how we put these signs together to construct complex structures that communicate our ideas and how we then encounter such structures and make sense of them by interpreting them through a process known as 'semiosis'.

# References

Dreyfus, H. L. (1998). Intelligence Without Representation, from *http://www.hfac.uh.edu/cogsci/dreyfus.html*

Dreyfus, H. L. (2004). A Phenomenology of Skill Acquisition as the basis for a Merleau-Pontian Nonrepresentationalist Cognitive Science, from http://ist-socrates.berkeley.edu/~hdreyfus/pdf/MerleauPontySkillCogSci.pdf

Gaver, W. W. (1991). Technology Affordances. Paper presented at CHI '91, New Orleans.

Gibson, J. J. (1965). The Comparison of Mediated Peception with Direct Perception *Purple Peril of J.J. Gibson*. unpublished manuscript, Cornell University http://huwi.org/gibson/mediated.php

Gibson, J. J. (1966). The Stick-in-Water Illusion (Revised) *Purple Peril of J.J Gibson*. unpublished manuscript, Cronell University *http://huwi.org/gibson/stick.php*

Gibson, J. J. (1969). The Psychology of Representation *Purple Peril of J.J. Gibson*. unpublished manuscript, Cornell University http://huwi.org/gibson/representation.php

Gibson, J. J. (1971). A Preliminary Decription and Classification of Affordances *Purple Peril of J.J. Gibson*. unpublished manuscript, Cornell University http://huwi.org/gibson/prelim.php

Gibson, J. J. (1974). A Note on the Relation Between Perceptual and Conceptual Knowledge *Purple Peril of J.J. Gibson*. unpublished manuscript, Cornell University

Gibson, J. J. (1979). *The Ecological Approach to Visual Perception*. Houghton-Mifflin Co., Boston.

Hartson, H. R. (2003). Cognitive, Physical, Sensory and Functional Affordances in Interaction Design. *Behaviour and Information Technology*, 22(5), 315–338.

Johnson, M. H. (2001). The Development and Neural Basis of Face Recognition: Comment and Speculation. *Infant and Child Development*, 10(31).

Le Grand, R., Mondloch, C. J., Maurer, D. and Brent, H. P. (2001). Early Visual Experience and Face Processing. *Nature,* 410(890).

Le Morvan, P. (2004). Arguments Against Direct Realism and How to Counter Them. *American Philosophical Quarterly*, 41(3), 221–234.

McGrenere, J. and Ho, W. (2000). Affordances: Clarifying and Evolving a Concept. Paper presented at Graphics Interface 2000, Monteal.

Merleau-Ponty, M. (1998). *Phenomenology of Perception*. Routledge, London.

Norman, D. A. (1988). *The Psychology of Everyday Things*. Basic Books, New York.

Norman, D. A. (1998). *The Design of Everyday Things*. The MIT Press, London.

Norman, D. A. (2004). Affordance, Conventions and Design, from http://www.jnd.org/dn.mss/affordance_conv.html

Norman, D. A. (2004). Affordances and Design, 2006, from *http://www.jnd.org/dn.mss/affordances_and.html*

Oliver, M. (2005). The Problem with Affordance. *E-Learning*, 2(4), 402–413.

Shannon, C. E. and Weaver, W. (1949). *A Mathematical Model of Communication.* University of Illinois Press, Urbana, IL.

Stamper, R. (2007). Stumbling across a "Soft Mathematics"? While Exploring some Issues of Law and Metaphysics. Paper presented at The International Conference of Organisational Semiotics ICOS2007, Sheffield.

Stamper, R. (in preparation). *Analysis of Perception and Meaning for Information Systems Engineering.*

# Chapter 5
# Semiotic Theory

## 5.1  Signs and Signification

If affordance essentially arises from the direct perception of the environment, as
embodied knowledge, then mediated knowledge, which relies on indirect second-
hand signification, must inherently be semiotic in character. In this chapter we will
look more closely at the semiotic theory in general and try to understand what
semiotics has to offer to help us theorize about interactive media.

As the study of sign systems, the basic aim of semiotic theory is to understand the
structure of sign systems in relation to the way they convey meaning. Semiotics takes
the view that signs can be organized within various media, to form texts that can convey
some kind of meaning. For example, Saussure posited that words, in order to convey meaning, consisted of two distinct parts. Firstly, the 'signified', that is the part
of the word that pertains to its meaning and secondly, the 'signifier', which is the
part of the word that is representative of that meaning (Saussure 1966).

The signified is considered by Saussure to be the concept that exists within the
mind, that we want to communicate. This may be a set of experiences, impressions
or perhaps feelings related to an object or situation, e.g., the mental representation of
what a dog is. This is intrinsically bound to the signifier which is representative
of that concept, e.g., when seen together, the letters D O G signify the concept of dog
in written English. Together, the signifier and the signified combine to become a sign
(Fig. 5.1)That is, a sign, according to Saussure, is what is experienced when someone
comes into contact with a set of stimuli that can be equated to a mental concept.

The common understanding taken from Saussure is that the signifier is the
physical phenomenal part of the sign and the signified is the meaning represented
by that physical phenomena, a definition that was elucidated by Louis Hjelmslev
some years later, by the introduction of form and substance into the description of
a sign (Hjelmslev 1961).

Essentially, Hjelmslev characterizes the substance of the signifier as the physical
materials of the medium, e.g., sound, light, wood, or stone. It is part of the perceptual
input that comes from the environment that must be processed in order to be interpreted as a sign (Gottdiener and Lagopoulos 1986). The form of the signifier is that
which is recognized through interpretative codes as a representation of something.

S.O'Neill, *Interactive Media: The Semiotics of Embodied Interaction,*
doi: 10.1007/978-1-84800-036-0, © Springer Science + Business Media, LLC 2008

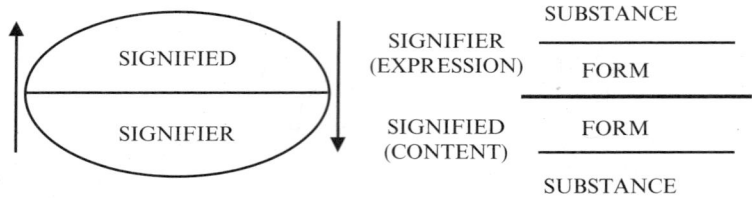

**Fig. 5.1** Comparison between Saussure's sign and Hjelmslev's sign

It is syntactic and structural. On the other side of the relationship, the form of the content is the way that concept has been coded, its semantic structure. The substance of the content is the amorphous concept in the mind, i.e., its meaning (Fig. 5.1).

One can think of all of this in terms of a statue of a figure from Greek mythology. The substance of expression is the stone that is used to produce it and the form of expression is the shape of the body that it takes on as a representation. The form of the content is the identity of the person that the statue represents, e.g., Zeus or Hermes, and the substances of content are the ideas that these two figures might represent. In the case of Zeus, it is the concept of the divine or all knowing, and for Hermes, it is the principle of transformation or contact between the heavens and the earth.

### 5.1.1 Peircean Semiotics

Alternatively, and without knowledge of Saussure, Charles Sanders Peirce developed an altogether different conception of the sign about the same time (towards the end of the nineteenth century).

Starting from a philosophical position imported from Emmanuel Kant, Peirce's semiotic theory is based on an essentially phenomenological approach to consciousness.

As his theory unfolds, Peirce gives an account of three different kinds of phenomenological experience, which provide the background to his conception of signification (Peirce 1931–1958).

Peirce's concept of 'Firstness' is the primary and ideal experience of a phenomenon that is without reference to any other subject or object whatsoever. When we are experiencing something but are unable to describe it, or identify it or what has caused it, then we are in a state of firstness. Firstness then, is an undifferentiated qualitative experience that we cannot name or give voice to.

Moving on from firstness, we experience the phenomenon that we do not recognize or cannot fully identify but which resists us in some way. This we experience as secondness. Secondness is where we begin to differentiate the 'us' from the 'not us', ourselves from the world around us, sensations of pain from causes of pain and actions from reactions. Effectively this means that there is some kind of mapping between some sensation and its cause or something and something else without any meaning coming into play; e.g., in the way that smoke signifies fire. The effect (smoke) has a direct cause (fire), there is a physical link between the signifier and the signified and no interpretative bit is needed to explain what is going on.

This brings us to 'Thirdness' or full-blown semiosis, where we have a 'representation' rendered in some kind of medium, which, when we encounter it, we 'interpret' and mentally make a link to the 'object' to which the representation refers. Thirdness is the experience of representational objects standing in for experiences of real objects; i.e., thirdness is the domain of signification. The process of something 'standing for some other thing', is managed by an interpretative mental process, including recall and recognition of those objects, and the meaning associated with them. The representational object does not need to have any direct reference to the object and can be a purely abstract symbol that is related by a set of functional rules.

Thus, Peirce's conception of a sign consists of three distinct parts: the 'object', the 'representamen' and the 'interpretant' (Figure 5.2). The object of a sign is the thing that is being represented, which is referred to, indirectly, by a representation of it, i.e., the 'representamen'. This process of reference is managed by a mental process that links the experience of the object with the experience of the representamen, e.g., a picture of a cat standing in for a real cat. For Peirce this mental process was best understood as 'Abductive reasoning' whereby a person's best guess, based on available information, results in an Interpretant (Cobley 1996; Peirce 1931–1958).

Peirce develops the concept of Semiosis further, by introducing the idea that an interpretant can in fact be a representamen in another representamen/object relationship, this other relationship also having its own interpretant. In other words, through some other previous semiotic experience, an interpretant can become a representamen in relation to an alternative interpretant, which in turn can become a representamen, and so on.

For example, the word 'Cats' might act as a referent to the two feline animals that I once had as pets. This word also carries with it another reference to my grandmother's love of cats, and a further reference to the Andrew Lloyd Webber musical of the same name. The reference to the musical furthermore carries with it a reference, for me, to London's West End, and London's West End carries a further

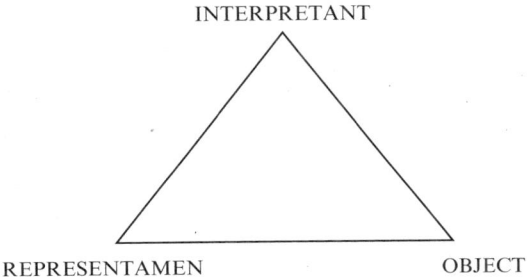

INTERPRETANT

REPRESENTAMEN                                      OBJECT

**Fig. 5.2**  Peirce's triadic sign

reference to another family member who was once an actor there, even though he never appeared in the aforementioned musical, or indeed for that matter ever owned any cats. Thus, the train of semiosis develops, one referent connecting an object to an interpretant and that interpretant acting as a further referent to another object, with its own interpretant.

Unlike Saussure, Peirce was less concerned with language and much more concerned with categorising the phenomenal qualities of different kinds of signs. While this proved to be very problematic for him, he did develop some very useful ideas about sign types. Building upon his notions of firstness, secondness and thirdness, Peirce developed the notions of icon, index and symbol as an initial sign type categorisation. These were expanded in great detail, but here we will concentrate only on the basics:

- **Icons:** Peirce describes iconic signs, in relation to firstness, as signs that represent their objects via a direct likeness or similarity. Essentially, icons have features or qualities that resemble those of the objects they represent; e.g., all pictures, paintings and photographs are essentially iconic because they attempt to faithfully represent a recognisable image of their subject matter.
- **Indices:** An index essentially 'indicates' something and is related to Peirce's concept of secondness. For example, the position of the shadow on a sundial indicates the time of day in relation to the position of the sun. A paw print made by a cat indicates the path that it has traveled. The symptoms of an illness are manifest indications of the infection causing them. There is a direct link between the object and the sign. Indices are signs or imprints often left in one physical entity, possibly a medium, by the passage of another physical entity that uses that medium. There is a clear connection here between the signifier and the signified, the form and the content.
- **Symbols:** Symbolic signs are signs that refer to their objects by virtue of a law or set of socially derived rules that cause the symbol to be interpreted as referring to that object. Thus, similarly to Saussure, Peirce views symbolic signs as conventional signs and wholly related to the notion of thirdness. Generally, symbolic signs have no relation to their object other than the accepted conventions agreed upon by a culture. They do not look like them nor have they any direct relation to them as indices do. Essentially, they are signs that have an arbitrary relationship to their objects. Words, books, and mathematical symbols are good examples of symbolic signs.

## 5.2   Context and Cultural Codes

Umberto Eco's "Theory of Semiotics" (Eco 1976) is a highly developed re-evaluation of the major branches of semiotics from both the Saussurean and Peircean schools of thought. Eco produces not so much a new definition of the sign but a definition of the sign that takes into account the myriad social, cultural and contextual issues that underlie every instance of the use of the sign. In doing so, Eco proposes a theory of semiotics in terms of the use of signs as acts of coding and decoding messages with reference to sets of culturally defined conventions, or codes. This socio-cultural aspect of semiotics and the importance of context in evaluating meaning are central to his theory.

Based on the work of Katz and Fodor, Eco develops a dynamic model of the semantic aspects of signification that takes into account the circumstances and contexts on which the denotation and connotation of signs are dependent. Eco's conception of signs as aspects of codes, which run along and across the various social groups which make up society as a whole, are based on the notion that for a sign to be understood the reader has to be 'in possession' of the correct code in order to interpret it. It is this coding and decoding of signs that Eco attempts to model in his revised Katz and Fodor (KF) model (Fig. 5.3).

In explanation: a sign vehicle/s-v/is a signifier which is formed by a set of syntactic markers (sm). This sign vehicle then has a meaning <<sememe>> that can be either a denotation **d** or a connotation **c** depending on the context (other signs within its system (**cont**)) and circumstances (signs outside of its specific system (**circ**)), with which it is encountered. The contextual and circumstantial parameters in which the sign vehicle is encountered affect the type of meaning that the sign vehicle may pertain to. In other words, the denotative and connotative meanings that a sign vehicle might have alter depending on when and where the sign vehicle is encountered (Eco, 1976, p 105).

For example, the word 'blue' might be encountered in relation to 'sky', 'grass' and 'feeling'. Each alternative word alters the meaning of blue, offering different denotations and connotations. 'Blue sky' simply denotes the colour of the sky. 'Blue grass' is a type of American folk music. 'Feeling blue' connotes an emotional state.

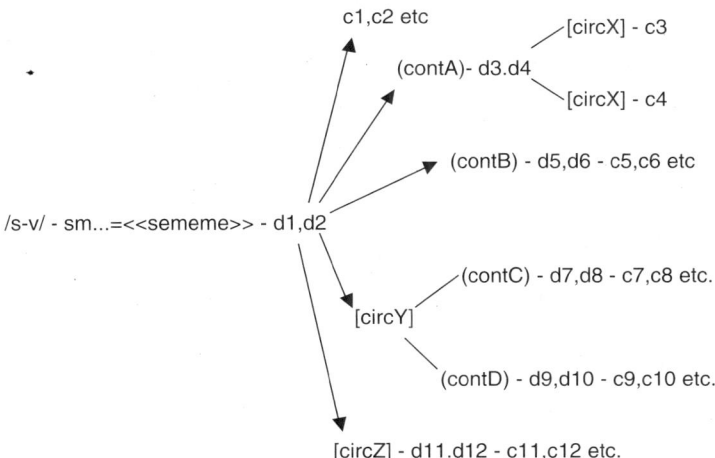

**Fig. 5.3** The revised Katz and Fodor (KF) model (Eco, 1976)

Social theories of semiotics are greatly concerned with the way in which semiotics has developed in relation to socio-cultural issues. For Umberto Eco, for example, meaning is no longer an individual construct, as in the arbitrary semiotics of Saussure. It is now seen as the result of a process in which an individual takes part in society through the coding and decoding of his/her relationship with the cultural values and societal norms of the time.

"Codes, insofar as they are accepted by a society, set up a 'cultural' world which is neither actual nor possible in the ontological sense; its existence is linked to a cultural order, which is the way in which a society thinks, speaks and, while speaking, explains the purport of its thought through other thoughts. Since it is through thinking and speaking that a society develops, expands and collapses, even when dealing with 'impossible' worlds, a theory of codes is very much concerned with the format of such 'cultural' worlds, and faces the basic problem of how to touch contents." (Eco 1976 p 61)

Daniel Chandler states, "A code is a set of practices familiar to users of the medium operating within a broad critical framework" (Chandler 2001 pp 147–148); they are not just the conventions by which we communicate; they are more correctly "systems of related conventions which operate in certain domains" (p 149). That is to say, certain codes are specific to certain social activities, realms of knowledge or encountered phenomena. Chandler offers three main groups of codes that are derived from the work of Umberto Eco, Michael Halliday, Gunther Kress and Theo van Leeuwen, which he identifies as particularly important:

- Interpretative codes: perceptual codes (Gestalt psychology), ideological codes.
- Textual codes: scientific codes, aesthetic codes, rhetorical codes, mass media codes, etc.
- Social codes: verbal language, bodily codes, commodity codes, and behavioral codes.

Interpretative codes have to be able to represent aspects of the world outside of their particular set of signs. They have to be able to represent objects and their relations in the world outside the representational system. In doing so, they offer a number of ways in which objects can be represented, and related to each other. Chandler's outline of perceptual codes brings with it notions from Gestalt psychology, which propose that human visual perception is predisposed to interpreting the world in a certain way. Indeed, from a semiotic perspective, concepts such as background/foreground, proximity, and similarity that structure our perceptual processes fit well with Kress and Van Leeuwen's notions of analysing visual images.

Textual codes are codes that have the capacity to form complex groups of signs or 'texts' that are coherent within themselves and within the context for which they were produced. For example, the visual grammar of Kress and Van Leeuwen offers the potential for different compositional arrangements that allow the realization of different textual meanings. Chandler puts it thus:

"Every text is a system of signs organised according to codes and subcodes which reflect certain values, attitudes, beliefs, assumptions and practices. Codes transcend single texts, linking them together in an interpretative framework, which is used by their producers and interpreters. In creating texts, we select and combine signs in relation to the codes, with which we are familiar. Codes help to simplify phenomena in order to make it easier to communicate experiences. In reading texts we interpret signs with reference to what seem to be appropriate codes. This helps to limit their possible meanings. Usually the appropriate codes are obvious, 'overdetermined' by all sorts of contextual cues. The medium employed clearly influences the choice of codes" (Chandler 2002 p 157–158).

In particular, Chandler tries to put across the way in which aspects of texts signify which particular codes should be used to decode them. Some of this is apparent in the medium. That is, certain aspects of a medium give us clues or afford us an insight into which codes are appropriate for decoding it. For example, in a film, the nature of the medium gives us clues about the way it has been put together, the types of shots used, the lighting, the genre (documentary, science fiction, film noir etc.) all give us clues about how we should interpret the film. Understanding the medium provides us with an understanding of how to decode it.

Perhaps it is Roland Barthes who is best known for his treatises on texts, codes and decoding, as in "Image Music Text", (Barthes 1977). Barthes explores many of these issues, opening up notions of text from a strictly literal understanding to encompass photography, graphic design, advertising and film. In "Mythologies" (Barthes 1972), for example, Barthes explores these ideas, moving towards an exploration of social codes by examining aspects of fashion, sport, films and other cultural domains. Barthes makes us explicitly aware of how, as Chandler puts it, "We communicate our social identities through the work we do, the way we look, the way we talk, the clothes we wear, our hairstyles etc." (Chandler 2001 p 154) resulting in social codes that Barthes labels as modern myths.

These social codes have to be able to manifest the relationship between the producer of a sign or complex of signs, and the receiver/reproducer of that sign. That is to say, they have to be able to manifest the particular social relationship between the producer, the receiver and the object represented (Kress and van Leeuwen 1996). The debate about whether these codes structure society or whether society structures these codes still goes on and is a central concern in the work of social semioticians such as Michael Halliday (Halliday 1978), Robert Hodge and Gunther Kress (Hodge and Kress 1988).

## 5.3 The Structure of Texts

It was Saussure who first proposed the idea that meaning was derived, not just from simple signifier/signified relationships in themselves, but from the differences between these relationships as understood in reference to the overall system of signification or *langue* (Saussure 1966). These differences operate in two different dimensions: the syntagmatic dimension and the paradigmatic dimension.

- **Syntagms:** Syntagms are combinations of signs that are put together in an organized way to produce some form of a meaningful whole. Sentences, for example, are syntagmatic, in that they are ordered combinations of signs written one after the other to produce a meaningful statement; e.g., 'bus stop' or 'the cat sat on the mat'. In this way, syntagms are often considered to be sequential in character, where meaning is derived temporally from 'chains' of signifiers, as in speech, music or dance. However, syntagms can be considered in terms of spatial relationships as well. Examples of 'spatial syntagms' exist in much of the visual arts, e.g., painting, sculpture and even architecture. As such, they exist as combinations of different shapes, forms and colours that are organized in different physical positions to produce some form of a meaningful or aesthetic whole (Chandler 2002; Kress and van Leeuwen 1996).
- **Paradigms:** Contrary to the common definition of a paradigm as an overarching theory or understanding of some particular subject (Kuhn 1962), a semiotic paradigm is a group of signifiers or signifieds (signs) that are in some way associated with one another or are members of the same overarching category, e.g., synonyms. In language, paradigms work as groups of words such as nouns or verbs that are used to substitute one another in the construction of sentences; e.g., in the sentence 'the cat sat on the mat' 'cat' is replaceable by 'dog' or 'man' and 'mat' is replaceable by 'rug' or even 'chair'. The semiotic analysis of paradigms concentrates on aspects of substitution, particularly on the connotations that derive from the associated words that are alternatives to a chosen signifier. What is important to think about here, is how a syntagm or text would be altered if certain words were exchanged for others from similar or even different categories. The 'commutation test' derived by Roman Jakobson (Chandler 2002) does exactly this. It is a particular technique used by semioticians that is aimed at uncovering paradigmatic themes that underlie the texts they are analysing.

### 5.3.1  Layers of Meaning

Other important aspects of the theories in semiotics are the concepts of 'denotation', 'connotation' and 'metalanguage'. Hjelmslev first formulated these concepts around his explanation of Saussure's sign as essentially 'denotative'. That is to say, that there is a one-to-one 'literal' relationship between the signifier and the signified. The term 'denotation' in general refers to a signifier/signified relationship that is instantly understandable with no ambiguity. It is a culturally agreed situation where an arbitrary sign or symbol is given a definition or literal meaning that is easily identifiable (Chandler 2002). Hjelmslev goes on to propose that beyond this there are other levels of meaning that occur when signs interact with each other or are experienced in different contexts.

- **Connotation:** Connotation is generally considered to be a secondary level of signification that, according to Hjemslev and Barthes, occurs when an initial denotative sign is taken as the signifier for another signified. This is possibly an infinite process that can give rise to many different connotations that, as Eco points out, are not only dependent on the initial denotation but also the circumstance and context in which the initial sign occurs (Eco 1976). Also, this connotation is dependent on the socio-cultural codes that an interpreter is able to use in order to read this extra level of meaning.

- **Metalanguage (Metaphor):** Another aspect of the so-called secondary level of meaning that occurs as part of signification is that of metalanguage. Metalanguage is identified by Hjelmslev and Barthes as an aspect of signification that occurs when an initial denotative sign (signifier and signified) is taken as the signified of a different signifier. This is the ground for 'figurative' or 'metaphorical' signification whereby a signified concept, referring to one particular domain, is described by signifiers from another, for example, 'the ship ploughed through the water' or 'the ship sliced through the water'. Each one refers to the same motion of the ship 'sailing' on the water but uses different signifiers from different domains of knowledge to describe the action. This sets up a metaphorical relationship between the domains of 'sailing' and 'ploughing'. Similarly, the signifier of 'ship' and the signified of 'shipness' are referred to metaphorically in the terms 'Starship Enterprise' from the television show Star Trek and 'ships of the desert' referring to camels. Indeed, in the case of the Starship Enterprise, the whole notion of ships and 'shipness' is transferred from one domain (the sea) to an entirely new one (outer space) and is used as a metalanguage to describe this new domain.

It is important to note here that metaphor and connotation are very closely linked, as they are both aspects of a second level of signification that is built onto an initial denotative level of signification. Connotation and metaphor offer the potential for additional meaning making beyond denotative principles, which is intrinsically linked to the cultural codes and semiospheres (domains of shared sign systems) which individuals take part in. Connotations and metaphors are not fixed meanings; they are entirely dependent on the contexts and circumstances in which codes are brought to bear on interpreting sign vehicles.

Going back to the example of the Greek statue mentioned earlier, the statue is denotative in as much as it stands as a physical expression of the conceptual content of Zeus. According to Barthes' Diagram (Fig. 5.4), the connotative aspects would be additional meanings above the denotative level where the statue of Zeus, as a whole, becomes an expression of the 'greatness', 'mysteriousness', and 'civilized'

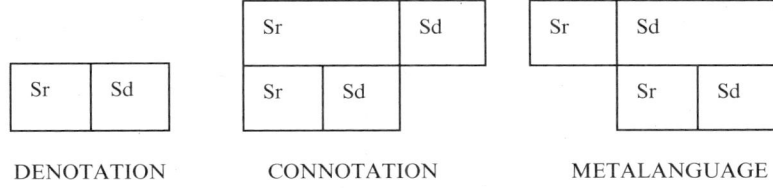

DENOTATION      CONNOTATION      METALANGUAGE

**Fig. 5.4** Barthes' model of denotation connotation and metalanguage

aspects of Greek culture. Alternatively, an example of metalanguage might occur when the qualities of the Zeus statue are attributed to someone who perhaps looks like the statue in some way. Thus, the statue becomes the metaphorical content for an expression describing that person.

## 5.4   Communication

Signs and symbols, words and texts in any media, are all really about communication at some level. Saussure's model of the 'speech circuit' is an early model of the communication process that occurs as two people talk. (Fig. 5.5), Essentially, it is a linear model of communication, whereby the listener comprehends what the speaker is saying through simply sharing the same set of cultural conventions of language. Effectively, Saussure views this process as transparent. In other words, because the two people communicating with each other share the same rules of language, the meaning that is transmitted by person A is the same as that received by person B.

This is a very naïve way of viewing communication. Later semioticians and communication theorists contend this point by highlighting the complex process of contextualisation and interpretation within the author/reader relationship (Chandler 2002; Barthes 1972, 1977). For example, Roland Barthes in particular was interested in the communication process. However, unlike Saussure he did not think of it as a transparent process. Drawing on the work of Shannon and Weaver (1949), Barthes shows not only how texts are messages sent from an author to a reader, which are susceptible to noise and miscommunication, but also that the reader is in control of interpreting the message (Fig. 5.6). In this way of thinking, texts are much more ambiguous and open to many different interpretative readings; they are opaque rather than transparent. Barthes gives the example of a press photograph as a

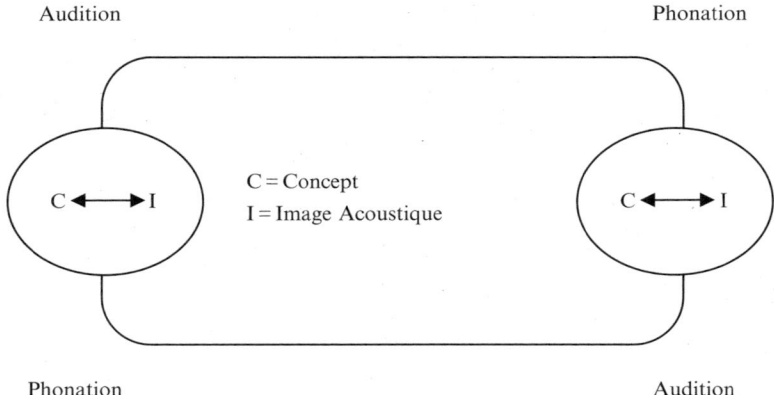

**Fig. 5.5**  Saussure's 'speech circuit' model of communication

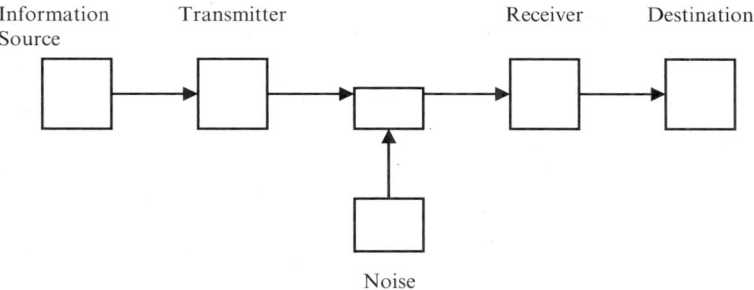

**Fig. 5.6** Shannon and Weaver's communication model

message, where the source of emission is the photographer and the technicians who lay out the pages and supply the text with the image. The channel of transmission is the material of the paper itself and the receiver is the general public who read the paper. It is however, in the reading of the paper that the meaning is constructed from all these component parts and it is not always the case that the original intentions of the photographer reach the reader.

In using Shannon and Weaver's model, Barthes actually manages to semiotically articulate the author/reader problem of their still simplistic view, by highlighting the opaque nature of the received message and the contextual elements that contribute to the interpretation of it. His exploration of denotation, connotation and metalanguage gives rise to a concern with the layers of meaning that arise within the reading process.

Indeed, Barthes looks deeply into these ideas in "Mythologies" (Barthes 1972) and "Image Music Text" (Barthes 1977) where he further explores the notion of connotation in relation to what he describes as the third level of meaning, that of modern 'myth' building. Particularly, he focuses on the notion of deconstructing 'texts' to explore the relationship between author and reader, in terms of denotation, connotation and metalanguage. For example, Barthes critically analyses aspects of popular culture, such as the perceived wholesomeness in an advertisement for pasta and the connoted superiority evident in haircuts from films depicting Romans.

## 5.5 Semiotics and Interactive Media

In Saussure's terms then, in a simple sense, we can understand the elements of an interface or aspects of interactive media as signs. The physical characteristics of a screen, for example, provide the means for signifiers to be represented during interaction, the signifieds of which have to be understood for a user to operate the machine. However, this conception of a signification is rather primitive for our needs, as it does not take into account the contextualisation and interpretation of meaning, nor does it provide any useful way of thinking about convergent media artifacts.

Issues of communication are also highly relevant to the semiotics of interactive media. Indeed, SERG have focused their entire research agenda around the issue of the communicability of interfaces. However, again Saussure's version of communication is far too simple to be applied to interactive media. The idea of the interface as 'the designer's deputy', developed by SERG, highlights how complex this issue is as it foregrounds not only the opaque nature of signification in general, but more specifically the way that computer interfaces are designed to represent information dynamically.

At the more structural level of the medium, some of the semiotic concepts outlined by Saussure do have a particular relevance to the development of a semiotics of interactive media. For example, interactive media interfaces are full of paradigmatic structures that are often articulated into syntagms through user interaction. Buttons and hyperlinks often have different states that change as the mouse is rolled over them or when they are clicked. Often this signifies, to the user, some form of functionality or different meaning from its original state. Similarly, the sequential and spatial syntagms as outlined above are exactly what Andersen refers to when he discusses the notions of sequential and concurrent chains of signs in computer interfaces. As such, these notions are essential in understanding interactive media, particularly interactive media that foregrounds symbolic operations and manipulation of the medium as signs.

Hjelmslev's ideas also provide a useful way of thinking about the forms and structure of digital signs. For example, if we consider a computer display, the pixels of the screen provide us with the substance of the expression. The graphical qualities of the symbols represented on the screen, e.g., colour, shape and structure, etc., provide the form of the expression. The form of the content is then what the structure can be identified with, e.g., a button to be pressed or words for us to read. And finally, the substance of the content is what the form means, e.g., a play button or an error message.

Another important idea to take from Hjelmslev comes from his theory about how signs provide layers of meaning for users as they interact. Most significations in screen based media tend to be designed to denote something, e.g., a button to be pressed or a graphic to denote a file type. However, screens are not just huge collections of denotative signs. The desk-top metaphor for instance has been used for over 20 years, as a way of contextualising these signs and providing an extra layer of meaning by which users can understand what certain buttons mean.

Metaphor then, is important to understanding interactive media. Connotation on the other hand has not really been considered in relation to interactive media. The focus in HCI has largely been to increase efficiency and usability by reducing ambiguity, thus removing the possibility for connotation. Thinking about the connotative aspects might provide new avenues for signification and further layers of interactive media. It might also give us an extra tool to help us understand how people interpret interactive media within the larger social context in which they appear.

In terms of sign types, Peirce's concept of iconicity is particularly relevant to the notions of immediacy in interactive media outlined by Bolter and Grusin (see Chapter 1) regarding the way in which they attempt to hide their mediating properties.

In opposition to that, the notion of symbolic signs is central to interactive media, particularly in relation to Bolter and Grusin's notion of hypermedia, which foregrounds the medium itself. Windows for example, are not iconic representations of actual windows but symbolic representations of the window concept. Also, the index is an interesting concept in relation to interactive media as it is not strictly identifiable in itself, but it is an essential part of most signs in interactive media, particularly symbolic signs. For instance, the line drawn on the virtual paper of a drawing package is an index of the movement of the users drawing hand, which is symbolically represented on screen by colored pixels. These sign types sit alongside those defined by Andersen. Sometimes overlapping, they potentially provide more leverage in understanding the relationships between the convergences of media types in interactive media applications.

De Souza draws heavily on Peirce's conception of a sign to develop the SERG approach to understanding signification with interactive media in screen-based interfaces. Indeed, Peirce's concept of how signification takes place through thirdness, where a representation is related to its object via an interpretant, is a much clearer idea than Saussure's signifier/signified dichotomy that is often misunderstood.

For SERG (Prates, de Souza and Barbosa 2000) a computer interface is a "one shot message" sent from a designer to a user, much as Barthes describes a newspaper article. The communication principle from author to reader is important here because while this one shot message is sent from one to the other, it is only through interacting with it, rather than simply reading it, that users encounter and transform the many other messages that are embedded in the interface. The one shot message acts as the designer's deputy, a dynamic text that communicates how it works through interaction, rather than just reading.

However, where SERG identify this concept of the interpretation of interactive media texts, they are not concerned with understanding the meaning making processes of users, nor are they concerned with establishing the myths or codes that are at work in interactive media objects. Rather, they are more concerned, as HCI experts, with trying to improve communication between the author and the reader, by trying to have an interface explain itself as it is used. Semiotic engineering then, is not so much about exploring the layers of meaning that users interpret while interacting as it is about usability evaluation. This approach then misses some of the opportunities that interactive media might offer in terms of user experience, and does not fully engage with the problem of meaning residing in user interpretations rather than in the interface. To paraphrase Barthes, we must consider the implications of the 'death of the designer', in order to fully understand interactive media.

Barthes' ideas then, echo our concern for understanding the interpretative process of interactive texts. This offers a radically different approach to interface design as it suggests that communicability cannot be guaranteed and that users play a far more significant role in interpreting interactive interfaces than just executing tasks to attain goals. Interactive media can be understood as a complex text that is not easily and straightforwardly understood. The interpretive process requires a user to draw a great deal from past experiences with all kinds of signs types in order to decipher the layers of meanings that arise during interaction. SERG's approach to communicability evaluation shares a basic understanding of these ideas as an underlying, if unrealized, principle.

If interpretation is important to understanding interactive media, then the semiotic concept of codes is particularly relevant to developing a semiotics of interactive media, because it identifies interactive media objects as texts that can be decoded or even recoded culturally by a user (reader) at the interface level (Freire 1995). It is important here, not to confuse cultural codes with binary code or programming, even though there is also something inherently semiotic about them.

Binary code and programming exist as undisclosed entities to most users and are only relevant as cultural codes to those people who have absorbed them, e.g., programmers or systems engineers, etc. While Manovich (Manovich 2001), contends that the domain of binary code and programming (namely software engineering) provides the potential for new languages that describe aspects of interactive media, he essentially agrees that interactive media come with the social and cultural coding that is appropriate to the old media from which they are originally derived. Of course, these older cultural codes, styles and genres impact on our understanding of interactive media, but the interactive qualities of the media (as outlined in chapter 1) alter these codes, resulting in new kinds of codes, relevant specifically to the culture of those involved in interactive media. A semiotics of interactive media, must at some level, be able to take this into account, perhaps in some way establishing interactive media 'mythologies', as Barthes might do were he alive today.

## 5.6 Summary

Saussure's original conception of a sign is far too simple for describing interactive media at any level, but the concepts of syntagms and paradigms are very useful in describing interactive structures such as interfaces, as Andersen's work has already highlighted. Indeed, these ideas might provide some leverage in helping us understand problems of remediation and convergence, firstly by helping us identify the kinds of semiotic structures that can simulate older media and secondly, by thinking about syntagmatic structures concurrently and sequentially across convergent media.

Hjelmslev's description of a sign is also useful in terms of helping us to understand the structural components of an interactive medium that supports signification. These qualities of the interactive medium, to a certain degree, give us some understanding as to how different older media types can be remediated or simulated via interactive technologies. The material may be different but the structure of signification remains somewhat similar.

Similarly, Barthes' extension of Hjelmslev's denotation, connotation and metalanguage ideas moves us to consider how layers of meaning can be embedded in the complex structures of interactive media texts when considered beyond the level of simple buttons and icons. Moreover, Barthes' ideas introduce a way to 'problematise' these new opaque interactive texts, highlighting problems of communication and usability that confront designers while foregrounding the interpretative processes that users brings to such encounters.

From the Peircean perspective, the focus is on the phenomenology of signification, i.e., signs as they are experienced. This is very useful as a starting point for
understanding how users (readers) might experience interactive media signs in the
wild, so to speak. The concepts of firstness, secondness and thirdness could prove
to be crucial to a semiotics of interactive media that might manifest in many different ways from screen based signification to tactile interaction and sensor based
interactive spaces. Not every kind of interaction is going to be based on thirdness.

Similarly, Peirce's categorisation of sign types provides an interesting way to
consider the signification possibilities of interactive media. For example, it is
highly likely that any attempt to relate these categories to current interactive signs
will highlight the impoverished nature of signification within the current interactive
medium. Screen based media in particular, despite their multimedia leanings,
provide only a few kinds of signifying phenomena compared to those embedded in
the real world. Considering Peirce's sign types in relation to future and emerging
technologies might allow designers to build new forms of signification in the interactive media of the future.

Eco's approach to semiotics is also of interest to our theory of interactive media.
Carrying on from Hjelmslev and Peirce, he foregrounds the social, contextual and
circumstantial aspects of meaning, attempting to bridge the gap between structural
and phenomenal positions. Contextual and circumstantial aspects of signification
again draw attention to the syntagmatic structure of convergent media signs. But,
more importantly they highlight the complex and sometimes subtle influence on
meaning that occurs as a result of composite media texts being interpreted by users
framed within socio-cultural situations.

All the semiotic concepts discussed in this chapter offer the potential for the
further understanding of the remediation of old media in all their new forms. Not
only do they offer ways of formalizing the descriptions of interactive media objects
or artifacts, they also offer a different perspective for understanding how meaning
is derived through interpretation and interaction with interactive media. However,
while these concepts offer the potential for the development of a semiotics of interactive media, it is not yet clear how their relationships with older media can be
applied to interactive media. We will look at this more closely in the next chapter.

# References

Barthes, R. (1972), *Mythologies*. Vintage, London
Barthes, R. (1977), *Image, Music, Text*. Fontana Press, London
Chandler, D. (2002), *Semiotics: The Basics*. Routledge, London
Cobley, P. (Ed.) (1996), *The Communication Theory Reader*. Routledge, London
Eco, U. (1976), *A Theory of Semiotics*. Indiana University Press, Indiana
Freire, M. M. (1995), A Socio-Cultural/Semiotic Interpretation of Intercommunication Mediated
    by Computers. Retrieved 08/10/02, 2002, from http://psych.hanover.edu/vygotsky/freire.html
Gottdiener, M. and Lagopoulos, A. (Eds.) (1986), *The City and the Sign*. Columbia University
    Press, New York
Halliday, M. A. K. (1978), *Language as Social Semiotic- The Social Interpretation of Language
    and Meaning*. Edward Arnold, London

Hjelmslev, L. (1961), *Prolegomena to a Theory of Language.* University of Wisconcin Press, Madison

Hodge, R. and Kress, G. (1988), *Social Semiotics.* Polity Press, Cambridge, England

Kress, G. and van Leeuwen, T. (1996), *Reading Images (The grammar of visual design).* Routledge, London

Kuhn, T. (1962), *The Structure of Scientific Revolutions.* University of Chicago Press, Chicago

Manovich, L. (2001), *The Language of New Media.* The MIT Press, Cambridge, Massachusetts

Peirce, C. S. (1931–1958), *Collected Papers of Charles Sanders Peirce.* Vol. 1–6. Harvard University Press, Cambridge

Prates, R. O., de Souza, C. S. and Barbosa, S. (2000), A method for evaluating the communicability of user interfaces. *Interactions,* 7, 31–38

Saussure, F. (1966), *Course in General Linguistics.* McGraw Hill, New York

Shannon, C. E. and Weaver, W. (1949). *A Mathematical Model of Communication.* University of Illinois Press, Urbana, IL.

# Chapter 6
# Semiotics and Screen Based Interaction

## 6.1 The Semiotic Screen

Having now armed ourselves with an understanding of some basic semiotic concepts, such as signs, syntagmatic structures, and layers of meaning, we shall now go on to explore how these ideas have been used to theorize about various aspects of visual (in our case screen-based) media. Here the focus will be on looking for ways in which semiotic theory can help us to understand the structure and properties of interactive screen-based media. In the initial sections, we will explore how semiotic theory has been applied to understanding subjects such as graphic design, visual images, and film. In the latter half of the chapter, we will take some of these ideas forward to a case study that explores the issue of the remediation of creative media.

### 6.1.1 Screen-based Media

Usually, when we think of screen-based media, our first thoughts are of television or maybe film and video. After all, television has been such an integral part of our media environment for so long that it has literally become part of the furniture. These days, with the advent of interactive digital TV and on-demand programing, we are seeing a transformation occur in the way in which we use our television screens. We now interact with menus and graphics on the screen in order to make choices about when we want to watch programs instead of having them programed for us. The processing and storage capacity of computerized media is affecting the way in which we interact with television.

More recently, with services like YouTube on the Internet, it has become difficult to determine where television ends and computers start. As a result, a great deal of our tele-visual media is now delivered through our personal computers (PCs) rather than our television sets.

As media convergence continues, the boundary between the two will only continue to become more blurred.

S.O'Neill, *Interactive Media: The Semiotics of Embodied Interaction*,
doi: 10.1007/978-1-84800-036-0, © Springer Science + Business Media, LLC 2008

Interestingly though, despite the closeness of the two, the kind of media usually delivered via the computer screen has not really been transferred back to the television. Office-based activities such as file storage, accounting records, and writing documents are still firmly rooted in our personal computers, and despite the fact that computers are becoming media-entertainment machines, televisions are not becoming an integral part of our day-to-day work.

Arguably, the reason for this comes down to strongly defined cultural differences between text-based paper media at work and tele-visual media (or film) for entertainment. These days, despite convergence, most of our interactions with computers are still focused around text-based activities such as manipulating spreadsheets and writing with word processors.

Even the Internet, though increasingly imbedded with movie clips and animations, is essentially still text based at some level (Fig. 6.1). It would seem then that

**Our Vision**

From interactive film and TV to online environments and from mobile devices to interactive homes, there is a growing demand for designers who can navigate the interactive media world confidently and creatively. Interactive media is one of the fastest growing sectors in the international economy. Studying Interactive Media Design at Dundee will help prepare you to join this rapidly evolving industry.

Studying with us, you will explore many kinds of interaction design and cutting-edge technologies. The world needs a new kind of designer to meet the amazing technical and creative challenges that new media technologies are opening up to us. It needs 'hybrids' - people who understand how to get technology to work for them and how to produce work that is usable, without losing sight of the importance of beauty, excitement and engagement. We offer you a challenging, fun, stimulating and well-resourced environment in which to become just such a person. The 21st century needs hybrid designers. Are you up for it?

Career prospects

Interactive media designers are found in many settings and industries; entertainment and interactive TV, product and industrial design, web-based commerce, e-learning, games, advertising, business and the public sector. Several of our current students have been successful in securing summer internships and placements with a wide range of companies including design centres, TV production companies, product manufacturing companies and new media development agencies.

The skills you will learn could also be transferred to a diverse range roles within these settings, for example content production in the entertainment business, project management, or training. They will equip you to work for organisations of all sizes, both in the UK and worldwide, or to use your IMD expertise as a platform for starting your own business.

News          View entire news archive

Search news archive

Jenny Kelloe (again) - IMD's first TV appearance
16th May 2007 @ 11:52

an apology from the Guardian...
15th May 2007 @ 13:56

Jenny Kelloe interviewed by Radio Scotland about her "Noise Bomb" degree project.
15th May 2007 @ 09:46

from IMD to the Royal College...
14th May 2007 @ 12:27

Phone|not Phone
14th May 2007 @ 10:44

Features

phone|not phone
A joint project between IMD and IPD Level 2 students which re-examines of the possibilities open to the most ubiquitous electronic device of today...

**Fig. 6.1** A screen shot from the Interactive Media Design website

the logic that still dominates interactive screen-based media is that of print media rather than that of the moving image.

The print medium, of course, draws its strength from the static page and the accompanying importance given to the layout, readability, and structure of its text and graphic images. This is particularly interesting, as there does not seem to be anything even remotely interactive about these elements at all. Obviously then, we are missing something important. The static elements of interactive media, its layout, forms, font colors, and graphics, play a huge part in establishing a frame of reference from which to engage with its interactive elements. Without the static elements to guide us on the screen, we would be lost in a maelstrom of interactive and dynamic elements. Nothing tells this story more clearly than those abominable early web pages that were full of animated 'gifs' and flashing banner advertisements, which plagued the eyes of the early adopters of the Internet.

The balance between good static layout and dynamic interactive elements is clearly an important part of any interface design. Therefore, screen graphics, interactive icons, symbols, and signs of all sorts are clearly the mainstay of interactive media. Along with buttons, mice (or mouses), and joysticks, they make up an integral part of any interactive interface or device that we might encounter today. The purpose of all these graphics is usually to provide us with a signifier for some element of functionality in the device/system that we are using, e.g., the triangle that signifies play on a video machine or software equivalent, and the little printer icon, which when clicked on, will print our document for us. The key aspect of the design of such graphics, then, has to be their ability to communicate their purpose to a user. From a usability perspective, this is the ground that many computer semiotics researchers have already been exploring (Andersen 1990; de Souza 2004).

However, it is not always as straightforward as assuming that a graphic might work in a singular, linear relationship with its function. Many other aspects of its makeup, its situation within a graphic structure as a whole, and the context in which it is viewed, can have an effect on its meaning.

Moreover, the functionality of graphics often works in a metaphorical way that attempts to imbue the virtual world with a similarity to the real world (e.g., the desktop metaphor), which does not always display the same logic or affordances that would be apparent in the real world.

The balance between information communication and affordance is a tricky one to get right, and more often than not the confusion over how affordance works has made this even more difficult. From our exploration so far, we have ascertained that affordances occur only when we can interact without having to think consciously about what we are doing. Unfortunately, most interactive interfaces do not give us this option and we find ourselves faced with numerous graphical elements that need to be interpreted in order to operate them. Here we will explore this problem further by looking at what makes a graphic work and by trying to understand how interactive media use them to communicate.

## 6.1.2   Graphics, Symbols, and Pictograms

The father of modern graphic design undoubtedly has to be Jacques Bertin, whose influential work of the 1960s and 1970s, *Semiology of Graphics* (Bertin 1983) and *Graphics and Graphic Information Processing* (Bertin 1977), amounted to a radical shake-up of the cartographic community of which he was very much a part.

Deeply influenced by Saussurian semiotics and the subsequent Paris school of semiotic thought, Bertin sought to redefine graphic traditions on the basis of semiotic theory. As such, Bertin drew a fundamental distinction between figurative or representational images, i.e., pictograms, and those of an abstract or symbolic nature, i.e., what he called "graphics".

For Bertin, figurative images are polysemic, i.e., ambiguous in that they possibly have more than one meaning, which places the interpretation of the image in the hands of the reader, possibly leading to confusion or problems in communication. Alternatively, for graphics Bertin proposes a monosemic system where all elements have a meaning attributed to them in the form of a legend or key, which is defined by the designer, well before the graphic is viewed, the idea being to give more control to the designer about what the elements of the graphic mean, thereby limiting its communicative possibilities and resulting in clear, denotative meaning.

Bertin goes on to propose the idea that "good graphics" consist of a number of variables that can be controlled by the designer to maximize their effect. For Bertin, the strength of graphics lies in the eye's ability to take in vast amounts of data in three dimensions at a glance.

> "In an instance of perception. Linear systems (e.g. music) communicate only a single sound or sign, whereas spatial systems, graphics among them, communicate in the same instance the relationships among three variables" [1]

Bertin defines these variables as the two planar dimensions of X and Y, in combination with the retinal variables of size, value, texture, color, orientation, and shape. These are equivalent to the Z dimension related to the eyes' ability to differentiate between types of graphic marks (see Fig. 6.2). As such, combinations of these marks can be used to convey the relationships between a large number of quantifiable data values. Edward Tufte has uncovered similar principles in his analysis of hundreds of graphical problems/solutions from all over the world. For example, the importance of "data density", maximizing "data ink", and the removal of "chart junk", all bear striking similarities to Bertin's ideas about retinal variables (Tufte 1990, 1997, 2001).

Bertin's semiology of graphics draws heavily on an understanding of the mechanics of optics and visual perception. As such, it is very close to the ideas of the Gestalt psychologists, which focus on the perceptual propensity of people to distinguish between various distinct forms among a mass of spatial data. This also ties in with some of Gibson's ideas about perceiving "invariant repertoires of behavior". As such, good graphics should allow us to perceive the difference between variant and invariant properties of colored dots and marks on paper (or screens) in order that we might understand the underlying meaning attributed to them via the key that we are given to decipher them.

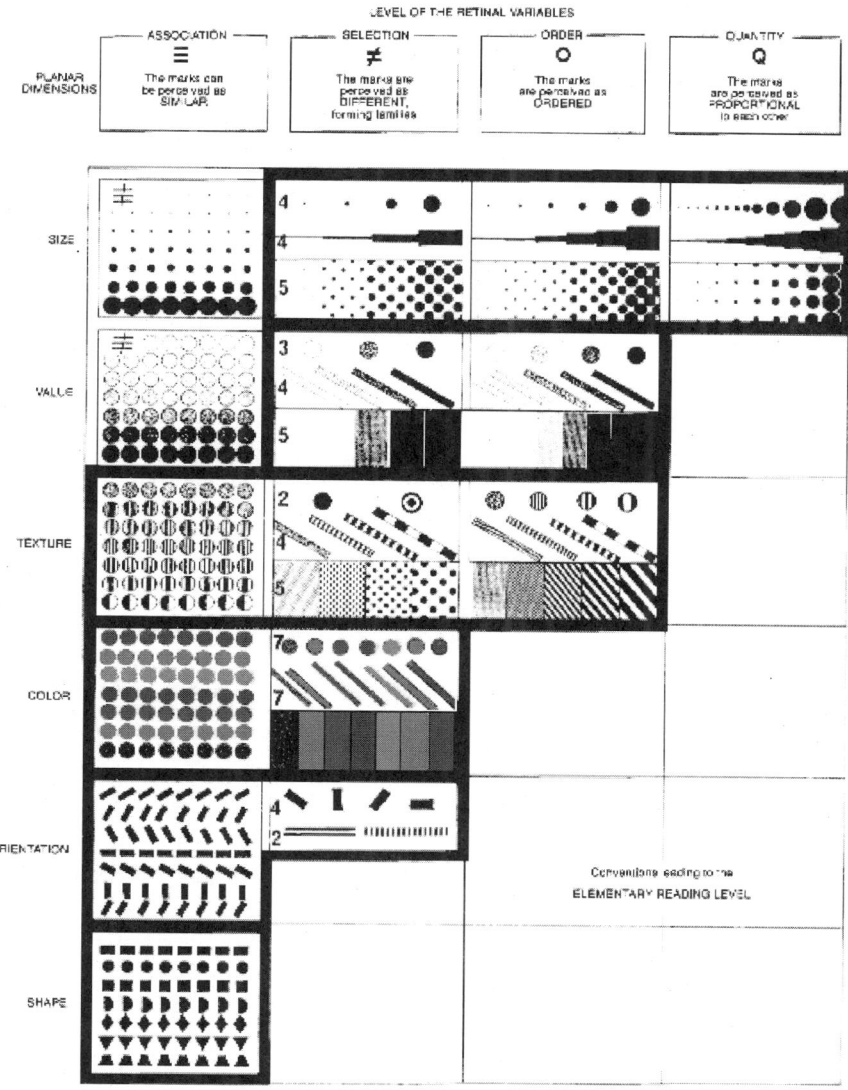

**Fig. 6.2** Bertin's system of graphics

In a sense, Bertin outlines the affordances of the graphic medium, highlighting the way in which properties such as line, shape, shade, color, etc., relate to our perceptual capacity as ways of communicating information. Controlling these properties of the medium allows the designer to set up a situation where differences in data can easily be perceived before they are meaningfully understood in light of the conceptual framework of a key.

Pictograms, on the other hand, are instantly identifiable in relation to a much looser set of cultural values that are associated with real-world objects (Barnard and Marcel 1984). Here, there is imprecision in the meaning with variations of form and a multitude of unique interpretations from reader to reader.

Perhaps a more useful way to think about the differences between graphics and pictograms is to apply the categories defined by Peirce as outlined in Chapter 4. In this respect, what Bertin considers to be a graphic can be considered as a Peircian symbol, that is to say, that it is utterly reliant on an understanding of agreed conventions and codes for its understanding. Bertin's figurative image is representational, as are Bernard and Marcel's pictograms. They both follow, more or less, what Peirce outlines as an icon. Iconic images are more likely to be understood in terms of cultural coding practices rooted in everyday experiences, whereas symbolic coding becomes the province of specialist domain codes that are often provided along with the graphic such as explanations of mathematical formulae. Beyond this, of course, we have Peirce's index, which is not mentioned explicitly in graphical terms, although the size of plots such as the height of a bar chart has an indexical relationship to the data being displayed.

Two of the key aspects that any graphical form (symbol or pictogram) requires to effectively communicate are legibility at a distance and legibility over time (Dewer 1999). This has proved to be particularly relevant in road safety signs and, more interestingly, in advertising. For instance, McQuarrie and Mick are interested in exploring the "artful deviations" of advertising images that work at different levels; statements, rhymes, puns, metaphors, tropes, and schemes are all explored in relation to levels of complexity and user rating. Their work is particularly focused on understanding user responses in decoding different types of images based on two particular levels of increasing complexity. They place schemes and tropes within the semiotic notions of over-coding and under-coding, respectively. Over-coded figures are generally less complex, resulting in reduced cognitive load, making them easier to understand and quicker to grasp. Under-coded figures are generally more complex than over-coded ones; so they require more cognitive activity to understand and therefore take longer for users to respond to. Interestingly, this extra cognitive load in understanding complex advertisements comes with its own reward, increasing the likelihood that users will remember and enjoy the advertisement. The down side to this is that advertisements that employ complex rhetorical tropes take longer to understand and are therefore not considered to be the best way to communicate to users in situations in which cognitive load is already high, e.g., when users are distracted such as when driving a car or performing some other activity (McQuarrie and Mick 1996).

In terms of interactive media, Bertin's ideas are probably most relevant to those involved with data visualization. His approach is aimed at developing a visual system that is based on the function of the eye in relation to visualizing quantifiable data. Much of his work focuses on developing easily readable statistical graphs and population mapping images. Indeed, Stuart Card (Card 2003) and others (Jackobson 2000) have already drawn on these ideas in relation to visualizing database information and building three-dimensional data visualization models. This type of interactive media relies on defining clear relationships between visual elements that represent information in "data space".

The terms and debates that surround the effectiveness of graphical communicability also seem totally relevant to the development of our understanding of interactive media because icons, indexes, and symbols seem to be exclusively what people interact with while using contemporary interactive media technology (Fig. 6.3).

Simply looking around the graphical elements of a word-processing interface is enough to make this explicit. Tool bars and drop-down menus are examples of none other than icons, indexes, and symbols. Indeed, a great deal of the visual aspects of interactive media is bound up with these semiotic definitions in relation to those of other theorists, e.g., Andersen and SERG.

In HCI, the importance of reducing cognitive load has been crucial in making interfaces more usable, and much of the work done here has followed the idea of simplifying graphical images or using metaphors within interfaces that mimic real-world behaviors. The really interesting thing that the advertising studies show is that understanding media of all sorts is not just about usability. Much of the pleasure and enjoyment that people get from advertising come from thinking and reflecting on the content presented. Following these ideas in interactive media where usability might be required, some of the overhead might be better off-loaded into the physical environment in a form that affords embodied interaction rather than thinking. This might leave room for more complex and interesting content that users could reflect upon and enjoy without having to think about how to move the interaction forward.

### 6.1.3   Visual Grammar

While graphics, symbols, and pictograms play an important role in making communication possible in interactive media, it is not enough to consider them individually. More often than not, we encounter graphics and symbols in groups alongside other

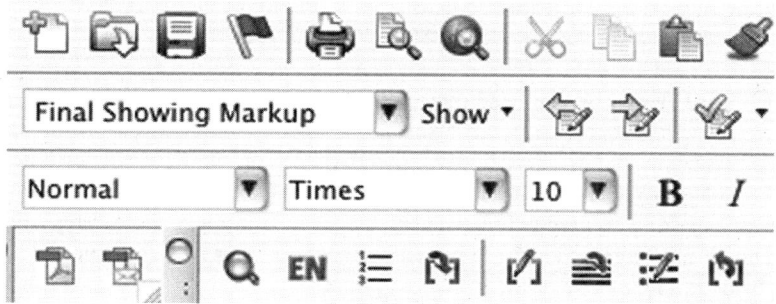

**Fig. 6.3**  Pictograms, symbols, and icons in a word-processing environment

elements such as text, images, and even video, which make up the interface. Arguably, these groupings of different signs can be considered as multimodal texts that are ultimately structured in some way, either spatially on the screen or sequentially in terms of how different elements are revealed to us over time during interaction.

In *Reading Images* Gunther Kress and Theo van Leeuwen concern themselves primarily with the task of isolating and defining the different methods of construction used in image making that allow meaning to be conveyed (Kress and van Leeuwen 1996). Their in-depth study of all kinds of image structures leads them away from traditional semiotic evaluation, in the sense of procuring meaning through the relationships between the various signifiers in an image and into a deeper concern with the syntactic construction of images as a whole.

This primary focus on "compositional structure" is then placed in the wider context of the process of representation in relation to the wider-still contexts of social, psychological, and political factors that come into play when an image is produced. Kress and van Leeuwen build on the notion of a producer's "intention" as the dominant factor in sign production, which is "motivated" against a background of necessary contexts, which remain an intrinsic part of any image that she or he may produce. This notion has a strong sociological basis in the work of Michael Halliday (Halliday 1978) and bears a relation to Eco's studies of context and circumstance (Eco 1976).

Kress and van Leeuwen go on to build a theory of sign production that focuses on the producer rather than on an overriding system. As they see it, a producer/sign maker has a meaning that he or she wants to express. This meaning is then clothed or "coded" into a form provided by a medium (substance), which is the most appropriate, given the context in which a model reader will witness it. This point of view does not deny the existence of an overriding system (i.e., a system of codes) but merely concentrates on the agency of the producer in choosing the form best suited to his or her purpose.

"Communication requires that participants make their messages maximally understandable in a particular context. They therefore choose forms of expression which they believe to be maximally transparent to other participants" (Kress and van Leeuwen 1996 p 11).

Visual grammar considers the composition of spatial syntagms with regard to the "informational value" of the contextual positioning of pictorial elements within an image. Developing a particularly Western perspective, Kress and van Leeuwen propose that the "left side" of an image is the "Given" side, the already known side: the start of an idea, as in the headline or opening paragraphs of a magazine article, for example. The right side is the "New" side, often a photograph in the case of magazines or newspapers. It usually demands attention or is problematic in some way. The left to right direction of reading also forms some kind of narrative that is linked to sequential syntagms. Obviously, this does not apply in cultures in which signs and symbols are arranged to be read up and down or from the back of a book to the front as in Chinese or other Asian cultures.

Furthermore, for Kress and van Leeuwen, elements that are spatially organized in the top section of images are considered to be "ideal", "good", or "whole", while elements that are in the lower sections of images are considered to be "real", "base", or generally more down to earth. This is particularly true of paintings that contain religious motifs. Finally, when a pictorial element is presented in the center of an image, it is presented as a nucleus of information around which all other elements become marginalized, subservient, or dependent. (Fig. 6.4).

These ideas are closely related to notions about embodied understanding that we have seen in metaphor theory (Lakoff and Johnson 1980, 1999), where the orientation metaphors in relation to conceptual understanding of the world are considered. The spatial organization of syntagms then derive much of their meaning in relation to bodily understanding and orientation in the world and there is a natural sense in which images exemplify these particular bodily derived concepts.

Other aspects of visual structure that Kress and van Leeuwen discuss, in terms of their importance to analysis, are the salience of objects, e.g., size, sharpness of focus, tonal contrast, color contrasts, and placement; framing, e.g., the degree by which units of information are demarcated as independent from others; and the liner/nonlinear composition of texts, e.g., the use of subheadings, emphatic devices, numbered lines, tables, diagrams, and so on, that encourage readers to scan the information instead of reading it in a sequential way. Hypertext is a perfect example of this type of thing.

From the size and shape of elements in images to their position and their relationship to one another, visual grammar offers us an understanding of syntagmatic compositional techniques, which is entirely appropriate for describing the display of screen-based information or, indeed, any concurrent grouping of visual elements. The idea that "Communication requires that participants make their messages maximally

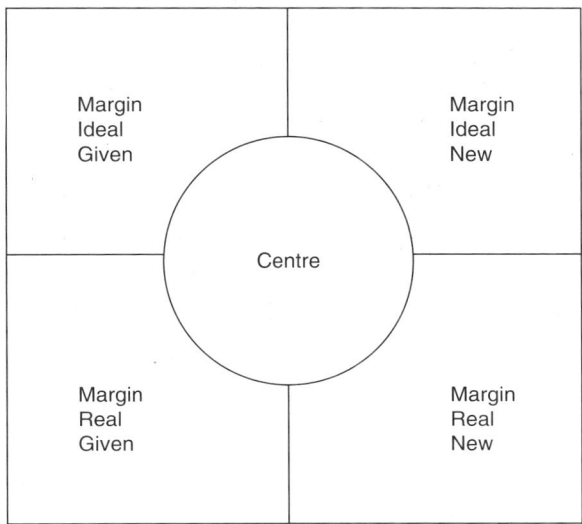

**Fig. 6.4** Kress and van Leeuwen's visual grammar (Kress and Van Leeuwen, 1996 p208)

understandable in a particular context" (Kress and van Leeuwen 1996) is particularly relevant to the SERG approach, where the aim is to design interfaces that communicate their message clearly to the user about how to use the system.

Visual grammar offers one way in which to make user interfaces maximally understood if it were used as an underlying framework for the form of websites for instance. Indeed, the left to right standard of "given" and "new" seems to have manifested itself in the "given" menu bars that control the delivery of "new" content in many web pages (Fig. 6.5).

### 6.1.4 Moving Images

As computers continue to collide with various media forms, we see an unprecedented range of media styles being reconfigured and remediated; e.g., the structure and layout of print media remains a central pillar of interactive media. This process of remediation continues with the transformation of how we relate to the moving image.

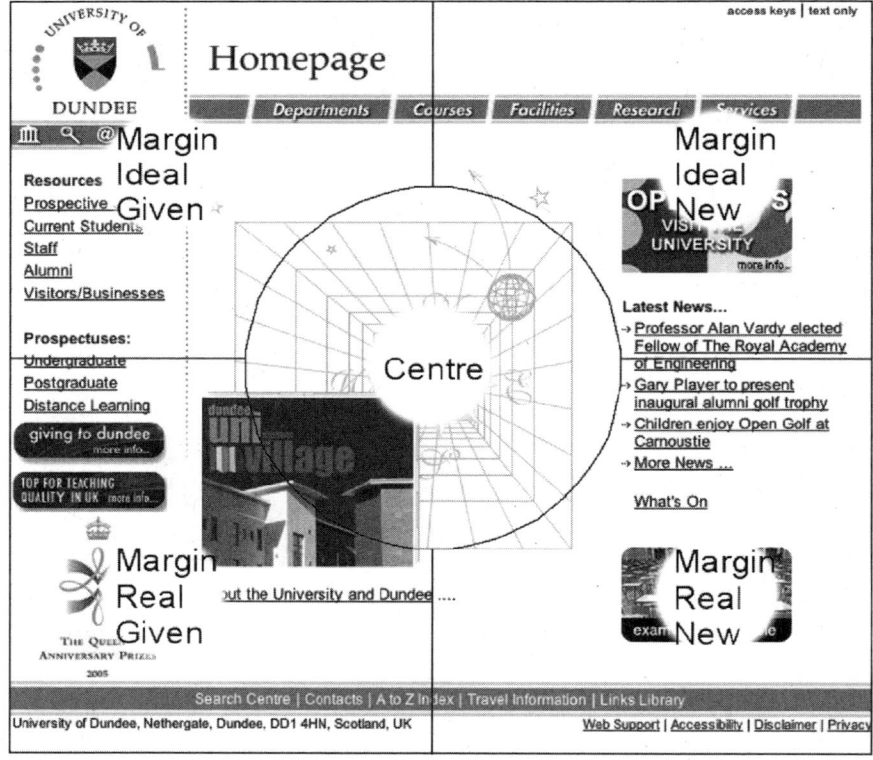

**Fig. 6.5** Webpage layout

Not only do we see interactive controls, such as play, rewind, and pause become graphical images on screen rather than physical buttons, we also see hybrid multi-media applications emerging in their own right. Just as the logic of the printed page still dominates how we lay out our interactive screens, the logic of film still dominates how we deal with moving images at the interface. Shots, pace, angle, and narrative structure have never been more important to understanding the moving image as they are in interactive media today.

The reason for this is that interactivity changes the way in which we access, construct, and view images, and we require a starting point from which to understand those changes. The multiple elements of interactive media that are now spatially compressed onto our screens form texts within texts. Movies these days often occupy only a small part of a screen, surrounded by text, graphics, and other images. Moreover, we often skip through them rather than watch them from the start, and we can jump from film to film as quickly as we like. Very rarely do we watch things in full-screen mode from beginning to end.

Moreover, the ability to access movies from different points leads us to the possibilities of establishing interactive opportunities for engaging with the story being presented. Rather like games, it is now possible for interactive movies to have multiple narrative threads and endings that are determined by the way in which the user interacts with the elements of the story. This multiplies the narrative structure of film and transforms the way we think about telling stories with digital media.

Arguably, multiple strands of meaning are present in every interactive application and this makes them difficult to understand and analyze. Nobody understands this problem better in terms of the moving image than Christian Metz.

Christian Metz (Metz 1974, 1986) is probably the best-known advocate of semiotic theory in relation to cinematic criticism. A particularly interesting feature of Metz's work is his explication of syntagms and paradigms in relation to film structures. For instance, he is particularly aware of the syntagmatic structures that exist in films, both the obvious temporal ones as well as the spatial ones. A significant aspect of this, to which he constantly returns, is the lack of the smallest semiotic unit in film. Metz considers this problem to be derived from the multiplicity of sign systems that have been assimilated into film due to its convergent nature. In visual terms, he proposes that "shots", in relation to language, are a type of smallest unit, which are more like statements than like individual words, this being a significant difference in the useful, identifiable smallest unit of film compared to the smallest unit of language.

His "Grande Syntagmatique", as it is known in its shortened form, is essentially a categorization of "shots" and sequences of shots that make up the rhetoric/grammar of film structure as he sees it. As such, in this revised category (Metz 1986) he proposes eight separate categories of syntagms that exist paradigmatically for filmmakers to select and structure narratives in filmmaking through the structuring of "shots":

- Autonomous shots: singular episodic plot periods
- Non-chronological sequences (parallel syntagms): contrasting sequences of alternating images structured A, B, A, B, etc. that are considered to present two different events or places existing at the same time

- Non-chronological sequences (bracketed syntagms): groups of shots that are all different but pertain to the same meaning without any reference to chronological order
- Chronological simultaneous syntagms (descriptive): sequences of events presented chronologically that pertain to the description of a place or events that are occurring simultaneously
- Alternate narrative syntagms: contrasting sequences of events presented alternately and pertaining to the chronological order of the plot
- Scene: a single succession of events taking place in one place, similar to the notion of the scene in theatre
- Episodic sequences: a chronologically ordered series of shots separated optically, by fades and wipes, etc., but related temporally to the plot line
- Ordinary sequences: sequences of shots that drive the narrative along but that miss out unimportant detail

Throughout all this, Metz constantly returns to the problem of the minimal unit, or lack of it, in film semiotics. Thus a semiotics of film requires an understanding of not just the rhetoric of filmmaking but also the nature of a medium that carries so many different sign systems in it, not the least, language itself, which has its own semiotic structures outside of film. In this respect, he points out that syntagms in film are constructed homogeneously and heterogeneously across channels, or "series" as he calls them (Metz 1974, p. 174). These include visual series, linguistic series, sound effect series, musical series, and credits. From this, he proposes that there are

- homogeneous temporal syntagms (sequences of signs within a specific channel, e.g., voice over),
- homogeneous simultaneous syntagms (signs in the image, i.e., the composition of visual grammar), and
- heterogeneous simultaneous syntagms (signs across channels at the same moment) and oblique syntagms (signs relating, for example, visual elements with speech that comes after it).

Metz goes on to discuss the problems of this in relation to decoding films. He focuses his attention on Hjelmslev's concepts of "form/material/substance" (Metz 1974, pp. 208–211) in relation to the problem of the film as a medium. In this way, he continues to develop the problem of the general semiotics of a film on the basis of the fact that film is in fact a meta-medium that brings different media together into one system. Metz seeks a general semiotic theory of film but finds that semiotic analysis has to take into account the different codes that come with each element of the material of expression that constitutes a film. Thus his Grande Syntagmatique focuses only on the image track and makes no attempt to understand the compositional structure of images or the oblique relationships between sound and moving images.

Furthermore, Metz explores the formal problems caused when one set of codes from one domain are transferred to a similar, yet very different, medium. For example, Metz points out that film, by dint of its recording nature, produces mechanical reproductions of reality. This results in analogous signs that bear an iconic relationship to the filmed object. This is possibly better understood as the concept of "immediacy" or fidelity, inherent in the iconic nature of photographic signs, as identified by Barthes. While this similarity is useful in understanding film, it is inherently problematic because of the temporal nature of the newer medium.

Film transforms the still image into a succession of moving images over time. The forms of the images are altered by the moving medium, which provides new information for the decoding of the medium as film. The medium is the message, as McLuhan once said (McLuhan 1994). This is true inasmuch as the medium of film essentially determines the type of messages that can be carried as content. In short, the semiotics of film is extremely complex because there are so many media components assembled together in one message.

## 6.2   Case Study: Remediating Creativity

In this section we will move on from our exploration of semiotic theory in relation to understanding interactive screen-based media and look at some examples of users interacting creatively with two different kinds of media. The aim of this is to compare and contrast interaction within a traditional artistic practice and that of a computerized arts practice. The purpose is to uncover some of the differences and similarities that each media form contains and to see if our semiotic ideas can help to explain what is going on during interaction in the real world. The study involves looking closely at the creative practice of two individuals, Owen and Dave.

Owen is a painter, i.e., he is a traditional artist who paints with oils on canvas. His studio environment includes an easel, canvases, a workbench, a mixing palette, paint, turpentine, various pots/cups, and a selection of differently sized brushes. While he paints, he interacts with these various artifacts in different ways. Often he mixes paint, applies it to the canvas, cleans his brushes, and changes brushes in quick succession. At other times, he takes long pauses in order to stand back to observe his work.

Dave is a designer who uses Photoshop, an industry-standard tool for manipulating and adjusting photographic images. His work is designed for use in new media, websites, CD-ROMs, etc. For the study, Dave worked on a photo-retouching job. He had a photograph of two people, a man and a woman, who were facing each other with their foreheads touching. Dave's job was to separate these faces into two separate images.

In the following sections we will compare and contrast the ways in which these two artists work and look at how they make sense of their interactions as well as how the two media, one a remediation of the other, shape the way in which they work.

### 6.2.1   Painting as Interaction

Owen starts from scratch on a brand new pre-primed canvas. Starting with a medium brush, he puts some turpentine on the canvas and then turns it upside down to evenly wet the surface. Taking a large brush, Owen then applies some blue paint straight from the palette onto the canvas. He then applies some green in the same fashion with the same brush. Owen then cleans and dries his brush.

Working from a sketch, Owen paints two dark shapes at either side of the canvas between the blue and green strips. He then paints in some darker foreground color, followed by lighter color in the middle of the painting. His initial intention here is to paint the sea, but as his brush touches the canvas he changes direction and paints the sky instead.

Using a smaller brush, he then paints in some detail, such as making the horizon line obvious and turning the two dark shapes into what look like islands. Throughout the painting process, Owen holds a selection of brushes in his right hand. Each one has a different purpose and they are often used in quick succession as he paints. He also uses his fingers from time to time for an unpredictable smudging effect. He often mixes paint on the palette but prefers to paint pure color straight onto the canvas "wet on wet" to produce the effects he is after.

The equipment that occupies Owen's work space are all linked together through the context of the activity of painting;this ranges from brushes and paints that are specially designed for painting as well as other tools such as cut-down plastic bottles, bits of wood, and old rags that he has appropriated from elsewhere.

In the images shown here (Fig. 6.6), it is possible to see how the elements of his medium are manipulated, arranged, and rearranged into concurrent and sequential structures that affect his process of interaction. Not only does the equipment of his space affect how he works, but as soon as he chooses to use one element, or combination of elements, this affects what he is doing. Once he has made a mark on the canvas, this in turn affects his choice of the next combination of elements.

Canvas blocked in,
Owen has brush in hand

Owen mixes paint off
camera

Owen starts painting
directly in the middle of ·
the canvas.

He stops and steps back

Then he starts painting
above the middle to the
left (the sky).

Owen uses broad strokes
to apply the white paint

**Fig. 6.6** The sequence of Owen's painting

For example, the sequence of events in which Owen loads his brush to paint the sea is affected by the concurrent relationship between what has already been painted on the canvas, in terms of an organized structure of marks, and the color being applied to the canvas in order to alter that structure. In relation to what is already on the canvas, Owen decides that the color he has chosen is better suited to painting the sky rather than the sea. Meanings occur and decisions are made on the basis of the relationships between existing marks and elements of the medium that are arranged about him. As a result, they emerge concurrently and sequentially as Owen interacts with them.

Essentially, Owen constructs sequential syntagms from the concurrent possibilities displayed in his environment. Taking a brush and mixing two colors of paint produces a new set of concurrent possibilities depending on the color of paint in relation to the painting. Similarly, when he paints a straight line, he uses a small brush and a straight edge because he knows that this particular structural combination of equipment in his medium will yield the result he is looking for in relation to the marks he has already made on the canvas.

## 6.2.2    Interaction as Painting

With the male face isolated, Dave proceeds to clean up the image. He selects a big brush from the brush palette and paints over the remaining areas of original background with white. The initial strokes of the brush alert him to the fact that it is not working, so he adjusts the flow rate and opacity to 100%. Dave then zooms in on the face. He then opens the brush palette and looks for a fairly small round brush with which he can get close to the face. Without disturbing the face image, Dave continues to clean up the background until no trace of the original is left. He then zooms out to get a good look at the image. He considers a few options here, concerning the lighting of the image and how best to solve the problem of the flat nose. Using the smudge tool along with another brush, Dave builds up the nose and then reshapes it using the eraser tool and various sizes of brush. To finish off the image, Dave chooses the blur tool and traces the edges of the face image, giving it a uniform quality.

In the images shown here (Fig. 6.7), as with Owen's, it is possible to see how the artifacts of his workspace are manipulated, and organized into concurrent and sequential syntagms of graphical images, icons, symbols, and indexes that affect the meaning-making process throughout the interaction. For example, where Dave tries to paint over the grey background, he checks that his brush is white but forgets to check the opacity of the brush. The concurrent/sequential relationship between these two signifiers is realized when he attempts to paint, and nothing happens. He, therefore, has to reorganize the syntagmatic relationship in light of the unwanted sequence of events. Of course, the Photoshop brush is not a physical object but a congregation of signs brought together on the screen in order to represent it. The representational version of a brush is actually quite complex, as it consists of a thin

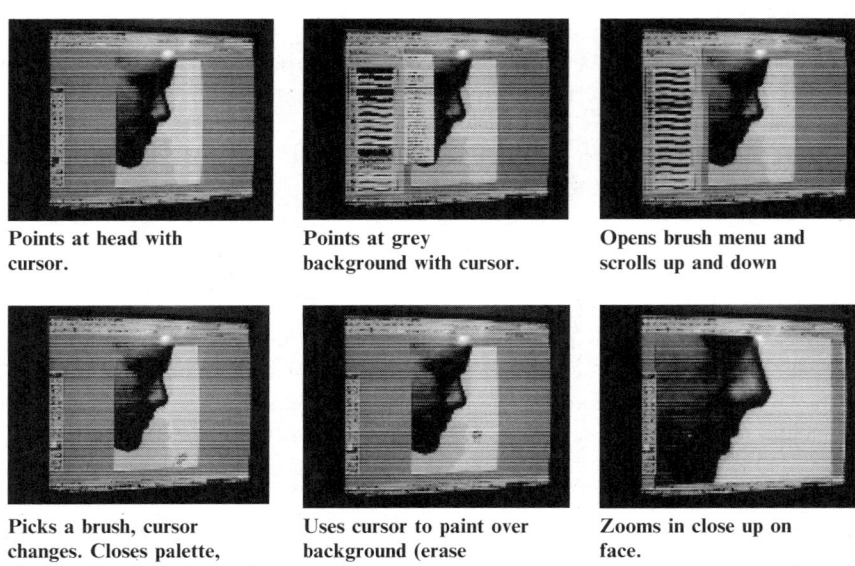

| | | |
|---|---|---|
| **Points at head with cursor.** | **Points at grey background with cursor.** | **Opens brush menu and scrolls up and down** |
| **Picks a brush, cursor changes. Closes palette, checks color. Tries to paint. Nothing happens. Changes opacity.** | **Uses cursor to paint over background (erase grey).** | **Zooms in close up on face.** |

**Fig. 6.7** The sequence of Dave's interaction

circle of a certain diameter on the screen coupled with information about the current color, opacity, brush style, flow rate, etc. It is not something that is easy to grasp like a real paint brush but something that is a dispersed concurrent graphical representation of the properties of a brush.

Indeed, the process of selecting a brush, the brush style, the size of brush, color, opacity, and flow rate amount to a sequentially structured syntagm just as in the study of the Owen painting. The difference here, of course, is that the interaction is with representational signs of the whole system rather than discrete objects. It is only when the syntagmatic structure is correctly and concurrently aligned through sequential activity that the brush is made manifest, and successful manipulation of the image can then take place. In other words, sequences of signs are manipulated to produce new concurrent configurations, which are, in turn, used to manipulate other concurrent signs on the screen.

What we see here then is that both artists are manipulating the artifacts within their workspaces in order to create images that signify something else to a viewer. Owen manipulates the physical things in his environment, while Dave manipulates the graphic signs and pictograms that represent those things as a simulation of the real-world activity. In both cases, combinations of elements are put together in order to act and progress through the process of creativity. However, in the representational world of Photoshop, the role of certain tools is converted from physical objects into complex structures of screen-based signs that represent concepts about how they can be used.

### 6.2.3   Zones of Interaction

As Owen progresses through the process of interaction, which is painting, what emerges from observing him work is a description of how he moves back and forth between three different "zones" of interaction, where different kinds of activity take place (Fig. 6.8). In Owen's case, there is a zone where he steps away from the canvas and away from the worktop where his utensils are. In this zone, Owen's activities are predominantly concerned with observing or reflecting on the canvas he is working on. Another zone that Owen inhabits is where he interacts with his medium. Here, he is often at the workbench mixing paint, cleaning his brushes, or changing his utensils, preparing for his painting activities. The final zone Owen occupies is right in front of the canvas. Here he is working on the painting. He is using his tools, or combination of tools, to produce his artwork.

Similar to Owen's, the observation of Dave's artistic practice again reveals three distinct zones of activity within which he works. Unlike Owen, however, they are not the physical spaces that he inhabits, they are the virtual spaces of Photoshop.

The first of Dave's zones is where he can view the entire picture he is working on. This is characterized by the "zoom out" facility in Photoshop and is analogous to the space that Owen occupies when he steps back from his painting. Dave's second zone is where he primes his tools ready for work.

Here he chooses brushes, adjusts their size, sets their opacity, and generally manipulates strings of signs in order to set the parameters of the virtual tools that Photoshop provides him with. This is analogous to Owen's utilities table and mixing palette.

The final zone that Dave occupies, like Owen's, is where he works on his chosen image. Here, he uses virtual tools (combinations of signs) to alter the image in

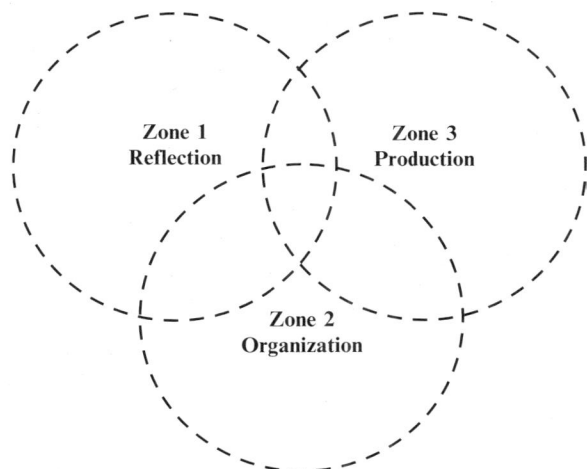

**Fig. 6.8**  A proposed model of zones of interaction

accordance with the parameters he has set for them. This zone is equivalent to Owen's canvas and is characterized by "zooming" in close to the image.

These three zones of interaction then seem to be the same in both types of interaction. They seem to be an important part of the creative process that allows for the organization of materials and tools (zone 2), the use of those materials and tools in the act of production (zone 3), and reflection upon the results of those activities as well as the current organizational situation (zone 1).

Looking at the sequence of his working pattern in the time chart (Fig. 6.9), it can be seen that Owen spends approximately 51% of his time in the production zone, which is 51% of his time actually spent painting. He then spends 26% of his time in the reflective zone, stepping back from and considering his work from a distance. Activities, such as mixing paint, changing, and cleaning his brushes, occur in the organizational zone and take up the remaining 23% of his time, during this interaction.

In one section, Owen moves in blocks between zones 1 and 3, and then he moves between zones 2 and 3. After this, he moves through each zone in succession for quite a period of time. This shows that early on he is working at the canvas and then stepping back to observe his work, then working again. In the second section, he is priming his tools, then working, then again priming his tools, and working again. Lastly, during the main section of his interaction, he is moving from contemplating the picture to priming his tools to working on the picture in a circular fashion.

In comparison (Fig. 6.10), Dave spends 46% of his time in zone 3 actually working on the image, 27% of his time setting the parameters of his tools, and 27% "zoomed" out of the working space looking at the image.

Interestingly, there is not a great deal of difference here between Dave and Owen, although there is a bit of a drop in time spent actually working in the production zone, which seems to have been taken up by spending time in the organizational zone.

As can be seen from the chart, in contrast to Owen, Dave moves back and forth across two zones one at a time rather than in a cyclical fashion. More often than not, he is moving between the organization and production zones rather than anything else. He also spends some time moving between reflection and production.

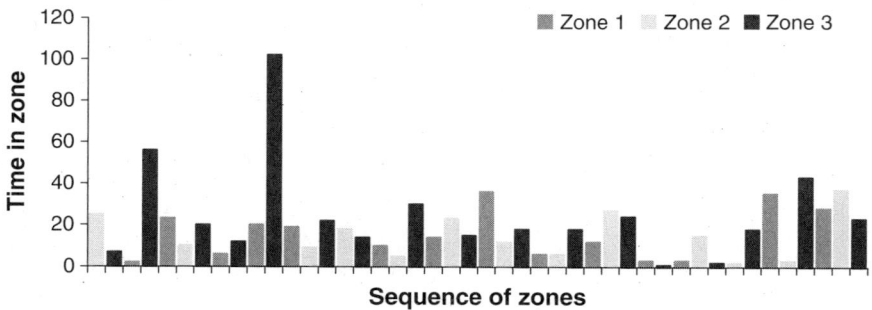

**Fig. 6.9** Owen's zone/time chart

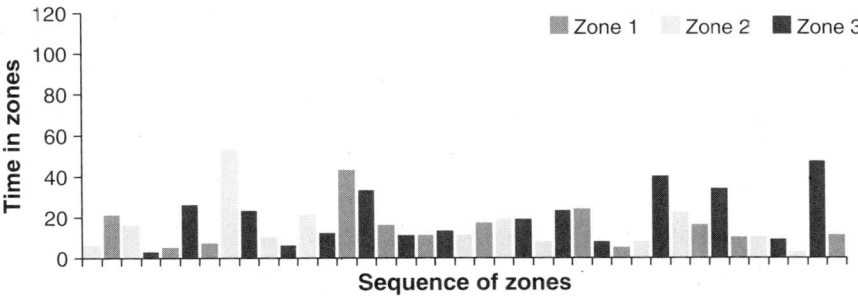

**Fig. 6.10** Dave's zone/time chart

Occasionally, he moves from organization to reflection and back again. This shows that he works in a way different from Owen's. Firstly he primes his tools, then looks at the image, then primes some more. He then works on the image, looks, then works some more. After this, he primes tools, works, primes tools, and works again, etc. He never moves in rapid succession across all three zones like Owen. Instead, he prefers to move back and forth across two zones at a time. Indeed, whether he prefers to do this or not is an interesting point. Arguably, this is not his choice. It is quite possible that this pattern of movement across these zones is a direct effect of the nature of the medium he is using. Given that he manipulates his medium through interpreting and structuring signs on a screen rather than actually handling real objects in the real world, it would seem to follow that he has to spend more time interpreting and organizing his screen elements than Owen does. He moves back and forth across zones arranging combinations of signs, testing them, and adjusting them until they do what he wants. For Owen, this process is much simpler, as he can simply change brushes with the flick of the wrist as he keeps things ready-to-hand as he paints.

### 6.2.4  Sense Making During Interaction

During the observations, both artists were asked to talk aloud about what they were doing, and in both cases their utterances were analyzed in relation to what they were doing as they moved through the emergent zones of interaction. While we will not spend too much time here going through this analysis, which is available elsewhere, (O'Neill 2005, 2006) it is worth making a few comments on the findings.

For example, Owen spends 26% of his time reflecting on his work. When he steps back from the canvas to observe his work, he is predominantly concerned with the colors he is using but there is an interesting shift to the connotative level of meaning in his utterances. Whole ranges of connotative meanings are revealed as he talks about how the painting is taking shape. Here, he is concerned with ensuring that the marks he is making in his medium convey the meaning he is trying to give to the picture. For instance, he talks about the islands, sea, and sky, as well as other ideas such as the effect of light he is trying to achieve or the time of day that the picture might evoke. Similarly with Dave, in his reflective zone, where he has "zoomed out" to look at the whole picture, whole ranges of connotative utterances occur. This suggests that it is the connotative power of the image that he is most concerned with as he "steps back" to assess his work, as no such level of connotation occurs in any other zone despite only spending 27% of his time here.

In the organizational zone, the connotative levels of meaning all but disappear. Here, as he cleans his brushes and mixes his paint, Owen's utterances become much more denotative of the artifacts he is using, again focusing on colors, brushes, lines, and tone. Owen spends 23% of his time here organizing and structuring his activities. There is, therefore, quite a high concentration of denotative reference here compared to the other zones where he spends more time. Interestingly, for Dave this zone appears to be similarly focused on ideas of organizing and manipulating the screen-based artifacts of his medium in a spatial way. He spends 27% of his time here involved in selecting and setting his tools in the correct way so as to make them effective, employing both denotative and metaphorical meanings to do so.

Owen spends most of his time (51%) engaged in the physical activity of painting in this production zone. While working, Owen is predominantly engaged in using his brushes and different colored paints to put something into or give something to the physical painting he is working on. The physical painting in itself is viewed as a container, not only for his activities and the paint he is using but also for the forms he creates such as islands and sea, etc. Owen's meaning-making process here seems to be much more metaphorical than in any of the other zones. Dave spends 46% of his time in this zone, which is characterized by a particularly high range of recurrent metaphors. This suggests that Dave understands his activities with the artifacts in this zone from a metaphorical point of view, not dissimilar to Owen. In particular, the recurrent reference to spatial metaphors and building activities suggests that these are significant underlying concepts that he brings to his interactions. However, this high level of metaphor also points towards the metaphorical design of the Photoshop software, which is successfully being interpreted by Dave.


## 6.2.5   Discussion

Signs of all sorts are easily identifiable in both these examples, particularly with the Photoshop users. For example, the symbols and icons such as the paintbrush or eraser on the screen represent the various tools that the artist might use. These are metaphorical representations of real objects that are graphically denoted in the interface. Dave chooses the brush tool because he knows that particular icon allows him to engage with that particular type of functionality in Photoshop. Similarly, for Owen the real objects themselves are information artifacts because they have information about them embedded in their form. Arguably, the physical equipment of Owen's medium afford him various different possibilities of interaction, which are quite different from that of the representational world of Photoshop. Much of what Dave has to do in Photoshop is to read, interpret, and organize the representational signs of Photoshop in such a way as to make them useful. This takes some time in terms of ensuring that the concurrent structures of signs are correctly aligned before painting can take place. For Owen the procedure is quite different. The thick, round sable brush or the 2-in. flat brush does different things because each is of a different shape and has different kinds of bristles. Owen recognizes this information and uses it to great effect in his work, allowing him to quickly manipulate his medium on the fly without having to invest in long sequences of organizational behavior before he paints.

Watching Owen work, it is easy to see evidence of a functional cycle as he strokes his brush across the canvas. His choice of brush, the color he mixes, the marks he makes, the shapes that appear in the painting, the adjustments in color, and tone that he makes, all come out of a continuous process of observing, considering, and acting on the elements in his painting environment. For Dave, too, this is quite similar. He zooms in and out of his work to see the changes he has made and to assess his work in order to know what to do next. They are both reading and interpreting the signs in their environments, including the ones they are making, in order to know how to proceed. However, Dave has to spend more time organizing his medium before he sets to work. This is evident in the way he cycles through his work. Unlike Owen, Dave moves through his work in phases, checking and rechecking that the representational structure of his medium is tuned correctly to deliver the kind of mark he is looking for. Owen, on the other hand, is able to move in a much more fluid cyclical manner, quickly setting his brush, painting, and reviewing the mark, before repeating the cycle. The functional cycle encompasses all three zones of activity, where the participants move to and from each zone in a fairly fluid and intuitive manner. Sometimes their intentions are realized and at other times unforeseen actions are forced upon them by the nature of the medium that they are using. It is this fluid sense-making activity that is central to interaction and results in the making of sequential syntagms or chains of signs out of all the concurrent ones that exist in the environment. Concurrent signs, in general, are the information artifacts that exist in the same space at any one time, forming the medium that the user interacts with. For Owen, these are his brushes and the types and colors of paints available to him in the arrangement of his workspace. For Dave, the concurrent signs are those that are programed into Photoshop, the various tools, filters, icons, menus, etc. that he has at his disposal. As each participant interacts with his chosen medium, different strings of signs emerge. For Owen, this can be seen in his mixing of paint or the positioning and adjustments of the elements in his painting. For Dave, sequential syntagms are even more apparent as screen upon screen of signs are manipulated throughout their interactions. Andersen's Concurrent/Sequential Paradigms are more than evident in all cases and SERG's idea of the designer's deputy is more than evident in the signs that make up the interactive medium of Photoshop.

One of the most striking things about these observational studies is the emergence of the three zones of interaction. In Owen's case, where he is painting in a real environment, the zones are completely obvious upon watching him. They are the physical and inhabitable spaces where he works. They are part of the nature of being a painter. In the case of the software-supported environment, clearly a desktop metaphor is at work in the design of the interface. There is a flat screen space where the image sits, which is the production zone, and a range of represented tools that surround it, which is the organizational zone, and the zoom facility supports a reflective zone, allowing the user to step back from or move closer to the image.

Dave and Owen both work mostly in the productive zone, that is, they both work a lot with the image itself. They select artifacts from the organizational zone in similar ways and they both use reflection to assess their work as it progresses. However, the way they move between zones is really quite different, as the process of structuring signs in Photoshop is much more complex than manipulating real paint. Effectively, the Photoshop user is inhabiting an information space constructed of signs (Benyon 2001), which mediate his interactions and is understood through different levels of meaning at different times during the interaction. The zones represent different aspects of the interaction process, such as reflection, organization, and production.

## 6.3   Summary

By considering the issues that are revealed in this case study in light of examining the work of Bertin, Metz, and the others, we begin to identify the problems we face in attempting to develop an understanding of interactive media. For example, through considering Metz's attempts to develop a semiotics of film, it becomes apparent that film uses structures and analytic frameworks that are derived from different media domains. In short, film is in itself a meta-medium as interactive media technology is today. In relation to developing our understanding of interactive media, this is an extremely relevant point to grasp.

Contemporary interactive media can be, as Manovich (Manovich 2001) contends, seen as a further development of the problems that Metz elucidates in his work. For example, the characteristics of interactive media outlined in Chapter 1 highlight the same sort of convergence of media forms and sign systems that Metz encounters in film. In understanding interaction with interactive media from a semiotic point of view, we can see from our case study that many different convergent media elements combine in spatial and sequential syntagmatic structures, resulting in new codes by which to understand them. This is quite a complex process.

Andersen's work, unlike Metz's, does provide a minimal unit of analysis in the form of his interactive sign types. However, this minimal unit is continually under threat owing to the expansion of interactive media, which introduces many more concurrent and sequential syntagmatic structures that are similar to those described by Metz. Andersen's model perhaps works best in closed operating systems that are clearly defined and symbolically graphical (Andersen 1999; May 2001; May and Andersen 2001). A fully defined understanding of the grammar of interactive media would be a very different matter, as, like film, it is composed of so many different media elements, as well as being uniquely interactive.

As Metz discovered with his proposal of the Grande Syntagmatique, a semiotic analysis of film, if taken to its normal stringent and exhaustive conclusions, becomes an extremely cumbersome and unwieldy undertaking. This is something that has the potential to occur in the detailed analysis of any given interactive media object, where homogeneous, heterogeneous, and oblique syntagmatic structures are constructed across convergent media elements, e.g., brush signs, flow rate, opacity, etc. Clearly, the level of abstraction to which semiotic analysis can be applied to interactive media must be considered. Very simply, semiotics could be applied to each different media element such as the graphical component, the video component, or the interface component, but still this would not account for oblique meanings across media elements.

Alternatively, semiotics could be employed in a much broader way to understand how meaning is established during interacting, rather than in trying to analyze all the aspects of the entire medium into its component parts. After all, it is the interactive component of this type of media that orchestrates all the others. Like Barthes, reader constructing meaning through the process of interpreting a text, it is only through interaction with this complex medium that users can construct meanings, and it is only through constructing meanings that users, such as Dave, are able to effectively manipulate the complex syntagmatic structures of media like Photoshop. This might be one way to avoid falling into the problems faced by Metz.

Essentially then, screen-based interactive media are extremely semiotic in character. The symbols, graphics, and pictograms, as well as the layout and structure of its emerging forms, are all related to the remediation of older convergent media, as the case study shows. The key difference is that it not only has to be perceived and interpreted to understand what it is but it also has to be used and manipulated to reveal what it does. The logic of immediacy is strong here in that much of the way in which interactive media is presented is often a simulation of previous, physical real-world media forms, e.g., drawing packages and word processing. However, the way in which those representations are conceptually structured often has to be very different form the older version, in order to take advantage of the computational aspects of remediation.

In the following chapter, we will extend our exploration from screen-based interaction to include interactive products and spaces and we shall look at another case study that explores some issues of interacting with virtual environments.

# References

Andersen, P. B. (1990) *A Theory of Computer Semiotics.* Cambridge University Press, Cambridge.

Andersen, P. B. (1999) Dynamic Semiotics and Hydrodynamics. An Exercise in Applied Semiotics. Paper presented at 7th International congress of the International Association for Semiotic Studies, Dresden.

Barnard, P. and Marcel, T. (1984) Representation and Understanding in the Use of Symbols and Pictograms. In: Easterby and Zwaga (Eds.), *Information Design.* Wiley, Chichester, pp. 37–75.

Bertin, J. (1977) *Graphics and Graphic Information Processing*. Walter de Gruyter, Berlin.

Bertin, J. (1983) *Semiology of Graphics*. The University of Wisconcin Press, Madison.

Benyon, D. (2001) The New HCI? Navigation of Information Space. Knowledge-Based Systems,14 (8), 425–430.

Card, S. (2003) Information Visualisation. In: J. A. Jacko and A. Sears (Eds.), *The Human-Computer Interaction Handbook: Fundamentals, Evolving Technologies and Emerging Applications*. Erlbaum, Hillside New Jersey, pp. 544–582.

de Souza, C. S. (2004) *The Semiotic Engineering of Human-Computer Interaction*. The MIT Press, Cambridge, MA.

Dewer, R. (1999) Design and Evaluation of Public Information Symbols. In: T. Boersema, H. C. M. Hoonhout and H. J. G. Zwaga (Eds.), *Visual Information for Everyday Use (Design and Research Perspectives)*. Taylor Francis Group, London.

Eco, U. (1976) *A Theory of Semiotics*. Indiana University Press, Indiana.

Halliday, M. A. K. (1978) *Language as Social Semiotic, The Social Interpretation of Language and Meaning*. Edward Arnold, London.

Jackobson, R. (Ed.). (2000) *Information Design*. The MIT Press, Cambridge, MA.

Kress, G. and van Leeuwen, T. (1996) *Reading Images (The Grammar of Visual Design)*. Routledge, London.

Lakoff, G. and Johnson, M. (1980) *Metaphors We Live By*. University of Chicago Press, Chicago.

Lakoff, G. and Johnson, M. (1999) *Philosophy of the Flesh*. Basic Books, New York.

Manovich, L. (2001) *The Language of New Media*. The MIT Press, Cambridge, MA.

May, M. (2001) Instrument Semiotics: A Semiotic Approach to Interface Components. *Knowledge-Based Systems*, 14 (8), 431–435.

May, M. and Andersen, P. B. (2001) Instrument Semiotics. In: K. Liu, R. J. Clarke, P. B. Andersen and R. K. Stamper (Eds.), *Information, Organisation and Technology. Studies in Organisational Semiotics*. Kluwer, Boston, pp.?

McLuhan, M. (1994) *Understanding Media: The Extensions of Man*. Routledge, London.

McQuarrie, E. and Mick, D. G. (1996) Figures of Rhetoric in Advertising Language. *Journal of Consumer Research*, 22 (4), 424–438.

Metz, C. (1974) *Language and Cinema*. Mouton, The Hague.

Metz, C. (1986) Problems of Denotation in the Fiction Film. In: P. Rosen (Ed.), *Narrative, Apparatus, Ideology, a Film Theory Reader*. Columbia University, New York.

O'Neill, S. J. (2005) Exploring a Semiotics of New Media. PhD Thesis, Napier University, Edinburgh.

O'Neill, S. J. (2006) Semiotics, Embodiment and Interactive Media. Paper presented at International Conference on Organizational Semiotics ICOS 2006, University of Campinas, Brazil.

Tufte, E. (1990) *Envisioning Information*. Graphics Press, Cheshire, Connecticut.

Tufte, E. (1997) *Visual Explanations*. Graphics Press, Cheshire, Connecticut.

Tufte, E. (2001) *The Visual Display of Quantative Information*. Graphics Press, Cheshire, Connecticut.

# Chapter 7
# Semiotics and Interactive Environments

## 7.1 Products and Spaces

Interactive media do not exist solely on screens. In fact, many of them are carried around by us, are distributed across our bodies, or rely on our bodies to make them work. A rapid increase in computing power, coupled with the miniaturization of electronic components, has resulted in a situation in which a great deal of the computing power is now spread over most of our everyday environment or has become mobilized.

Many of the products we carry around in our pockets now are more powerful than the supercomputers of a decade ago. Where once this type of computing power was the reserve of the military, it is now employed to store, retrieve, play, send, and reproduce our digital media. The things that used to occupy space in our homes, such as musical recordings, photographs, film clips, movies, files and documents, can all now be carried around with us or be accessed from numerous entry points to our personal networks. We are, almost, permanently plugged into the media-sphere that surrounds us.

For example, we use our phones not only to talk, but to message text, take pictures, organize our calendars, and send important data to one another, all while listening to the radio or our favorite MP3s. Mobile phones bear little resemblance to the static phones of 10 or 20 years ago. While they still allow us to perform the same basic activity, they have transformed from an object with a single function into the 21st century media equivalent of a "Swiss Army Knife". Moreover, form following function, as it does, this transformation in functionality has led to a change in the way phones become manifest. Candy bars, clamshells, and sliders are all new physical forms that these devices take. Of course, the position of our mouths and ears has not changed over the same period of time, so you would expect the shape of phones to remain somewhat constrained by this.

However, hands-free sets and Bluetooth technology have actually allowed us to split the phone into completely separate parts (Fig. 7.1). This has allowed us to distribute them across our bodies and our environment. With a Bluetooth hands-free set you do not even have to pick up the phone to answer it anymore. You simply press the button and can speak to whoever is calling you, while the phone itself

S.O'Neill, *Interactive Media: The Semiotics of Embodied Interaction*,
doi: 10.1007/978-1-84800-036-0, © Springer Science + Business Media, LLC 2008

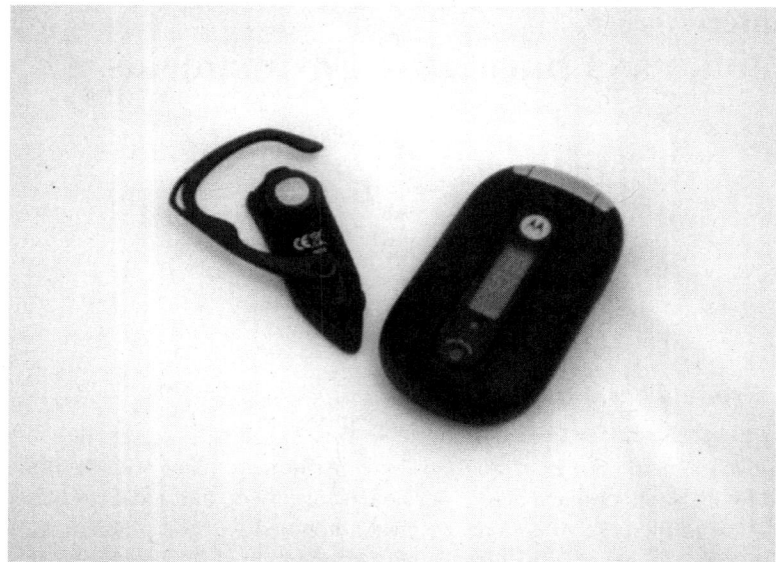

**Fig. 7.1** Mobile phone and Bluetooth headset

remains in your pocket or bag. Likewise, cars enabled with Bluetooth allow you to use your phone in a similar way. The car's stereo system and the phone synchronize so that whenever someone calls you, the stereo switches to the speakerphone mode and you simply speak as you drive. The function of the phone remains, but its form has changed dramatically as the function has been distributed throughout our environment in new ways.

Indeed, many of the activities that we are involved in on a daily basis are transformed as interactive media become embedded in our everyday lives. Take my own personal media network, for example. It consists of a static computer in my study (linked to the Internet), a wireless laptop, a mobile phone and an iPod. All these devices are synchronized through the wireless network I have in my home. I can take pictures with my phone and pass them, via Bluetooth, to my computer and share them with my laptop. I can also upload these pictures to the Internet (maybe Bebo or Flikr) so that my friends can see them or download them as they wish. Moreover, not only can I access files from my computer with my laptop, but I can also access the servers at work (where I store more information) so that I can work at home if I want to. Indeed, my calendar is synchronized across all three locations as well as my mobile phone, should I need to know at a moment's notice what I am doing next Wednesday.

I also have easy access to information that is stored somewhere in California on a server that synchronizes my "electronic briefcase" for me. I could quite easily go into any Internet café and use a machine to download and use any of that information wherever I am in the world. I also carry some information on a USB stick, just in case. Furthermore, the music on my iPod is synchronized to my computer and my iPod has an attachment that allows me to play the music on it as if it were my own FM radio station. All I have to do to use it in my car is to tune my car radio to the same frequency that my iPod is transmitting on. I can also access and play other people's music that happens to be logged onto the network at work from the comfort of my own home.

As a result of all this connectivity, my work practice has changed dramatically. I can work at home, on the train, or in some hotel room in Brazil should work take me there (and it has). I can move information around easily. I can store and retrieve it across a number of locations, which means I do not always have to carry important documents with me. All I need is access. Home world, work world, entertainment and friends' world are all collapsing into one as they become increasingly technologized. Work is no longer a place so much as a frame of mind that one has to establish in order to get something done.

With all this convergence and merging of media and activities across our environment, we are often left wondering how to make sense of it all. Here we will consider how our embodied semiotic approach relates to products and architecture in a way that might help us understand how we interact with media in these new ways.

### 7.1.1   Product Semiotics

Interestingly, by exploring the structure of products in semiotic terms, Susan Vihma manages to articulate the parts of designed products that can be viewed as communicative of its purpose and function. In this way, she categorizes aspects of designed products in functional terms within a semiotic framework that sees a designed product as a bundle of concurrent messages or text, not unlike Barthes (Vihma 1995).

Underlying Vihma's approach is a clear understanding of the social attitudes to products that are central to an individual's social development in a culture already heavily dependent on products in every day use. She is acutely aware of the role of human cognition in the use of objects, and she realizes the connection between cognitive development and socio-cultural issues. Furthermore, Vihma's semiotic approach focuses on the relationship between signs that are distributed on a mass social level and signs that are encountered daily by individuals seeking to perform specific tasks. For Vihma, the designed product sits central to these issues because of its ubiquitous place in society and its ability to communicate its function through its form as a sign.

The mobile phone is an excellent example of such a product (Fig. 7.2). Its ubiquitous character, size, shape, and color immediately signify what it is, even though many different forms of the phone exist. Moreover, and particularly interesting here, is how phones signify their function when we hear them for the first time. All phones used to make the same kind of noise to alert us to an incoming call. However, these days, mobile phones use all sorts of bleeps, twangs, tunes, or comedy

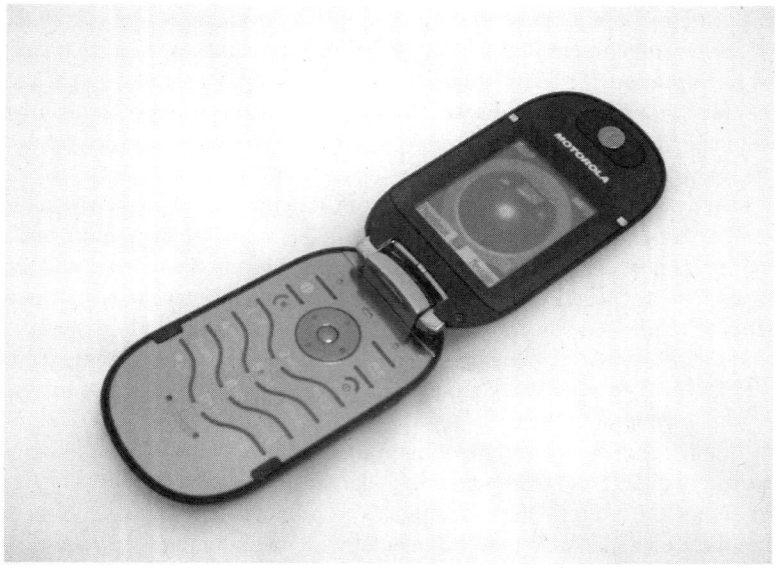

**Fig. 7.2** Signs and symbols on a mobile phone

sound bites as ring tones. The choice of ring tone as signifier has become a personal issue and yet hearing unusual ring tones has become part of our everyday experience, and despite the myriad tones that are out there, we almost always identify them as signifiers of incoming calls.

In Vihma's work there is a strong relationship between the form of an object and the material of which it is constructed. She sees this relationship as fundamental to what the product can communicate. Vihma draws on this notion of affordance to explain the central issues of design in terms of form and function. She extends the purely perceptual notions of affordance of an object by linking it to the human need to interact with its environment.

"When people move around in the environment, they do not perceive color and form as such on surfaces; instead they perceive the affordance of various surfaces and lay-outs of surfaces in space... People do not perceive good form, abstract form, mathematically elegant form as such in their everyday environments. What is seen is rather different opportunities to act, such as walking, sitting, resting, climbing, moving, etc." (Vihma 1995, p. 49)

Vihma takes this relationship between humans and objects further by characterizing the world of objects as signs that communicate their function. This ties in particularly well with our understanding of the place of affordance in relation to signification, where the affordances of certain materials provide the mechanisms by which ideas, in this case the function of the object itself, can be mediated. It also ties in very well with McLuhan's ideas about the mediated environment and Heidegger's notions about equipment.

Taking this point of view further, Vihma then develops a working semiotic model of product design based on a Peircean conception modified from Max Bense, where a product sits at the centre of two axes. For example, "semantics" and "material" provide the ends of one axis with a product at the centre as formed matter that has become meaningful. The other axis that crosses this one relates "syntax" to "pragmatics", with a product in the middle as purpose articulated into the components of construction that serve that purpose. Product design then is about making sure that the right material is chosen to fulfill the pragmatic functions of a device and that the syntactic structure of the device, e.g., handles, grips, buttons, noises, etc., communicate this functionality in a meaningful way.

Following on from this, Vihma goes on to develop, much as Kress and van Leeuwen do for visual semiotics, a taxonomy of the major functional aspects of product design in relation to Peirce's categories of Icon, Index, and Symbol. These range from the tradition of form in a product's development, through color and style, to the sound of use and noise of a product. Then Vihma uses these categories to talk about design issues across a number of design products such as household irons, phone boxes, etc. Using them to comment on the difference between a product's perceived functionality and its actual functionality, Vihma manages to successfully highlight the differences between good and bad design through semiotic comparison.

In terms of our understanding of interactive media, Vihma develops a product semiotics that focuses on the role products play in society as much as their physical make-up. Vihma also looks at issues of communicability and usability in terms of signs, which also remain a fundamental concern of human–computer interaction (HCI). It is particularly interesting to see how she negotiates the relationship between affordance and the semiotic threshold. For Vihma, the materials of the world afford certain activities that allow products to emerge, but in the process of working with these materials to produce products, the jump is made across the threshold as objects are given form and structure that communicate their functionality. In other words, products are formed into signs or groups of signs that mediate the knowledge of how to use them. In good product design, that knowledge is embodied in the form of the object itself, making it as clearly available to perception as possible.

## 7.1.2 Architectural Semiotics

Architectural semiotics has largely risen out of the social concerns of semioticians during the 1970s in relating people to their environment and vice versa. It stands against the traditional cognitive approach to human understanding of environment, developed over a decade earlier by Kevin Lynch in *The Image of the City* (Lynch 1960).

According to Gottdiener (Gottdiener and Lagopoulos 1986), Lynch's ideas brought about a more human approach to environmental design. However,

Gottdiener argues that the cognitive basis to this approach results in a fundamental weakness inherent in favoring perception rather than conception of an environment. Gottdiener credits Lynch as the first person to bring attention to these differences but then goes on to develop the conceptual side in relation to semiotic theory:

"The relation of people to the city goes beyond perceptual recognition and introduces the role of ideology. In short, the inhabitant of the city does not adapt to an environment, rather residents play a role in the production and use of the urban milieu through urban practices." (Gottdiener and Lagopoulos 1986, p. 7)

We must be careful here with terminology again, as perception in this sense is used in the traditional cognitive sense and not in Gibson's sense. However, the distinction Gottdiener makes is really one of engaging with an environment not only by perceiving it but also by being able to read and understand it as a grouping of signs. Here, Gottdiener focuses his attention on the social construction of space, which is the result of the interplay between different cultural groups and the ways in which they relate both to one another and their environment. This "conception" of space, rather than perception of space, is built upon Hjelmslev's definition of the sign. Particularly, Gottdiener focuses on the form/substance relationship within the signifier. Gottdiener sees this as fundamental to understanding the way people relate to their environments.

The substance of the signifier for Gottdiener relates to the physical existence of spatial elements, the objects themselves. The form part of the signifier is how that physical substance appears to an individual, which is dependent upon the knowledge Cognitive Type (CTs) or codes she has with which to make sense of them. For example, the substance of a set of stairs in a plaza affords climbing, as we perceive the upward nature of their physical configuration. For a pedestrian, the form of the stairs offers the opportunity to walk up or down them depending on orientation. For a 16-year-old BMX fanatic or "skater", the stair offers the possibility of a number of stylistic variations of "air time" as he attempts to jump them. This is not simply the affordance offered by an environment; this affordance, coupled with a cultural reading and the prerequisite cultural equipment, makes an activity possible. According to Gottdiener,

"Urban structures act as stimuli because they have become symbols and not because they support behavior by facilitating movement." (Gottdiener and Lagopoulos 1986, p. 8)

Again, this is an interesting exploration of the location of the semiotic threshold. The forms of buildings not only afford certain activities because of the nature of the material they are made of, but they also signify different functions to different groups of people who read the environment in different ways depending on their cultural perspective.

Like Gottdiener, Eco views architecture as spatially embodied forms that communicate their function as a result of the social and cultural forces that have brought them into being (Eco 1986). In short, architectural forms are signs that communicate their use. Whereas Gottdiener stresses the social aspects of reading the environment based on the possession of codes, Eco favors the notion of denotation and connotation as primary and secondary messages. (Writing after Eco, Gottdiener's conception amounts to a far more flexible and sophisticated variation of Eco's ideas).

"The Principle that form follows function might be restated: the form of the object must, besides making the function possible, denote that function clearly enough to make it practicable as well as desirable, clearly enough to dispose one to the actions through which it would be fulfilled." (Eco 1986, p.63)

Eco also defines the specific architectural grammar that operates at different levels within a building. For instance, at the construction level, a building amounts to a congregation of beams, columns, slates, floors, etc. Here nothing is communicated apart from what can be termed "Technical Codes". The second level, as Eco sees it, is the syntactic level where spatial types become articulated, e.g., stairways in relation to floors, windows in relation to walls, roofing in relation to floor plans, etc., and these amount to a set of grammatical architectural rules where roofs are always at the top of a building and stairs never go through windows. The third level of codes is the semantic level, where architectural elements such as roofs and stairs denote and connote different functions on different semantic levels, e.g., from the primary function of a roof to keep off the rain, to the grandeur of a cathedral dome, to the expected sociological behavior of being underneath that dome. This is perhaps the level that the BMX rider operates at in relation to his or her decoding of the environment as a potential play park.

Eco's primary contribution to architectural semiotics comes from these definitions of type, particularly the restrictive rules he uncovers within his second level of syntactic codes. Here, Eco defines architectural forms and, indeed, the practice of architecture from the point of view of architectural codes:

"Establish not generative possibilities but ready-made solutions, not open forms for extemporary 'speech' but fossilised forms – at best 'figures of speech', or schemes providing for formulaic presentation of the unexpected (as a complement to the system of established, identified, and never really disturbed expectations), rather than relationships from which communication varying in information content as determined by the 'speaker' could be improvised." (Eco 1986, p. 76)

Eco then defines architecture as the rhetorical play of already existing figurative forms, an organizing activity rather than a truly creative one. However, Eco is quick to point out that architecture still manages to renew its forms from time to time and that originality in architecture derives from the architect's ability to bring new ideas from other disciplines into the way in which traditional architectural forms are organized.

Eco's semiotic appraisal of architecture then, like Vihma's product semiotics, grasps quite clearly the semiotic nature of spatial elements in their relation to communicating their function. Eco's inclusion of the notion of architect as "speaker" also furthers the idea of spatial organization in terms of semiotic messages that are designed into the form of the space itself. Both Gottdiener and Eco are very aware of the semiotic capacity that architecture has in terms of form and function. Each of them, in their own terms, defines the environment as a group of messages or text that can only be read by a user in terms of the socio-cultural codes that they have at their disposal.

This is particularly interesting in relation to the example of my own personal network space presented earlier. From Eco' perspective, it is clear that this space is made up of constituent parts such as the physical elements of my house, the office, my computer, laptop, phone, servers, etc. It is also made up of the component parts that connect these elements together, e.g., the hard-wired connection to the Internet and the wireless capacities of other elements. However, much of the functionality of these elements remains hidden in the software that makes them function. It is, therefore, only through the reading and organization of these elements represented symbolically on screens that I am able to read and interpret the function of these network elements. Indeed, as we have seen with screen-based media, much of what is communicated here is extremely symbolic or abstract in nature. This makes the perceptual connection from the virtual to the real quite difficult. It is also what makes this kind of distributed information space possible at all.

According to Eco, then, through manipulating the configuration of these architectural network elements and the software that make them functional, I could probably reconfigure my network to include other devices and store information in other locations. What is more difficult to see, form this explanation, is how I might move around this space using the elements for my own ends. Architectural semiotics seems limited to describing the form and structure of the materials and how they communicate rather than how they are actually used.

### 7.1.3  Wayfinding

In terms of understanding how we move around and navigate through our environment, the work of Romedi Passini (Passini 1992, 1999) stands as a landmark in the development of wayfinding theory and in the development of information design to support this task. Passini takes an essentially cognitive approach to wayfinding activities, which is based on understanding two cognitive models:

- The linear sequential model – which is based on an egocentric view of an individual moving through space
- The spatial model – which is based on a non-egocentric view of the organizational structure of a place, or places, in relation to one another

Passini proposes that wayfinding can be considered a cognitive process that involves three key components: (a) the ability to make mental maps of the world around us, (b) the ability to make decisions related to the information in the mental maps, and (c) the ability to execute these decisions in the form of action in the world that moves us around the environment (Passini, 1992, p 46).

Of course, Gibson's perspective would be entirely different here, as it would show that, as we directly perceive the environment we pick up information about it. This process of pick-up in relation to our own physical characteristics and motivation reveals the affordances of the environment to us and we act on them accordingly. Interestingly though, within the environment rich with signs and information that is mediated to us, an element of thinking must come into play in terms of finding our way around. Interestingly, Passini develops an active model of wayfinding based on the decisions people make in relation to both the cognitive map they have of a place

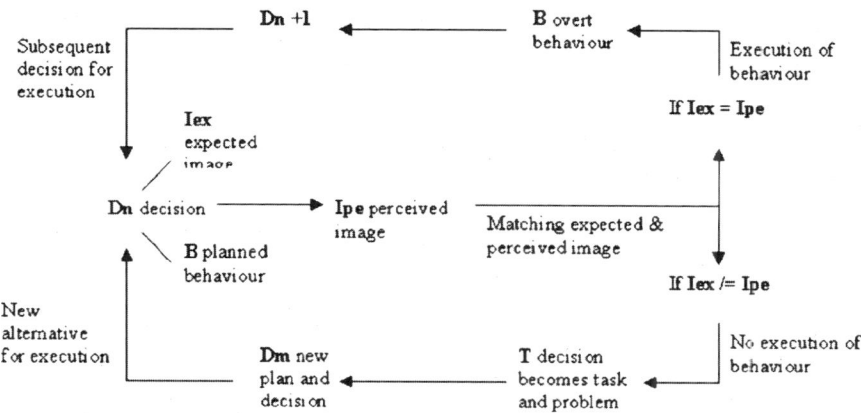

**Fig. 7.3** Wayfinding in architecture, after Passini (1992)

and the information they pick up from the environment (Fig. 7.3). This moves the position of the cognitive map from a stable picture of an environment to one in flux where the map is constantly changing in relation to information that is acquired and information that is forgotten (Passini 1992). His wayfinding model also shows the importance of the difference between the expected image, i.e., that in the mind, and the perceived image in making decisions.

Again we find ourselves encountering the problem of where to locate the semiotic threshold. It seems that in terms of wayfinding we are engaged in an unready-to-hand way of being, where we are sometimes moving around and picking up information about our environment in an online way where we do not have to think about it but which helps us orient ourselves. At the same time, we are doing something with this information in an offline sense. We are thinking about it and using it to plan where we will go after the next corner, for example. Much of this information is picked up through reading the signage placed in the environment, which requires us to interpret and make sense of its meaning. Wayfinding then is, in fact, a highly taxing activity with high cognitive overhead. This is why information is off-loaded back into the environment in the form of signs and maps.

In terms of information design this is interesting because both Passini and Michael O'Neill (O'Neill 1999) propose that the two cognitive models should be taken into account when designing not only wayfinding support materials such as signage and maps but also actual buildings themselves. This approach is aimed at bringing the expected image and the perceived image closer together, or at least providing the correct information at a potential decision point in a building. The more information that can be pushed towards the affordance end of our embodied semiotic spectrum, the less cognitively demanding will it be to find our way. It is perhaps quite telling then that it was within the cartographic community of France that Bertin's ideas had the greatest impact in terms of representing the various types of information required in map-making.

## 7.1.4  Wayfinding, Architecture, and Interactive Media

In wayfinding, Passini identifies two types of structures in the way that people acquire mental models of their environments, on the basis of their interactions as they move through it. Spatial models are derived from the relationships between buildings/places, as they exist in space, and sequential models are derived from buildings and places in relation to moving from point A to point B. These two types of mental models encourage the viewpoint of Benyon (Benyon 2000, 2001; Benyon and Hook 1997) that HCI can be abstracted in terms of navigating through "information space".

For Benyon, there is a strong connection between the way people understand the actual physical structure/signage of buildings and the information structures of computer interfaces. The position and type of information that are constructed in both buildings and websites, for example, take both a physical form and the form of a sign at the same time. Indeed, Benyon argues, not dissimilarly to Gottdiener (1986), that a semiotic analysis of space reveals many different subjective perspectives on space, which require to be interpreted in relation to context, cultural background, and the goals of individuals (Benyon 2001, p 428).

This he places as central to understanding both real and virtual environments. Moreover, Benyon also proposes that the extension of this concept is particularly applicable to information systems in which a user's orientation and navigation are essential to facilitate effective interaction. From an architectural perspective, this is related to Eco's levels of meaning and architectural rhetoric. The ability of users to recognize and understand the common forms in the structures of buildings is what allows them to navigate through them. Similarly, the ability of users to recognize the grammar of interactive media sign systems is what allows them to interact. Furthermore, it is this ability of the user to read these structural elements in relation to particular social knowledge that allows the user to interact with both real spaces and information spaces in different ways, e.g., the BMX rider and the hacker both appropriate spaces for their own use.

For interactive media, this is relevant to many emerging technologies that are shifting the location of our interactions, particularly the effect of the embedded devices of ubiquitous computing on the nature of information spaces, augmented reality systems, and virtual environments. If the very substance of our world, as in the forms of architecture, can be articulated as messages and texts by semiotic theory, then HCI would do well to understand the implications of this within the realm of interactive media. For example, embedded interactive elements are always going to have to be understood within the physical context in which they are situated. In such cases, the forms and structures of buildings play a huge part in helping us to understand that we can interact with them. Sensor-controlled doors that are smart enough to let the people carrying ID cards in and not those that are not carrying them, means that the cognitive load of having to remember passwords is off-loaded onto the environment. The open door signifies that we are welcome, and the locked door signifies that we are not.

Moreover, smart buildings that react to heat and movement can be programed to perform all sorts of energy-saving tasks such as switch lights on and off, regulate heating, and even boot up other systems ready for use, when you come in. While all this automation reduces the load on us, unfortunately it tends to also remove it from our view. Thus, we are often left with a sense that we have no control over what the system is doing. This can only contribute to the view that the medium we use to automate such tasks determines how we inhabit the spaces of our media-rich environment. Of course, the people that make and program the equipment ultimately determine this, but as layer upon layer of mediating technology become the backdrop to our interactions with the world, those of us without these skills often feel left out of the loop.

## 7.2  Case Study: The BENOGO Project

Having explored some of the aspects of semiotics that are related to understanding interactive spaces, in this section we will now focus on examining the construction of virtual environments as a way to show how some of these semiotic ideas can be employed to understand them. In particular we will concentrate, as we did earlier in Chapter 5, on comparing the real with the virtual, in order to establish how the medium works and which aspects of semiotics help describe the signification that takes place within them.

### *7.2.1  Recreating a Botanic Garden*

The study presented here is part of the BENOGO project, which was a European funded project that concentrated on trying to understand the concept of "presence". The BENOGO project was unique in that it used real-time Image Based Rendering (IBR) technology to create the visual component of the virtual environments that allowed physical movement within a restricted designated Region of Exploration (REX), which provided full 360-degree head movement and stereo ocular depth of field (Fig. 7.4).

As part of the BENOGO project, studies were undertaken to improve the fidelity of the medium as a representational tool for providing simulated virtual experiences of real-world places. The central idea motivating this aspect of presence research was to be able to "be in these places without going there" (Be-no-go). Studies from this project are well documented in the research literature (see, for example, O'Neill and Benyon 2003; Benyon et al. 2006; Turner et al. 2003).

The study presented here focuses on how to re-create the experience of being in a botanic garden. Like the study outlined in Chapter 5, an observational talk-aloud approach was used to gather data about users' experiences of both real-world places and their virtual equivalents. In the particular study outlined here (O'Neill and

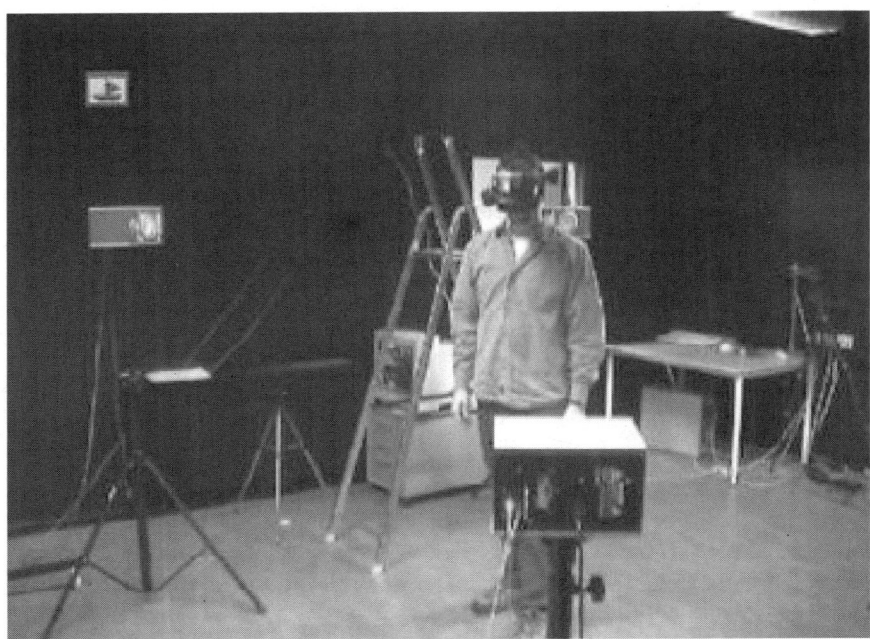

**Fig. 7.4** Using the BENOGO equipment

Benyon, 2003), 10 participants took part in the virtual section, while only half that number took part in the benchmarking activities in the real world.

The aim of this study was to uncover how users interpreted their surroundings by looking for the significant aspects of the environment that both enhanced the feeling of presence, i.e., made the virtual environment (VE) seem real, while also uncovering technical problems that got in the way of this experience.

Observational videos were taken that captured the users' point of view as they talked about and made sense of their surroundings. The videos were then viewed a number of times to promote immersion in the data, and a transcript of participants' comments was rendered along with notes on aspects of visual, audio, and timing of events. Analysis of the talk-aloud method resulted in the recurrence of a number of factors consistently in all the sessions. Broadly speaking, these were grouped into the three main categories that the talk-aloud questions explored:

- **The descriptive level of the environment**: recognizable objects and features of the environment, such as trees, plants, bridge, etc.
- **Significance**: The personal subjective engagement with the environment: feelings of calmness, pleasantness, lack of atmosphere and humidity, memories of holidays, etc.
- **Realness**: The technical limitations of the environment: cables, head-mounted display (HMD), resolution, etc.

Additionally, there were two other main areas of interest that arose from the talk-aloud sessions that were not considered before the tests, Movement and Sound. The next few short sections give some examples of user utterances and a brief description of how they were interpreted along with the video footage.

### 7.2.1.1 Descriptions, Things, and Objects

In the VE, the types of elements that people could see were obviously identifiable despite the resolution problems that arose owing to the technical limitations. Interestingly, participants often identified these technical problems as things that they could see in this descriptive section as if they were objects in the environment (e.g., "I can see stereo"). Every single participant commented on a computer-generated sculpture that had been added to the world and how odd it looked. These things were thus obviously present in the experience of the virtual world but did not seem to enhance the feeling of being there. (Note: participants are labeled R-real, B-BENOGO).

"I see a garden, with a bridge and an object, looks like coming from a leaf, staying in the middle, then I see the sun on the leaves. I hear some water. I see the roof." Participant B2.

"There is no moisture in the air, in my breathing or sensing on my skin. That's one of the things I'm missing." Participant B10.

In the real botanical garden, similar types of description occurred when participants identified particular objects such as trees, plants, water, the building, etc. (Fig. 7.5).

**Fig. 7.5** The BENOGO botanical environment

As well as these, a number of other things were highlighted in the descriptions of the real world. Fish, birds, signposts, heat, humidity, and people were all existent in the real world but not in the VE. The only time any of these things was mentioned in the VE was to point out their absence.

### 7.2.1.2 Significance and Memory

In terms of personal responses to the environments, it was in the real world that much more reference to significance and memory occurred. Participants were often reminded of other places that they had been to: other botanical gardens, gardens in general, or places with hot climates. Cultural references to films such as the Jungle Book, Tarzan, and general jungle films were mentioned, and personal memories of holidays, family members, and, in the case of two Greek participants, home were also mentioned.

"It reminds me of Kew Gardens I went there when I was younger, the other thing is the heat and the condensation it reminds me of a shower. Its very relaxing and quiet." Participant R1.

In the VE very little of this type of data was uncovered. There were some mentions of memories of other botanical gardens and holidays but very little that was as vivid as those in the real environment. In the VE there were a few mentions of games and gaming-related comments that were not present in the real environment.

"It reminds me of a place, a museum in Copenhagen which has a kind of indoor garden like this. It's not the same actually but it sounds very much the same... it reminds me of being on a holiday in a different place. Actually it doesn't remind me of a rain forest although it could be but there's too much light in here." Participant B10.

### 7.2.1.3 Realness

In the VE, comments about realness were almost always couched in relative terms. Most people understood or pinpointed resolution problems that made the visuals seem unreal. At the same time, most of the participants said that it "looked pretty real" particularly in relation to other types of VR.

"I think the way I see through the glass in here or whatever, is a bit blurry especially when I move quickly, but I think that it looks like a place that is here and I am looking through something." Participant B14.

In the real environment the same thing happened but this time in reverse. Everybody understood that they were in a real environment and that they could see real things, but the man-made construction of the physical environment brought out comments such as "fake" or "unnatural" that seemed to impinge upon participants' sense of realness.

"It is an artificially created real place. Everything around me is real I can touch it. It is tangible." Participant R1.

This is an interesting situation that became quite crucial in enhancing the virtual environment. By establishing that the "real" botanic garden felt fake in some way, the designers were able to get closer to that feeling than that of trying to re-create something completely natural.

### 7.2.1.4    Movement

Participants in the real world had much more freedom to move around the environment than in the virtual world. In the VE, attempts to move and mentions of wanting to move were quite common across most participants but these were physically restricted by the cables of the HMD, and technically by the REX of the images that made up the environment.

"I get the feeling of being attracted to walking over the bridge or trying to step down on some other place maybe walk round, to explore it even more. This possibility of being able to move around this place would enhance the feeling of being there." Participant B10.

A crucial aspect of improving the virtual world became clear in that the REX had to be increased to give a greater sense of being in the environment. Moving around involves the use of the body to explore. This embodied activity is very important in terms of making someone feel present in an environment. Without it, the exclusion of the body makes users feel they are simply looking at pictures or through a window at a world they are separated from.

### 7.2.1.5    Sound

Sound also featured quite highly in both environments. In the VE, many participants commented on the sound and its suitability to the visuals. However, many realized that the sound was not necessarily connected to the visuals even though there was something directional about it. Comments often arose about cars outside, birds, and the noise of water in the environment. These were sometimes accompanied by comments about the water not moving visually while it sounded like it was, or no movement in the trees where birds might be. In the real environment, sound comments were restricted to comments on the water, the humidifier being turned off and on, and the sense of quiet in the space.

"Sound, sound is very spatial it's location based." Participant B8.

"I can hear this bird's cry somewhere in the soundscape. So I, for a while, actually try to locate the bird. It seems to be impossible for me." Participant B10.

Linking up the sound with the visuals also became key to improving the user experience of the virtual world. While the images clearly displayed elements of the real world, the sounds often signified different things. In subsequent versions, a soundscape was developed that was tailored to fit more closely with the images.

## 7.2.2   Discussion

The first significant thing to come out of this analysis is what is revealed by the denotative level of meaning that occurs in the utterances of the participants. The evident split into two main types of denotation reveals the difference between the depicted world of the VE and the medium that supports this environment. The depicted world is revealed in the denotations that refer to the pictorial elements such as the bridge, the plants, water, etc. The technical world, or the supporting medium, is revealed in the denotations that refer to things like distortions, stereo/depth, monitors, etc.

In relation to aspects of semiotic theory, the images in the VE bear an iconic resemblance to the real things that they represent. In this way they are signs that represent real things. Taken as a whole, the VE is a group of concurrent iconic signs that represents a real place in a quite obvious semiotic way. While the structure of the environment might not be the same architecturally as the real one, the aim of the VE is to make it appear so. As the images bear such an iconic resemblance to the real features of the environment, the constituent components, i.e., trees, water, path, bridge, etc., can be read in a way similar to the real environment.

Interestingly, the technical elements of the medium are also experienced as part of the environment as much as the pictorial elements of the VE itself. In other words, the participants are equally aware of the medium that delivers the content as they are of the content itself. This ties in with the semiotic notion of the substance/form of the medium highlighted by Gottdiener. In this case, the substance of the medium is the computational software, the database of digital images, and the real-time rendering of the images on the dual screen of the HMD. The form is essentially the way in which the images come together to reveal a virtual world and the content therein.

However, the key to establishing a successful sense of presence in the VE is to try and minimize the experience of the medium, leaving only the content. In relation to presence research, this is a common problem that is known as the "illusion of non-mediation". Semiotic theory here helps us to establish how form and substance are related and how, like many real spaces, the substances of the material used to make them can often be hidden behind the content that they aim to portray. Of course, architecture often reveals the nature of the substance of construction, but for virtual worlds to succeed it must remain hidden.

Tied in with this notion of the form and substance of the images is the problem of movement and the role of the body. While most interactive technologies rely on following hyperlinks or navigating around information, virtual worlds usually attempt to make us feel immersed in the content of the environment so that we feel we can move around in it, as if it were a space that we occupy from a first person perspective. In this particular example, the REX is quite limited, so only a small amount of movement is possible. This is a result of the computational power needed to manipulate a massive database of images rather than having a virtual model of the place. What we gain is better fidelity in the iconic images, but what we lose is the ability to move around much in the environment.

The limited nature of this particular media makes it impossible to identify any manipulated sequential chains of signs in the environment. For, while it is evident that the VE can be considered one large group of concurrent signs rendered in the images, these signs in themselves cannot be manipulated in the same way that the symbols and indices of hypermedia can or indeed the stuff of the real world can. They have no interactive component to them that allows them to be manipulated in any way. As such, we can see that in the pursuit of immediacy, which attempts to hide the medium itself in order to promote presence, this particular VE had to restrict the interactive possibilities available to the users.

However, what is interesting about this is that the images themselves are rendered in such a way in real time to make us believe that we are actually immersed in a virtual world. In actuality, two composite images only are ever revealed at a time in the HMD, but the computer calculates the position of each image relative to the user, providing us with the right image of the place as we look around. The logic of way-finding is at work here, as it is by looking around and interpreting the information in the images that we can get a sense of where we might move to in the VE. Many of the participants expressed a desire to explore the environment further by walking around the paths and over the bridge. With more images and an extended REX, as some of the later versions of this environment used, this became entirely possible, and users were able to find their way around the virtual version of the real place.

Perhaps more than anything, it is the connotative aspects of user utterances that reveal how participants decode the signs that make up the VE. While there is a range of different memories and associations that are evoked during immersion in the environment, many of them are related quite clearly to the depicted scene. Here, the environment of the depicted botanical garden triggers a sense-making semiosis that allows cultural references to jungle movies or memories of holidays to take place. These can generally be grouped into three main areas: references to nature such as rainforest, animals, birds, warm atmosphere, and smells; references to a pleasant, quiet experience; references to the desire to move around or engage with the environment in some way.

The lack of metaphorical utterances used to describe the environment is also interesting. It seems to suggest that interaction with "immediacy" type media, which is purely iconic, requires less metaphorical understanding. Perhaps this is because the iconic nature of this type of medium appears to be more natural, supporting the illusion of non-mediation, whereas hypermediacy is largely symbolic in construction, confronting one with the medium itself, as Bolter and Grusin suggest (Bolter and Grusin 1999).

## 7.2.3   In Relation to Presence

Two widely accepted definitions of presence are "the subjective experience of being in one place or environment, even when one is physically situated in another" (Witmer and Singer 1998) or "the perceptual illusion of non-mediation" (Lombard and Ditton 1997). In this study, what is revealed about presence, as defined here, is that presence is a continually shifting of attention to what is experienced while immersed in a VE. This cannot but include elements of experiencing the medium itself, as the medium is the material that is formed to produce the illusory world. Without getting embroiled in a discussion of definitions of a sense of presence here, it is enough to say that the successful illusion of non-mediation (i.e., a perfect environment of immediacy) would be the removal of all the technical aspects of the medium that disturbs the experience of being in the depicted pictorial space of the VE. The ongoing and problematic question that is at the heart of presence research is how to make this possible. To that question, there is no answer offerred here. However, what this level of semiotic exploration reveals is the way the phenomena encountered by participants is denoted and made sense of as part of their "immediate" environment. This offers a potential method for measuring presence, which is evident in the relationship between the levels of recurrence of elements in the VE and the elements of the technical world. In the denotative data here, there is a high level of recurrence in elements of the VE and a low recurrence of elements intruding from the technical medium, perhaps suggesting that there is more content than medium, which should promote a better sense of presence in the VE.

### 7.2.4   Immediacy and Zones of Interaction

Bolter and Grusin (1999) make it quite clear that hypermedia confront the user with the fractured and multiple aspects of the medium directly, whereas immediacy is about providing one holistic singular representation of reality. In this study, while the zones of interaction described in Chapter 5 do not arise in the same manner, they can be identified as part of the mediating experience. The split between the immediate world of the VE and the medium that supports it is particularly relevant here. As discussed already, the world of the VE is the world of pictorial space represented by the photographs that make up the environment. The world of the medium, the monitors, the distortions, the HMD, etc. is the world that allows the creation of the pictorial space. Here, unlike the pictures that Owen and Dave worked on, the participants of the study are asked to "inhabit" the pictorial space in some way as if it were a real world. This is the basis of all VEs and it is at the core of issues of immediacy and presence identified earlier.

In the previous study, the organizational zone (zone 2) is identified as the tools, brushes, paint, etc., virtual or otherwise, that are manipulated throughout interaction. In this respect then, the world of the medium that supports immediacy is the real world of the equipment that tries to erase itself during the process of mediation. The organizational zone cannot be identified easily because, unlike hypermedia systems, immediacy systems try to hide it. Denotative utterances that highlight distortions, dynamic range, or the field of view reveal this aspect of the medium.

In considering the pictorial space of immediacy, it is important to consider how participants interacted with media in Chapter 5. What needs to be remembered is the way in which Owen and Dave were able to "step back" from the pictorial space into a reflective zone, or become engaged in the production zone, as they wished. With the attempted suppression of the medium in VEs, what happens is an immediate coming together of the pictorial space of production and the space of reflection.

This then forces participants to inhabit the productive space in an essentially reflective manner, where interaction is restricted (Fig. 7.6).

This is arguably supported to some degree by the masses of connotative utterances provided by the participants when they are asked about the associations they have with the environment. They are simply looking at it and thinking about it. They are reading it, not manipulating it or changing it.

This position might be reversed if the medium was designed to support a tele-presence activity such as controlling a bomb disposal robot, where the medium acts as a conduit to couple a real-world user with a real-world robotic device acting under the control of the user. The aim here is to ensure that the user and the robot inhabit the same real shared space despite great distance.

## 7.3  Summary

What this study has highlighted, in a way similar to the one about the artists, is the relative difference in the richness between real-world physical interactions with media and interactions with simulated media. Clearly, the signs of the simulated

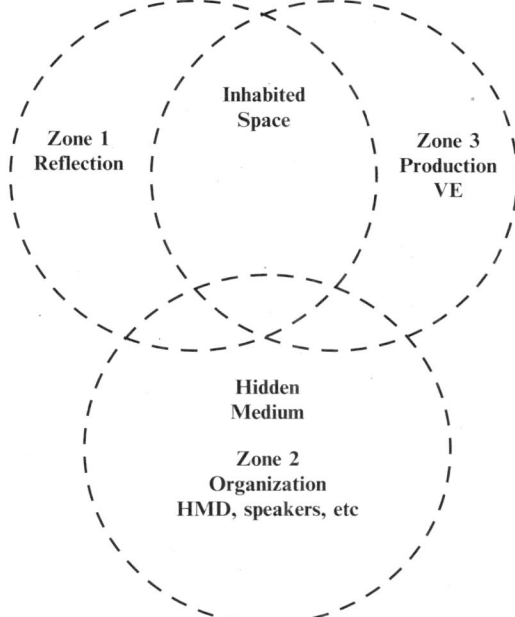

**Fig. 7.6** Adjusted zones of interaction in a virtual environment

botanic garden represent aspects of the real world very effectively, as elements in the environment were quite easily recognized, despite resolution limitations.

Interestingly, in both cases an extra level of connotative meanings appears as users interpret their surroundings, but this seems to be more prevalent in the real world as users walk about and physically interact with the stuff that surrounds them. Indeed, in the example presented here, the body is effectively excluded from interacting with the environment, by limiting movements to control only what is displayed on the screen as the user moves around. There is no possibility of manipulating the actual elements represented in the environment: they can only be looked at.

Undoubtedly, this has something to do with the restrictions placed on the perceptual process of users who are forced to engage with an impoverished iconic representation of the world rather than the real thing. Semiotic theory is helpful in describing interactions with this kind of media, by helping to make apparent the distinction between form and substance and the nature of iconic immediacy. We find we have gone full circle with the re-emergence of the importance of the body in interaction.

In the following part of this book we will re-engage with the issues of embodiment and return to thinking about how best we can integrate some of the important ideas that we have uncovered in these last few chapters. Most importantly, we will look at how the phenomenology of Heiddeger and ideas from semiotics come together with our understanding of Gibson's theories of perception to provide a framework that describes the continuum of interaction possibilities we have looked at so far.

# References

Benyon, D. (2000). Beyond the Metaphor of Navigation in Information Space. Paper presented at CHI 2000, April 1–6, The Hague, Netherlands

Benyon, D. (2001). The new HCI? Navigation of information space. *Knowledge-Based Systems,* 14(8), 425–430

Benyon, D. and Hook, K. (1997). Navigation in Information Spaces: supporting the individual. Paper presented at INTERACT'97, July 14–18, Sydney, Australia

Benyon, D., Smyth, M., O'Neill, S., McCall, R. and Carroll, F. (2006). The place probe: Exploring a sense of place in real and virtual environments. *Presence: Teleoperators and Virtual Environments,* 15(6), 668–987

Eco, U. (1986). Function and sign: Semiotics of architecture. In: Gottdiener, M. and Lagopoulos, A. (Eds.), *The City and the Sign.* Columbia University Press, New York

Gottdiener, M. and Lagopoulos, A. (Eds.), (1986). *The City and the Sign.* Columbia University Press, New York

Lombard, M. and Ditton, T. (1997). At the heart of it all: The concept of presence. *Journal of Computer-Mediated Communication,* 2, 3

Lynch, K. (1960). *The Image of the City.* The MIT Press, Cambridge, Massachusetts

O'Neill, M. (1999). Theory and Research in Design of 'You are Here' Maps. In: T. Boersema, H. C. M. Hoonhout and H. J. G. Zwaga (Eds.), *Visual Information for Everyday Use (Design and Research Perspectives).* Taylor and Francis, London

O'Neill, S. and Benyon, D. (2003). A semiotic Approach to Investigating Presence. Paper presented at COSIGN-2003, September 10–12, University of Teeside, Middlesborough

Passini, R. (1992). *Wayfinding in Architechture.* Reinhold, New York

Passini, R. (1999). Wayfinding: Backbone of graphic support systems. In: T. Boersema, H. C. M. Hoonhout and H. J. G. Zwaga (Eds.), *Visual Information for Everyday Use (Design and research perspectives).* Taylor and Francis, London

Turner, S., Turner, P., Carroll, F., O'Neill, S., Benyon, D., McCall, R. and Smyth, M. (2003). Re-creating the Botanics: Towards a Sense of Place in Virtual Environments. Paper presented at The 3rd UK Environmental Psychology Conference, June 23–25, Aberdeen, UK

Vihma, S. (1995). *Products as Representations – A semiotic and aesthetic study of design products.* University of Art and Design Helsinki, Helsinki

Witmer, B. G. and Singer, M. J. (1998). Measuring presence in virtual environments: A presence questionnaire. *Presence: Teleoperators and Virtual Environments,* 7(3), 225–240

# Chapter 8
# Being-with-Media

## 8.1 Preparing the Ground for Developing a Theory

In Chapter 3 we established that affordance has its roots in direct perception, which seems to fit best with the theories of embodiment that the phenomenologists have developed, rather than those from cognitive psychology. In Chapters 4–6, we looked at mediated perception in relation to semiotics, which specializes in theorizing about how signification takes place and how meanings are attributed to signs. What we have not done yet is to establish the relationship between embodied knowing, signification and representational cognition that have emerged from our initial explorations of these key areas. The way to start this is to consider the foundations of these approaches in order to establish a firm footing for bringing some of these ideas together.

As we have seen, phenomenology, semiotics and cognitive psychology are completely different schools of thought, with different areas of interest and research agendas. However, this simple division belies the complexity of their relationship. While phenomenology focuses on theorizing about the nature of being-in-the-world as a way of solving certain epistemological problems about the contents of consciousness, semiotics explores the problems of sign systems, communication of knowledge and the process of interpretation and attributing meaning to experiences. Additionally, cognitive approaches tend to look at the way in which these processes are carried out in the mind/brain. Where they overlap is at the point where mediated sign systems, such as spoken and visual languages, become an irreducible aspect of our surrounding phenomenal environment; i.e., the act of communicating produces 'artifacts' in-the-world that we encounter through our perceptual and cognitive functions in order to interpret them.

This becomes ever more apparent when we start to consider that nearly every aspect of our environment is now designed in some way. For example, architectural design is the manifestation of someone's ideas about our living and working spaces, interior designers create physical expressions of ideas about our seats, our desks and the colors of our walls, and software designers create expressions that manifest as the software that we use to communicate our own ideas to one another via email, text or videophone.

S.O'Neill, *Interactive Media: The Semiotics of Embodied Interaction*, doi: 10.1007/978-1-84800-036-0, © Springer Science + Business Media, LLC 2008

More and more, it appears that we live in a preconceived, designed world, and more and more it is difficult to distinguish what constitutes the difference between an authentic 'real' experience and an inauthentic 'anti-real' experience of that world. For example, are our experiences of new interactive devices authentic empirical experiences of our natural surroundings, or are they inauthentic experiences of some ideas mediated through the physical form that the device takes? By exploring the relationship between embodied knowledge, semiotics and cognition, in this chapter and the next, we hope to be able to establish a set of ideas that allow us to answer these kinds of questions.

### 8.1.1   The Problem of Reality

Realists insist that the external world is something that exists independently of our ability to know about it and that the only way we can know about it is through our empirical sensory perceptions of it. Thus we can never truly know everything about reality because our perceptual capacities are limited. They also insist that our knowledge of reality (the statements we can make about it) must be bivalent, i.e., logically true or false and that those statements are ultimately verifiable against evidence from the real world. However, the realist position often lacks the ability to show how we gain access to knowing that reality exists in the first place, as it is generally linked with a weak form of dualism, which insists on a split between mental phenomena and the physical material of our bodies and the world around us. In the conventional view of perception, our senses are notoriously unreliable because cognitive processes are always involved in the interpretation of sensory data. Therefore, it is not possible to 'know for sure' that our interpretation of reality is correct because we do not necessarily have direct access to it.

One solution to the problem has been the use of the scientific method, e.g., positive realism, to gather objective empirical evidence that either supports or refutes hypotheses about reality. Of course, empirical evidence that supports our hypotheses can always be brought into question by empirical evidence that is contradictory. For realists then, our knowledge of reality is always in a position to be challenged; empirical evidence supports theories that are our 'best guesses' about reality, but never proves them beyond a shadow of doubt.

Opposing this view, anti-realists argue that reality is, at least in some way, dependent on our cognitive abilities, i.e., in the act of perceiving the world we create our sense of reality. Born of essentially 'idealist' and 'constructivist' positions (which insist on the necessity of a mentally interpretive component to create reality), the anti-realist approach ensures that reality is something that is empirically accessible to us in that it is never beyond our cognitive capability (Blaauw and Pritchard 2005). While this solves the problem of access to reality, it plants the seed of 'relativism' in that nothing we know can ever be considered to be a true picture of reality because each and every one of us will have a different perspective on that reality. The upshot of this is that it is therefore not possible, from an anti-realist position, to assert that there is any such thing as a universally objective reality that we all share. Thus anti-realist thought insists that our knowledge (statements) about reality can only ever be true or false in ideal situations or in situations that are relative to one another.

Gibson's theory of ecological perception is of course wedded to the notion of direct realism, a special case of realism that states that through direct perception we are always availed of access to the true nature of things, even though we can perceive them in different ways at different times. Of course we always experience these things in relation to ourselves, but key for Gibson are two basic facts: That our perceptual capacities have evolved in relation to surviving in this very same real environment and there is no aspect of perceiving the real world that draws on any conceptualization or representation that might be stored in the mind. Of course this might happen at the cognitive level of interpretation, particularly in relation to understanding mediated knowledge, but it is not an aspect of direct perception. Thus Gibson maintains a realist position that avoids dualism.

Interestingly, Heidegger is often thought to be very much of an anti-realist because of his ontological commitment to the idea that human activity is essentially a cultural phenomenon and that science in particular is a culturally embedded practice. However, as Wheeler points out, this is not necessarily the correct way to understand Heidegger's ideas:

"Unlike our everyday practices, scientific practices do not themselves determine the nature of the entities they reveal. Scientific practices paradigmatically reveal the mathematically describable causal properties of entities, properties that, as the present-at-hand, are precisely not related to any particular network of everyday significance. Of course when one does science, one uses tools... and those tools are equipmental entities. Nevertheless, the entities that are uncovered by the use of those tools are not part of the relevant involvement-network. Thus, the Real are independent of everyday significance." (Wheeler 2005, p. 153)

Scientific method has to begin from some kind of 'theory laden' position that makes certain assumptions about the world, but it is not necessarily the case that these assumptions are the same as those we employ in our everyday smooth coping of encountering ready-to-hand as a network of equipment. Indeed, Heidegger gives science special status as a present-at-hand way of being that allows us access to the real properties of the world even if we start from incorrect 'theory laden' commitments. Should the outcomes of such misguided scientific endeavors prove to be flawed, this will become apparent, through hypothesis testing, in the difficulties faced by the theories that attempt to explain the evidence from experimentation. Eventually new theories will have to be found, ones that explain the scientific data much better than the originals. Heidegger then, can be considered very much of a realist in relation to the philosophy of science, while perhaps maintaining his commitment to the socially constructed aspects of our everyday world.

Considering the problem of the real in relation to semiotics, it becomes apparent that early semiotic thought such as Saussure's structuralism sits within a naïve deterministic realism where our statements, i.e., use of words, are bivalent and therefore an accurate reflection of reality. In contrast to this, European semiotic theory as it stands today in its post-structuralist form, sits well within an anti-realist position. The reason for this can be found in the linguistic turn of philosophers such as Wittgenstein and Derrida as well as the whole social-scientific revolt against the failed materialistic positivism that attempted to explain social phenomena through strict scientific method. These days, much of semiotic theory is at pains to disassociate itself from its structuralist past to the point of adopting constructionist stances that emphasize the role of sign systems in the construction of reality (Chandler 2002, p. 215).

This goes beyond the notion of perception shaping our experiences in cognition and moves towards the idea that not only our ability to think, but also our ability to perceive, is dependent on the conceptual frameworks that we have already learned from our peers. Such a position argues that the cognitive structures with which we interpret our empirical sense experiences are socially constructed and are specific to our particular history and location in space and time. Chandler continues:

"Assertions which may seem 'natural' may in fact be generated by the ways in which sign systems operate in our discourse communities. Acknowledging the mediation of signs need not involve a denial of external physical reality – we may argue that although things may exist independently of signs we know them only through the mediation of signs and see only what our sign systems allow us to see... Semioticians argue that signs are related to their signifieds by social conventions, which we learn. We become so used to such conventions in our use of various media that they seem 'natural', and it can be difficult for us to realize the conventional nature of such relationships. When we take these relationships for granted we treat the signified as unmediated or 'transparent', as when we interpret television or photography as 'a window on the world'. Semiotics demonstrates that the 'transparency' of the medium is illusory." (Chandler 2002, p. 215)

The semiotic position then is that the only way that we can know anything about anything is by making inferences about our sensory experiences in terms of what we already know (i.e., other inferential semiotic experiences that are derived from the store of representations that we keep in our heads as memories). This is an essentially anti-realist position, coupled with a weak form of dualism.

Semiotics also suggests that it is power and politics that play a determining role in establishing and maintaining the 'naturalized' conventions by which we interpret and construct our realities. It thus becomes incredibly important to be able to identify and differentiate between competing versions of reality that are constructed in our intellectual, ideological and political discourses. As mediation expands and permeates all aspects of our lives we must ask ourselves how we know we are living our lives and by whose rules.

"Signs do not just 'convey' meanings, but constitute a medium in which meanings are *constructed*. Semiotics helps us to realize that meaning is not passively absorbed but arises only in the active process of interpretation." (Chandler 2002, p. 217)

This is exactly the relativistic, anti-realist position that sets up the legitimization problem of scientific method that theorists such as Lyotard and Feyerabend identify with and which has become a central pillar of post-modernist thought (Feyerabend 1975; Lyotard 1984). Such extreme relativism argues for the free play of signs in representations of the world, each representation having its own natural position, each position seemingly as valid as the next. Relativism thus undermines any use of the scientific method as a way of progressing our knowledge about the world, by denying that we have access to any such real thing.

## 8.1.2 Clearing the Conceptual Ground

In relation to understanding interactive media this leaves us with a problem. On the face of it, the ecological theory of perception and Heidegger's description of science in general are both arguably by and large realist in their philosophical underpinnings. Semiotics on the other hand appears to be staunchly anti-realist in its position. So what can we do about it? One way might be to simply opt for a Saussurian structuralist approach to semiotics that maintains its realist roots. However, this provides its own problems. The fact that we would have to abandon much of the semiotic theory that has emerged over the last 50 years notwithstanding, Saussure's notion of perception is heavily dependent on the idea of the signifier as a sound-image that acts as a representation of perceptual phenomena in the mind. Thus, it is incompatible with the ecological approach to perception, which is our starting point for understanding how we perceive the world.

The alternative approach then, is to appeal to the Peircean strand of semiotics as a route to realism. The difficulty here is that Peirce's writings are so dense and fragmented in places that it is hard to determine exactly the thrust of his thesis. The basis of his semiotics is essentially phenomenological in character; in other words, he is mostly concerned with understanding what various forms of experience feel like from an internal perspective. This would seem to fit, to some degree, with the phenomenological positions we have seen so far from Heidegger and Merleau-Ponty. Moreover, while Peirce's theories are derived from Kant's transcendental idealism, Peirce comes out time and again against idealism, holding that reality is something that exists independent of the mind.

So far so good; we now have our way into exploring the problem of relating the ecological theory of perception to the phenomenology of being and to the study of sign systems in the form semiotics. We have prepared the ground by eliminating what might possibly have seemed like incompatibilities in the first instance. However, we have not yet successfully shown how these theories are compatible or what we get when we bring them together.

The key to solving this fundamental problem is in understanding the relationship between perception and conception. In other words, in developing a theory that takes into account how veridical perceptual experiences of the 'real' world that are derived through direct perception become stored, represented or re-perceived in our minds as knowledge. Furthermore this theory also has to take into account how this knowledge is fed back into the world as mediated representations that signify that same knowledge in our heads, allowing us to communicate and socially construct the everyday world of our reality. This is no small task, as it will still run into anti-realist trouble if we are not careful.

## 8.2 Bringing It All Together

Gibson's ecological theory of perception relies on the idea that direct perception is a fundamental process for engaging with the world that does not involve any kind of representational knowledge stored in the mind. It does not deny that this kind of knowledge might exist, just that it plays no part in perceiving the world. There are three main aspects to Gibson's theory:

1. Direct perception that works without the inclusion of representational knowledge.
2. Knowledge itself, representational or otherwise, that is part of other higher cognitive processes, e.g., thinking, imagining, etc.
3. Mediated perception, as distinct from direct perception, in that it provides us with information about the world at second hand. To some degree knowledge must be brought to bear on understanding, although the perceiving media is still direct.

Heidegger's phenomenological description of being-in-the world makes a clear distinction between how we experience the world in an everyday sense as a 'ready-to hand' network of equipment through which we smoothly cope with our surroundings, and our experience of the world as 'present-at-hand', where we reflect upon our experiences, which are disclosed to us in an entirely different, often objective, mode of thinking. Sometimes, perhaps more often than not, we find ourselves in a situation between these two modes of being, where we experience the world as unready-to-hand, i.e., where we only partially cope smoothly as we struggle to master or understand our situation.

In his attempt to relate Heidegger's ideas to cognitive science, Wheeler proposes that ready-to-hand experiences are a kind of on-line perceptual experience where the world is very much present and taking part in an embodied and embedded form of non-representational cognition, whereas he characterizes present-at-hand experiences as a kind of off-line experience where, away from the direct input of perception, we are manipulating mental representations as thoughts in our minds. So from our understanding of Heidegger we can establish three different modes of being:

1. Ready-to-hand: The mode of smooth coping and mastery of everyday tasks involving the equipment of the world as we find it.
2. Unready-to-hand: The mode of being where we are learning to cope with the world around us, or where we encounter some new situation in which we have only partial mastery or understanding.
3. Present-at-hand: The mode of being where we experience the world from a reflective, thoughtful state of mind, that draws on our knowledge of different experiences.

Peirce's phenomenology of experience that leads to his theory of semiotics also produces three clearly distinct descriptions of how we encounter the world. While his theory of semiotics outlines various types of signification, the categories of signs he identifies are all fundamentally based on these three modes of experience:

1. Firstness is purely and simply described by Peirce as the qualitative feeling we have of being conscious in a primal state. It is a state of flux, of fleeting undifferentiated sensations that are not tied to any clear perception, representation or concept. It is a state of pure possibility, that has the potential to form habits.
2. Secondness is the state of perceiving. It is not full-blown signification but proto-semiotic. In secondness the ego encounters the other (an external real world that forces itself upon us continually as constraints). In encountering the other, the ego becomes aware of itself, its limitations and capabilities.
3. Thirdness is the state of full-blown semiosis where we encounter not only the other in the form of an external world but representamens that stand in for absent aspects of that world. It is the category of mediated relations that form signs composed of a representation, the object being represented and an interpretation of what the representation is representing.

It would be nice to think that these three groups of three entities could map quite straightforwardly onto one another. Sadly, of course, it is not quite as straightforward as that. In order to make connections between these three different ways of explaining our relationship with the world, we must of course draw direct comparisons between them all but we must also establish that the connections we do make hold as tenable propositions. Obviously not everything will be compatible or fit neatly together. However, as we move to explore the relationships of these three groups of ideas we will draw on the work of other theorists to clarify what we mean and attempt to establish the extent of a spectrum of ideas that might constitute the basis of an embodied semiotic approach to understanding interactive media.

## 8.3 Throwness and the Mediating Environment

Heidegger's insight into how we inhabit and act upon the world through two essentially different but complementary ways of being, offers us some leverage with which to theorize about our relationship with media and our practices of mediation in general. On one hand, our ready-to-hand relationship to the world leads us to act directly on the world and then reflect upon the results after the fact. On the other, we start by reflecting on the situation that surrounds us and act upon those results in order to alter them.

The deeply embedded and embodied nature of our existence in the world results in these two modes of interacting with the world and as Heidegger states, we begin first in the state of experiencing by 'doing'. We are thus deeply entwined with the material of the world because our bodies too are material in existence. The very nature of our bodily existence affects the world around us. We take from our environment food and shelter. We leave behind footprints where we have walked, crumbs from our bread, heat from our bodies. These acts are inscribed on our surroundings without our thinking about them, they are the result of our bodily inhabiting the world around us and they are, in the first instance, unintentional.

In relation to the central themes of both McLuhan's theories about the media environment and Gibson's ecological theory of perception, Heidegger described the situation of 'thrownness', where we are born into a world constructed by the activities of previous generations of inhabitants. As one generation replaces another, we find ourselves living in an already adapted 'naturalized' environment, where the paths they have inscribed on the world become our immediate surroundings and the backdrop for our own perceptual and conceptual relationships with the world. In this way, the media that surround us become the 'norm', the 'everyday' and the 'mundane'.

For the most part, we are largely unaware of that which surrounds us. Our environment goes unnoticed as the background to our daily lives. But there is an interesting tension in the relationship between ourselves and our immediate environment. As we develop, we automatically manipulate and transform our environment beyond attaining our immediate needs for survival. The world becomes increasingly inscribed with the paths and structures of generation upon generation in layers of media that get thicker as time goes on. As a result, we must in turn not just fashion the world that surrounds us but 'refashion' that which has been left behind by others, in order to make it our own. Interactive media are an excellent example of this, if we think of them in terms of the perspective of remediation introduced in Chapter 2.

## 8.4   Authenticity and Mediation

Related to the concepts of 'Ready-to-hand' and 'Present-to-hand' are the concepts of 'authentic' and 'inauthentic' being. For Heidegger, 'authentic' being comes about through experiencing the world as ready-to-hand in its firstness, its primary authentically disclosed state in a direct one to one relationship with a natural environment without any mediation. 'Inauthentic' being then, for Heidegger, is the experience of being-in-the-world that is predominantly based on being thrown into a pre-inscribed world; i.e., it is an experience of living in a media-saturated world where most of our experiences are second hand. Both 'authentic' and 'inauthentic' experiences can occur in relation to both ready-to-hand and present-at-hand modes of being. That is, we can experience the natural world and the mediated world from the perspective of doing things with it or thinking about it.

Interestingly these ideas bear similar characteristics to those discussed earlier in relation to Gibson's theory of ecological perception. What Heidegger describes as authentic experience bears all the hallmarks of direct perception whereas inauthentic experience seems very similar to Gibson's outline of mediated perception.

Of course it is not so simple as to just make a direct comparison between the two. One has to take into account the relationship between Heidegger's description of modes of being and Gibson's tentative distinctions between direct perception and internalized re-perception processes (autostimulation). In a general sense, it would not seem out of line to point out that what Heidegger describes as ready-to-hand looks very similar to Gibson's ideas of experiencing the world through direct perception. Both theories consider the body as the fundamental basis for our relationship with the world and both theories describe an active being both perceiving and doing things in the world as the primary way in which we encounter it. We have already drawn the same comparisons (Chapter 4) with Merleau-Ponty's phenomenological approach that takes the role of the body as paramount.

It is, however, important to point out that some confusion may arise in Gibson's delineation of the difference between direct perception and mediated perception. If ready-to-hand experience is related to direct perception, does it mean that it is distinct from mediated perception? The answer is, no. From Heidegger's perspective it is of course possible to have Ready-to-hand experiences of both the natural environment and the mediated environment (think about interacting with various media as equipment). The distinction he makes is between authentic and inauthentic disclosure of the world. While Gibson is a little vague here, we have already seen in our deeper exploration of this problem that direct perception has to be involved in the perception of the natural environment and of materials that afford the mediation of contents during signification. Thus, it can be argued, Gibson's notion of direct perception is very similar to Heidegger's notion of ready-to-hand, but the distinction must be maintained in experiencing an authentic natural environment and an inauthentic mediated environment.

The other important aspect to consider here is how Heidegger's notion of Present-at-hand relates to Gibson's theories of internalization. Both ideas describe a process of thinking rather than doing and both ideas suggest that this is not the primary mode in which we encounter the world. Where Gibson suggests that thinking is a specially adapted learning of perception that has been internalized in order to manifest verbalization or visualization in the mind, Heidegger is less concerned with describing the processes that occur in terms of cognition and rather focuses on the way in which the phenomena of thought are disclosed to consciousness through thinking. This is simply a matter of difference in approach and level of description that occurs in relation to different methods of analysis, i.e., Gibson being a psychologist and Heidegger being a phenomenologist.

Importantly though, there is something to be said for more closely examining the relationship between thinking and mediation in both Gibson's and Heidegger's theories. Both theories describe what is essentially a form of offline cognition, i.e., it is not based on direct perception of the surrounding environment (although direct perception or interaction with the world in a ready-to-hand way may actually be occurring at the same time).

The hypothesis is that while interacting directly or in a ready-to-hand fashion one does not need to think about what one is doing; it is simply a matter of perceiving and acting as a continuous loop of smooth coping. As soon as something becomes difficult to do, or perhaps mediated content is encountered that needs to be understood in order to progress with coping, thinking enters the scene.

For Heidegger this is the switch to experiencing something as present-at-hand; for Gibson it is drawing on our learned capacities to re-perceive knowledge from previous experiences. In the case of understanding media, perhaps reading a passage in an instruction manual while performing a difficult task, such as replacing an oil filter in a car, we perceive and use the manual in a direct and ready-to-hand fashion but we are engaged cognitively in understanding the content presented through the medium of writing. Once we have established, through reading and thinking, what the next course of action is, we then move on to act it out in the world. Of course this is recognizable as essentially akin to the model of computational descriptions of representational cognition and task-based problem solving. However, what we learn from both Gibson and Heidegger in this instance is that this kind of thinking is a special kind of cognitive process that emerges from our embodied interactions with the world, rather than, as has previously been thought by other theorists, the primary way in which we engage with the world.

Whether this kind of cognition is representational or not is still up for debate. Indeed, while Gibson proposes an alternative view based on an extension of direct perception to internalized processes, representations may well yet prove to be an important part of the picture. What seems clear however, from both Heidegger and Gibson, is that they play a much smaller part in our everyday interactions with the world than was previously thought.

Thinking is a special case of interacting with the world and when the world affords us smooth coping we do not have to think. Arguably one of the ways in which the world requires us to think is in understanding and interpreting mediated communications. If we think of the rich sources of content mediated by books or by films and television programs, we are generally compelled to witness them in a reflective frame of mind. Reading is less a doing activity than a reflective thinking activity and thus it involves our internal thought processes, whatever they may be, more than our smooth coping practices. Of course we must turn the pages and perceive the characters on the page, but these elements seem to disappear in the act of reading as the content is revealed to us, just as the hammer disappears in the act of hammering.

A curious aspect of relating Gibson to Heidegger becomes apparent when we consider how inauthentic or mediated experience is, in relation to this reflective mode of being present-at-hand. It would seem to make sense, given the need for reflective thought in terms of understanding mediated content, that thinking is in some respects a fundamentally inauthentic activity, when we are engaged with thinking about mediated material. Similarly, of course, when we are engaged in making physical representations of our thoughts, i.e., placing them out in the world either through writing, speaking or drawing, we are making further inauthentic media elements to be thought about. Thus we cannot help but inhabit an inauthentic mediated environment.

## 8.5 Being, Affordance and Mediation

So how does all this help us understand media, especially interactive media? Learning from both Gibson and Heidegger's descriptions of both direct perception and ready-to-hand mode of being, we can see that Media (as the material of the world that affords the mediation of some form of content) must essentially disappear from our conscious attention in order for us to be able to concentrate on the content which is embedded in it, unless we want to know something about the qualities of the mediating material itself, in which case we focus our attention on it and we are able to think about that rather than the content.

Offline thinking, in Wheeler's description (Wheeler 2005), is a purely mental activity; it is utterly representational in nature. There are no physical entities involved in this process, only representational elements or signifiers. However, as Wheeler argues further, physical entities outside the mind can support online cognition, by providing vehicles to literally hold our thoughts by fixing them in our perceptual field.

From what we have seen so far, this is only possible through mediating materials that exhibit invariant repertoires of behavior (affordances) that allow us to impress our thoughts and ideas into them. In doing so we no longer strain to hold our attention to them in our minds, we simply attend to them as part of our environment, which is cognitively less demanding. Therefore, the physical form of the material we chose to mediate our thoughts with must not interfere with our thinking. It must disappear from our consciousness. We do not want to think about the form, we usually just want the content. In this way our ideas become manifest as artifacts that inhabit the world, e.g., speech, dance, poems, paintings, books, etc, as well as beds, houses, doors, cars, and computers. The former are entities that signify meaning for us; they mediate our ideas and our knowledge, allowing us to communicate. The latter are also entities that mediate our ideas but in general they are born of our physical bodily needs and habits and exemplify knowledge in action rather than knowledge in communication.

Physical engagement with the entities of our world can afford us possibilities of interaction when they allow us to act without having to think about what we are doing. Ideas are mediated by physical entities that afford us the possibility to think about the content of the medium rather than the medium itself. In this sense the affordance is in the qualities of the medium that have become naturalized to our perception, that carry or represent some other form or idea. In short this is signification.

Here we should bear in mind that the painter Mark Rothko argued that the intentional act of inscribing an idea into the material that surrounds us is a biological necessity for human kind, an "extension of oneself into the perceptible environment" (Rothko, 2004 p. 8). Consider simply the first acts, the primitive acts, of marking the world around us intentionally, e.g., territorial markings, cave paintings, tribal body painting, in short, the fundamental graphic act described by Gibson. In this sense the act of intentionally marking the world fulfils the need to express one's self or to affirm one's own existence in the world by having the world bear witness to one's acts.

This is of course a fundamental aspect of our relationship with the world around us. However, there is perhaps a deeper way to understand this relationship between bodies, minds and mediation. The realization that we can intentionally mark the world around us, allows us to give form to our thoughts and experiences. In marking the world we no longer have to think. Instead we can look. In giving form to our ideas we no longer have to hold them in our heads. The world can hold them for us. In line with Gibson's notion of Affordance, mediation is possible because as we intentionally give form to an idea by inscribing the material world around us, we give that idea the properties of an 'invariant repertoire of behavior'; thus an idea achieves the kind of stability that the mind cannot give it. A medium provides us a continual perceptual stimulus directly related to our perceptual capacities, which in turn reduces cognitive load by performing the act of fixing the idea for us.

With the idea out in the world formed by a medium, we are more readily able to engage with it, not just in an intellectual present-at-hand way, but in a ready-to-hand way. Arguably, all acts of mediation must to some extent be ready-to-hand acts of skilled smooth coping, as in order to intentionally inscribe a medium with an idea one has to have developed some kind of embodied know-how about the world that allows this to take place.

Interacting with media of all kinds then falls between these two modes of being. On one hand we perceive and encounter our media-rich environment directly, we manipulate it and transform it through our-ready-to-hand mode of being. On the other hand, we are constantly viewing, reading and interpreting mediated information through the reflective mode of encountering it as present-at-hand. At the same time we move between these two modes of being as we inscribe, interpret, transcribe and transform our mediated environment. In a very clear sense we are deeply entwined physically with the media in our environment and in another we are constantly making, and making sense of, the inscriptions that the media environment affords us.

## 8.6  Summary

What we have seen in this chapter is an attempt to clear the conceptual ground, in order to establish a firm footing for exploring the relationships between some very different theories. The problem of reality has been explored and a position that allows for a direct realist approach has been established in order to accommodate Gibson's theories of ecological perception as the starting point for our theorizing. From here we have examined, in more detail, the relationship between Gibson's ideas and those of the phenomenologists, in particular those of Heidegger. In this way we have been able to compare and contrast these different theories in order to establish where they overlap. This has resulted in some interesting theoretical leverage, which helps to explain our embodied relationship to our media- rich environment and the central role that the body takes in interacting with and inscribing onto the stuff of the world as media. In the following chapter we will look more deeply into the relationship between semiotics and theories of embodiment, as well as theories of embodied cognition, which will move us toward a framework for understanding interactive media that takes into account the role of the body, as well as providing an explanation of representational cognition.

# References

Blaauw, M. and Pritchard, D. (2005) *Epistemology A-Z.* Edinburgh University Press, Edinburgh.

Chandler, D. (2002) *Semiotics: The Basics.* Routledge, London.

Feyerabend, P. (1975) *Against Method: Outline of an Anarchistic Theory of Knowledge.* New Left Books, London.

Lyotard, J.-F. (1984) *The Postmodern Condition: A Report on Knowledge.* Manchester University Press, Manchester.

Rothko, M. (2004) *The Artist's Reality: Philosophies of Art.* Yale University Press, New Haven.

Wheeler, M. (2005) *Reconstructing the Cognitive World: The Next Step.* The MIT Press, Cambridge, MA.

# Chapter 9
# Embodied Semiotics

## 9.1  Non-representational Interaction in a Thoughtless World

As we have already seen, it is quite possible to relate Gibson's view of direct perception to that of Heidegger's ready-to-hand mode of being. Both theories attempt to describe a primary way of interacting with the world that is based on the emergent relationship between the body and the environment it inhabits. As such, all the points from Gibson's theory identified above seem to fit across Heidegger's description of being as ready-to-hand, but what of semiotics? How does semiotics relate to this mode of being?

Interestingly, it is not so much the Peircean concept of firstness that seems to fit here, but rather that of secondness. While firstness describes, to a certain extent, the undifferentiated continuum of sensation that Gibson describes as the flux of environmental energy, it quickly becomes apparent that in bringing body and world together, semiotic theory must move to secondness. It is in secondness that Peirce describes how the "ego" fist encounters the "other", i.e., the not itself, and in doing so is made aware of what itself is.

In essence then, the emergent process of being that perceives affordances and experiences the world as ready-to-hand is best described in semiotic terms as the proto-semiotic relationship between the ego and the other. Thus, the second point identified in Peircean semiotics seems to fit best with Gibson's theory of perception and Heiddeger's primary mode of being, in terms of describing the same phenomena from different theoretical perspectives. To extend this notion further, it is perhaps useful to consider the work of the biologist and proto-semiotician Jacob von Uexküll (Sebeok 1979).

Primarily, von Uexküll was concerned with how organisms relate to their environments and the biological factors that determine what an environment means to an organism. According to Thomas Sebeok, the most important thing that von Uexkull attempted to do was to reconnect the phenomenal world, as experienced by a living thing, back to the reality of the environment in which it exists, from a biological perspective (Sebeok 1979, p 196)

This is achieved through describing what von Uexkull termed the 'Umwelt', which is the world that an organism perceives in as much as that perception is the

S.O'Neill, *Interactive Media: The Semiotics of Embodied Interaction*,
doi: 10.1007/978-1-84800-036-0, © Springer Science + Business Media, LLC 2008

organization of sensation into recognizable environmental elements, or signs, which may be good, bad, or of no consequence to the organism (Deely 1990, 2001). The fundamental underpinning factor of this perceptual process is the genetic makeup of the organism, which defines its sensory/perceptual capacity, as a matter of species. The main idea behind the concept of the Umwelt is that each aspect of this proto-semiotic phenomenal environment has a functional meaning for the organism and that it is created, or emerges, as the organism actively engages with the real world around it. Embedded in this concept is the notion that, as a result, it is not possible to separate minds, bodies, and worlds because they all contribute to the process of a meaningful existence (Sharov 2001, p 211).

Drawing on Uexkull's work, Sebeok makes it evident that semiotics is not, as first suggested by Saussure, an arbitrary conventional process but that semiotics is present throughout the animal kingdom, and that humans in particular can be considered to be "semiotic animals" at a fundamental level, i.e., the level of the body. Uexkull's focus on signification works at a genetic level, where an organism is programed in its bodily makeup to decode the "signs in its environment" as a matter of survival through a perception/action loop.

As an organism interacts with the world, meaningful decoding takes place on the basis of the relationship between the organism's genetic codes (i.e., what it is programed to do in order to survive) and the makeup of the environment. The important thing to remember is that the organism is an essential part of the environment, not something distinct from it. The nature of the environment affects the survival of the organism and the organism affects the nature of the environment. In the complex case of human beings, we live in a world that has been vastly altered by our cognitive abilities such that we inhabit not only the empirical world of physical entities but also the world of sign systems, which are a direct result of our cumulative interactions with the world (and each other) over time. Thus, the relationship between the subject and the object is dealt with in a pragmatic way, where external phenomena are experienced as signs that are meaningful to an organism and there is no separation of the two (Sharov 2001).

The similarities between Gibson's theory of perception and von Uexkull's Umwelt theory are really quite striking. What von Uexkull describes as an organism's Umwelt is in effect its ecological niche, which is made up of the physical properties of the organism and the physical properties of the environment brought together through interaction. An Umwelt then, can also be described as an emergent collection of affordances that the environment provides in relation to an organism's perceptual capacities.

We have to be very careful here to disentangle some terminology. While the similarities are undoubtedly self-evident, it is important to clarify exactly what von Uexkull means in terms of signification. Confusion is inevitable if we incorrectly assume that the kinds of signs von Uexkull is talking about are similar to those perceived in mediation, or as some form of representational view of mind a la Norman. Von Uexkull does not intend any cognitive processes to be involved in his descriptions of Umwelts. Primarily concerned with describing the Umwelts of bees, insects, birds, and other animals (Clark 1997), the kind of signification von Uexkull is talking about is species-specific and natural in character. He does not intend for us to think that ideas and interpretation are brought into the perceptual process. He simply suggests that organisms already have an "inbuilt" primary semiotic component as part of their genetic physical makeup, which interprets the world in a meaningful way through the perceptual process. This then brings his ideas even closer to those of Gibson.

Unfortunately, given the history of semiotics (which tends to draw on representational theories of mind) and the lack of clarity in establishing the limits of the semiotic threshold, (i.e., where true signification begins and proto-semiotics ends), some semioticians have taken von Uexkul to mean that signification is what occurs at all levels of perception. Thomas Sebeok, for example, makes the jump from direct perception to mental models, via von Uexkull theories, in claiming that organisms do not necessarily perceive things as they really are, but that they perceive signs that are interpreted in relation to their genetic blueprint. This process of interpretation results in mental models of the world that in turn are made sense of via other signs that act as further interpretants (Sebeok 1979 p 195).

We are not so quick to establish the same sort of link here because it is predicated on the assumption of a representational theory of mind, which we are, at least in relation to perception, attempting to avoid. Our aim is to clarify how several different theories might be related to one another at the point where they describe the same elements of interactive media. For us then, it is particularly important to firmly understand how perceptual experience of the world moves towards knowledge and the possibility of signification before making a link to higher cognitive functions.

According to Peirce, signification occurs as thirdness, so the distinction between secondness and thirdness is crucial here. In this respect, it is important to note that Gibson's distinction between the immediate perceptual experience of the world that surrounds us and the second-hand experience of media, is in fact, unbeknown to Gibson, the same distinction drawn by semioticians to describe the location of the semiotic threshold. It has never been exactly clear how it is possible to cross the semiotic threshold and for direct experience to become either knowledge in the mind as memory (possibly representational) or how it becomes represented back in the world. It is to these issues that we now must turn.

## 9.2   The Problem of the Semiotic Threshold

The problem, in semiotic terms, has always been where to place the threshold between the empirical experience of the continuum of authentic reality and the mediated experience of signs composed by an author and interpreted by a reader (inauthentic reality). While there are many different strands of semiotic theory, it is only in Peircian semiotics (and versions of semiotics based on Peirce) that an attempt has been made to address this semiotic problem in relation to the experience of different kinds of phenomena.

When Umberto Eco talks of a "continuum" in his books on semiotic theory, what he alludes to is the idea of a "presemiotic experience", i.e., an experience of the undifferentiated continuum of sensation, or as he further claims, what Kant would describe as sensations within the manifold of intuition, where direct empirical experience of the world is all undifferentiated sensation and therefore nothing can really be signified (Eco 1976, 1999).

The problem, of course, is how to get from sensations in the manifold of intuition to higher cognitive function, i.e., pure semiotic experience, concepts, ideas, etc. The question is: What is it that moves us from experiencing the world from below the semiotic threshold to beyond it, in our higher cognitive functions?

For Gibson, this is explored in the idea of re-perceiving as a form of internal auto-stimulation of the perceptual capacities. Gibson thus attempts to avoid a representationalist theory of mind entirely by describing thinking as an extension of practiced perceiving, rather than the storage and retrieval of coded representations of previous experiences. This perspective avoids the problem of explaining how perceptual experiences of the real world are transformed into coded representations because it maintains that there is no change in *kind* between perceptual experiences and those that are re-experienced as memories.

Semiotics, on the other hand, must still struggle with the specter of representationalism, which accompanies much of the European school of thinking. Even in Peirce, there remains the notion that interpretants are somehow stored in memory and then called upon, by association, to shed light on the meaning of representamens. This is a problem that is difficult to avoid.

## 9.2.1   Semiosic Primitives and Embodied Schemas

In semiotics, the transition from perceptual experience to full-blown semiotic experience of representational mind is often described as a jump across the semiotic threshold, but it is not clear as to how this process occurs. One approach is to consider what are called semiosic primitives, which act as the schematic background for the translation of perceptual experience into cognitive representations. Umberto Eco explains:

"Let us think of a being placed in an elementary environment, before it comes into contact with others of its kind. However it decides to name them, this being will have to acquire some fundamental "notions" (no matter how it might later decide to organize them into systems of categories, or in any case into units of content. It will have to have a notion of high and low (essential for its corporeal equilibrium); of standing upright or laying down; of some physiological operations, such as swallowing or excreting; of walking, sleeping, seeing, hearing; of precieving thermic, olfactory, or gustatory sensations; of feeling pain or relief; of clapping hands. Thrusting a finger into some soft material, hitting, gathering, rubbing, scratching, and so on... however it comes to name these fundamental experiences, they are certainly original" (Eco 1999 p 144).

For Eco, these semiosic primitives act as the schematic background to all our higher cognitive functions. These bodily originated primatives provide the stepping stone across the semiotic threshold, from the perceptual experience of the undifferentiated continuum of the world, to higher cognitive function, by acting as a primitive embodied framework of reference from which semiotic inferences can be drawn.

Eco is careful to avoid the debate about what goes on inside the "black-box" of the mind, claiming that it is not so important in semiotics to know how the mind does what it does, at the wet-wear level, but rather to describe, in a more satisfactory way, how experience becomes knowledge. Therefore, he does not describe what form these semiosic primitives take in the mind, but perhaps we can find a similar description elsewhere.

### 9.2.2  Semiotics and Embodied Cognition

Interestingly, in both *Metaphors We Live By* (Lakoff and Johnson 1980) and *The Philosophy of the Flesh* (Lakoff and Johnson 1999) Lakoff and Johnson also argue for the "embodiment of mind", where consciousness operates in a figurative way that is entirely dependent on the existence and activities of the body. They propose that, at a deep level, there are links between the motor functions of the body, active perception, and neural networks, which develop in relation to these processes engaging in activity in the environment. The relationship between mind and body is therefore hard-wired within the brain where physical connections allow the development of metaphorical modeling processes, based on motor activity (Lakoff and Johnson 1999). This is echoed in Allot's view of the evolutionary development of language (Allot 1992, 1994) where the central view is that the human capacity for language is hard-wired into our brains as the perceptual and primal motivating functions of our genetic makeup.

To back this up, Lakoff and Johnson give countless examples of everyday metaphorical conceptualizations that take the bodily experience of existing in the world as their base domain. From this, they derive a number of categories for body-based metaphorical understanding of the world we inhabit called image schemas, some of which are shown in (Figure 9.1).

Others include

- The centre – periphery schema
- The cycle schema
- The part – whole schema
- The verticality schema

What Lakoff and Johnson essentially propose is an understanding of cognition that not only relies on having a body to move around and perceive a world, but more radically, a cognition that is fundamentally related to the sensory motor capacity of the human body as a basis, not only for perception, but also for conceptualization (Brandt 2000). They propose that it is the same bodily structures that move us around and allow us to act in the world that allow us to think. Furthermore, they

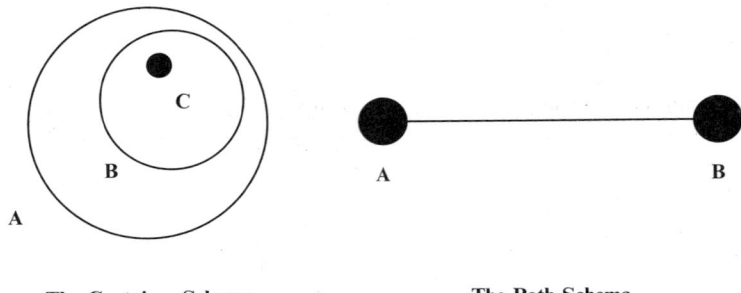

The Container Schema                          The Path Schema

**Fig. 9.1** Some examples of Image Schemas

propose that complex cognitive activity is built up from a number of combinations of these primary metaphorical embodied thinking building blocks. Thinking and meaning-making is a continual process whereby we are always comparing our experiences against our previous experiences, from one domain to another, in a metaphorical way, where the very nature of our embodied existence gives us grounds for understanding.

At the basic level, it appears that both semiosic primitives and low-level embodied schemas are describing the same sort of thing. That is to say, because we have bodies, which act in the world through perception/action loops, we already have knowledge embedded in our very physical being about how we relate to the world. We are physically aware of up and down, of inside and out. We are also aware of wet and dry, near and far, and a whole host of other comparative experiential sensations that we perceive day in and day out. These perceptual experiences create the bedrock for our thoughts as we are pushed and pulled by the world from what Mearleau-Ponty described as our optimum point of equilibrium.

Perhaps then, this outline of primary semiotic schemas, as embodied in the active perceptual neural networks of the brain, can also be viewed as the corporeal components of Gibson's perceptual system, which is not only involved in direct perception of the world, but is trained, through practice, to internalize its processes. So long as they are considered to be part of the perceptual system, rather than free-floating representational concepts in the mind, there is no reason to believe that Gibson's description of internalization could not be compatible with this notion of embodied schemata and semiosic primitives.

Furthermore, the very nature of these embodied primitives, which are derived and maintained through the pressures of the evolutionary process at a genetic level, ensure a connection to reality because they are born out of millennia of testing in the crucible of surviving in the material world. They are not, as a strong realist position might require, deterministically direct connections to reality. Neither, as anti-realists propose, are they free-floating signifiers that bear no relation to reality whatsoever. While higher cognitive interpretation of perceptual input may still be necessary in order to have knowledge about reality, the semiotic inference that is necessary to know anything might only be made possible by the existence of these primary embodied schemas. They are not previous knowledge of a conceptual kind, free-floating in the mind. They are primary interpretants ultimately anchored by their embodied perception capacities, to experiences of the real world.

### 9.2.3 A Motor Theory of Language

A further development of these ideas can be found in the bio-semiotic research inspired by von Uexkull and Sebeok, which explores a motor-theory basis for the development of language (Allot 1992, 1994). The theory is based on functional ideas similar to Uexkull's, but focuses on the motor activity at a neural level, which is not that dissimilar to the work of Lakoff and Johnson. The theory suggests that as humans have evolved and become more sophisticated, the modeling systems and motor patterns for activities like movement have, over time, been transferred to activities involving the production of sound resulting in speech (Allot 1992).

The important idea to grasp here is that speech becomes possible as a result of the interconnection between the genetically inherited neural structures of the organism and the given ecological niche that it inhabits, each one affecting the other. As we have evolved, for example, our perceptual capacities have developed in relation to the structure of the world around us and those other beings that also impinge upon/share our habitat. The motor patterns and habits we evolved for moving around our environment are physiologically and neurologically connected to our capacity for speech. Movements associated with breathing, for example, are central to both acting in the environment and speaking about it. At some point, so the theory goes, these connections allowed us to begin to communicate vocally in a very basic sense about our environment. Over time, this has evolved into the complexities of speech we hear today.

This is entirely in line with Uexkull's idea of the Umwelt, which Deely places as "central to semiotics" (Deely 2001). However, Deely goes further. His argument is that language has so altered the human Umwelt that humans can no longer be seen to exist in a "semiotic web based only on biology" (Deely 2001). The motor-theory argument takes this into account through the link between perception and action, stating that within this continual functional process, language is simply an extension of the perceptual modeling capacity turned into action within the Umwelt.

Deely's conception of the Lebenswelt (used to describe the language-infused semiotic world of humans) is to a greater or lesser degree a glorified Umwelt, equivalent to and working in the same way as the one proposed by Allot (Allot, 1994). Kalevi Kull identifies this conception of the semiotic world of humans as a set of interconnected Umwelts or Semiospheres, which bear a marked resemblance to both Eco's and Halliday's conceptions of social codes, as well as Brier's cyber-semiotic model (Brier 2001).

In essence, what is important to grasp here is that we not only experience the world biologically in terms of perception/action loops, but that we also live within the production and interpretation of mediated cultural signs (such as language) that we experience as part of the world around us. The mediated signs that we encounter are possible only because we perceive and act in the world that allows us to manifest our ideas in the form of signification, be it language, painting, or whatever. What semiotics describes as the distinction between secondness and thirdness, i.e., the semiotic threshold, is essentially the same as what Gibson describes as the distinction between direct perception and mediated perception. It is also essentially the same distinction made by Heidegger in terms of his description of authentic and inauthentic experience. There is also room to consider being ready-to-hand and present-at-hand, in relation to the semiotic threshold, if we explore further a semiotic understanding of cognition.

## 9.3   Semiosis, Embodied Cognition, and Conceptual Blending

In semiotics, Peirce's concept of thirdness is the location of genuine signification or full-blown semiotic experience. What this refers to is the point where a representamen, referent, or representation is put in place of a real object, in order to stand in or signify it, e.g., the word "cat" stands in for a real cat during conversation.

The object and the representamen (signifier) standing in for the object are then brought together and related to one another by what Peirce calls an interpretant (signified). The interpretant is usually thought to be an element in the mind, such as a memory or representation of previous experiences, e.g., previous experiences of the word "cat" with experiences of "real cats" that are called upon to make sense of this particular use of the "cat" signifier. This process of triangulation brings the real world of objects, the mediated world of signifiers, and the world of the mind together in order to make sense of a particular act of signification.

Clearly then, the interpretant is something in the mind that makes sense of the sign in the medium (the representamen). Peirce also suggests that such interpretants, as mental content of some sort, can act as representamens in their own right, i.e., mental content behaves representationally by standing in for some other external object. Thus hearing the word cat, might conjure up an image of a cat, which in turn acts as a representation in the mind of what a cat looks like. This representation in turn is made sense of by a further interpretant, e.g., it might make one think of a neighbor's cat, or the time you were once scratched by a cat. Each memory that is associated with this internal representation then can give rise to further interpretants and representamens. This is what Peirce describes as the process of unlimited semiosis, where chains of representamens are linked together through association in the mind.

Obviously, this is a description of some kind of higher cognitive process, i.e., thinking, imagining, or daydreaming, which occurs in the mind and involves representations of real objects. However, while this describes a representational mechanism in the mind, it does not necessarily follow that this mechanism is the same as that proposed by representationalism, which takes a more abstract view of representation, where sensory experiences from perception are coded into some kind of computationally useful data that is stored and retrieved in the brain. There is no reason to believe that semiosis follows this logic; indeed, semiotics does not seek to understand the workings of the brain, but wishes to describe how we make sense of mediated signs. The way in which the brain manifests representamens and interpretants is essentially irrelevant to semiotics. Gibson's view of self-stimulation would work equally well as a way for the mind to re-perceive past experiences, giving rise to mental content.

Interestingly, Umberto Eco describes such elements as mental schemas, or cognitive types (CTs), which are not necessarily images or bits of abstract data but descriptions of how to reconstruct images or similar, previously-experienced perceptions. These cognitive types are derived from direct experience of the world through primary semiosic primitives, resulting in slightly more complex mental structures or memories that ultimately come together to form associated domains of knowledge that allow us to recognize further similar experiences. Likewise, Eco argues that it is not important for semiotics to understand the workings inside the black-box of the mind, and that even so we can postulate the existence of CTs in the mind (however they may be constituted) by the very fact that they function by producing some kind of output, i.e., signification that we can intersubjectively check by relating token to type. (Eco 1999, pp134–136)

Similar ideas can be found in a slightly different form in cognitive linguistics (Brandt 2000; Fauconier and Turner 1998; Imaz and Benyon 2007), where mental schemas are conceived as being like conceptual spaces or domains of knowledge that contain many different features that are about something or the other. Fauconier and Turner's main concern is with describing how concepts can combine in the mind as "Conceptual Integration" or "blends", whereby distinct conceptual domains are activated simultaneously and connections across the domains are formed, resulting in new conceptualizations.

Whereas Lakoff and Johnson's metaphor theory concentrates on proving the link between source and target domains via primary embodied metaphorical constructs, Conceptual Integration explores the blending of higher-order mental concepts that result in new conceptualizations (Figure 9.2).

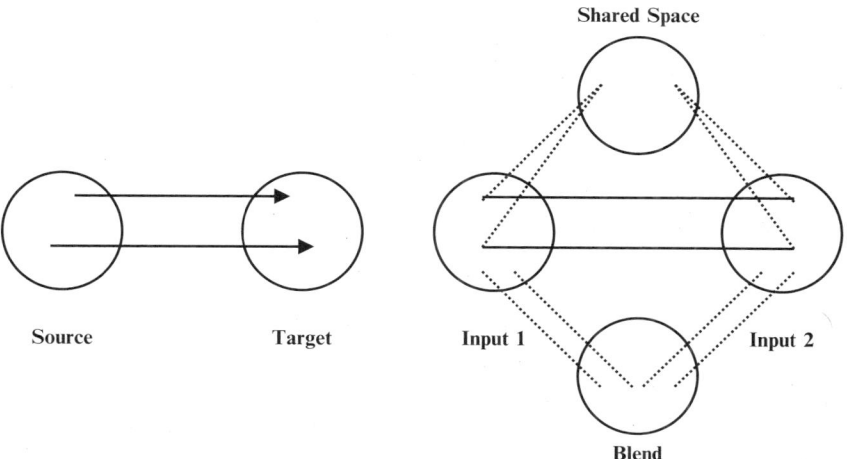

**Fig. 9.2** Comparing Metaphor Theory with Conceptual Blending

Fauconier and Turner propose that conceptual integration is a fundamental cognitive process similar to metaphor theory, sharing a common embodied origin, but which often results in the creation of new knowledge, rather than only figuratively understanding one domain in terms of another.

In this way, Fauconier and Turner account for our ability to solve problems, devise riddles, and tell jokes (Ungerer and Schmid, 2006). What they describe is an essentially creative process that brings associated ideas together in order to invent new ones. Excellent examples of conceptual integration can be found in any fantastical or mythical beast you can think of, such as Pegasus the winged horse or the gryphon, which is half eagle, half lion; think also of any of the weird creatures painted by Hieronymus Bosch or Dali's surrealist paintings.

### 9.3.1  Blending as Semiosis

While the arguments still rage between advocates of the metaphor theory and the conceptual blending theory as to their relationship and which is better or more accurate, the important thing here is to understand their relationship to semiotics.

Suppose, for example, that we agree that we are endowed with bodily-derived primary schemas as described by Lakoff and Johnson (in the form of the semiosic primitives, described by Eco). They claim that the cognitive process that allows cognition is essentially metaphorical and at some level made possible through the motor pathways of the brain that control bodily function, being employed or triggered in relation to new incoming stimuli or the self-stimulation of thought. Thus, the bodily understanding from a primary schema is mapped directly onto a new domain of experience, giving us a way in which to conceptualize about the new things we experience in the world, e.g., describing feeling happy as up, sad as down, or metaphorically personifying the front of a car with the face of a person.

Fauconier and Turner claim that it works differently from this. In their version, the bodily understanding of a primary domain is not metaphorically mapped onto another but shares some common features with some other domain of stimulus, a generic space. It is quite possible that this similarity might be the triggering of physical motor pathways in the brain, allowing for the sensation of one thing to be "like" the sensation of another. Of course, these two domains also have other features that are mutually exclusive. However, Fauconier and Turner claim that through this process of association the uncommon features are blended together to form a new conceptually integrated space. For instance, the personified car is possible as headlights and radiator grill share some spatial relationship that is similar to those of the eyes and mouth in a face. Bringing the two together allows the blending of dissimilar elements such as wheels and limbs.

From a semiotic point of view all this looks surprisingly familiar. Peircean semiosis relies on what appears to be a very similar process. For example, the word "boat" can be used to refer (stand in for) to some kind of "ocean going object". The word "ship" might also equally be used for the same purpose. Similarly, the word "vessel" can also be used to stand in for the same "ocean going object". The words boat, ship and vessel can each stand in for one another and for some kind of ocean going object because they conceptually share some kind of paradigmatic generic space. Similarly, if we bring together the concepts of ship and plow, we can combine the use of those words to describe each other's domains in a metaphorical sense because they share something of the same conceptual structure, i.e., moving through a substance in a cutting motion; thus a picture of a ship on high seas can be described as plowing through the water. The meaning of the word "plowing" becomes an interpretant that describes what the ship is doing. It is the process of association of a representamen and an interpretant that makes this possible. The Peircean notion of semiosis actually describes the same processes described by Fauconier and Turner. Similarly, the metaphorical process described by Lakoff and Johnson bears a marked resemblance to these same ideas. While higher cognitive function can blend concepts together, the argument here is that the free-floating nature of higher cognitive function is possible only through embodied schemas. The semiotic inferences made possible by these schemas are the seat of semiosis – primary interpretants that combine together through blending, to produce the infinite semiotic possibilities.

## 9.4   The Spectrum of Embodied Semiotics

A good way to understand the relationship between all these ideas might be to lay them all out along an axis that describes a spectrum of embodied semiotic relationships. If we take Peirce's explanation of firstness, secondness, and thirdness as the initial structure for this spectrum, we can then see, for example, where Heidegger's ways of being such as ready-to-hand, unready-to-hand, and present-at-hand, or Gibson's direct perception, also lie along this axis. The other explanatory theories such as the metaphor theory and the Umwlet theory can also be located along this axis, giving us a visual map of their relationship to other ideas. It is not expected that the relationships will fit neatly into allotted spaces along this axis, but that they will overlap with one another, as different approaches include and exclude different elements and ideas. However, this mapping across theories allows us to establish the extent to which different theories describe similar topics and how they might combine to form an overall framework to help our understanding of interactive media.

In exploring the relationship between these various theories, what emerges is a set of groupings or stages, where different theories provide explanatory power over sections of the continuum. Where they overlap provides the conceptual glue to bring such a framework into existence. As such, it is not then a theory in itself, but a marshalling of other theories in order to provide explanatory power for understanding how we inhabit, interact with, and make sense of our mediated environment. This is complex and attempts to show, in particular, the importance of understanding where embodied cognition gives over to semiosis and representational cognition, and vice-versa, across the semiotic threshold.

Interestingly, this dividing up of the continuum of interaction can be related to the findings of observational studies conducted by the author, which explore how creative people work with both old and new interactive media (O'Neill 2005; 2006). In these studies, what emerged through observation was the way in which users moved through different "zones of interaction" as part of their creative process. Three zones were identified: a reflective zone, an organizational zone, and a productive zone. Creative users seemed to engage with their chosen medium by moving from one zone to another, depending on what was required during the creative process. For example, sometimes they would be reflecting on the work they had been making, sometimes they would be organizing the elements of their medium in order to prepare for action, and at other times they would be acting directly by using the medium to form the object of their intention, e.g., a representation or product. At the time it was not clear how to theorize about why these zones of interaction emerged. However, now that we have explored the issue of interaction from many different perspectives, the diagram (Figure 9.3) and the descriptions below help to clarify what they represent.

### Stage 1: Pure Experience

Peircean firstness. The pure authentic experience of the undifferentiated continuum of sensation in being. Pure possibility, the necessary primary condition of an autopoeitic system, ready to respond to an external world but as yet not exposed to it. Søren Brier's primary chaotic level of continuity, quality and potentiality, with a tendency to take habits.

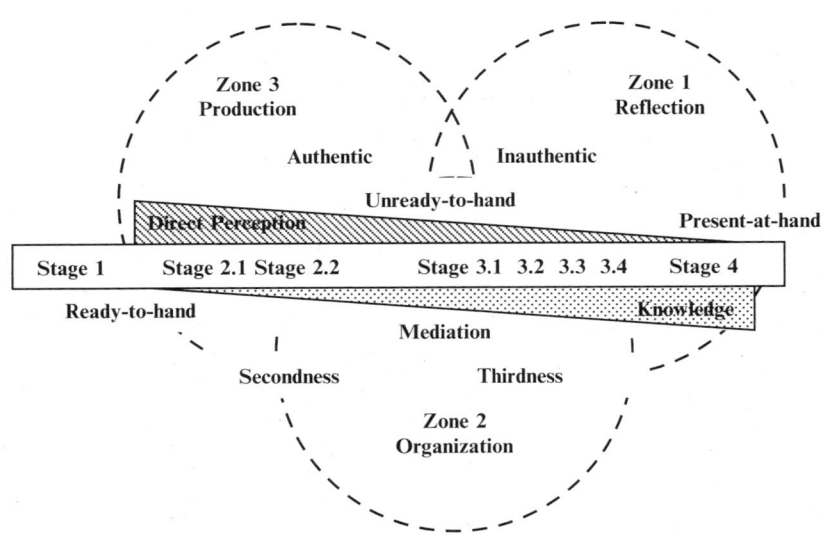

**Fig. 9.3** The Continuum of Interaction across the Zones (Note that zones 1 and 3 have swapped positions)

## Stage 2.1: Tight Coupling

Peircean Secondness, where the ego meets the other. The home of Gibson's ecological theory of direct perception, where the coupling of an organism to an environment results in embodied, non-representational cognition, affordances and a species-specific Umwelt. Our primary way of being which experiences the world authentically as ready-to-hand, in acts of smooth coping. This also describes the production zone of the creative process outlined above.

It is important to understand that we are, from a semiotic perspective, an already existing embodied bundle of (genetic) codes that has been thrown into an already existing coded world. Secondly, we need to understand the relationship between this bundle of codes, which is us, and the world that surrounds us, a world that shapes and forms us as we shape and form it. At the centre of this is an autopoeitic functional cycle, tightly and structurally coupled to a world out of which it evolved, an autopoeitic system/organism that is driven by an implacable necessity for survival and reproduction.

## Stage 2.2: Primitive Embodied Schemas

Brier's "Causal level of material natural forces", and the basis of Eco's primary iconism, where something is impressed on something, e.g., a master pattern is pressed into the sand of a mould and an impression is left in the sand, a reflection of an opposite form of negative space. The sand has taken on some of the formal characteristics of the master. Primary iconism is "the natural willingness of something to correspond to something else" (Eco 1999 p 107), e.g., the chemical characteristics of photographic paper, sensitive to light, that has a natural willingness to correspond to the image impressed upon it.

"To understand higher cultural phenomena, which clearly do not spring from nothing, it is necessary to assume that certain 'material bases of signification' exist, and these bases lie precisely in this disposition to meet and interact that we can see as the first manifestation…of primary iconism" (Eco 1999 p 107).

The development of bodily schemas or semiosic primitives that are manifest in the motor circuits which develop as we interact with the world around us. Thus we develop embodied understanding of the world such as up–down, in–out, on–under, etc. These bodily manifest basic schemas guarantee a relationship to reality because they are physically derived from our relationship to our environment and are pre-cognitive. These are the basic building blocks of cognition and what makes inference/semiosis possible in the first instance, as primary interpretants.

## Stage 3.1: Internalization

Peircean thirdness begins. Self-stimulation stands in for direct perceptual experience. Active practice becomes imitation, a way to recreate previous events. Practice is also internalized. Recognition and the comparison of internalized practiced processes with new experience result in new knowledge about the world. Semiosic primitives are brought into play as a way of recognizing and differentiating further between ego and environment. Initial Cognitive Types are formed from direct experience, interpreted through embodied schemas. The first step is taken to cross the semiotic threshold as signification begins as part of internal processes of visualization and thinking.

### Stage 3.2: Semiosis and Imagination

Conceptualization and conceptual blending, extending the semiotic process internally as described by Peirce's notion of unlimited semiosis. Internalized Cognitive Types interpret direct experience through comparison and differentiation. They also interpret other internalized Cognitive Types. Metaphorical mapping and conceptual blending take place and new Cognitive Types are formed that are not directly related to external experience. The imagination is born.

### Stage 3.3: Expression

The functional cycle results in sense-making through activity. Activities are practiced as a way of re-creating events for perception. Cognitive Types are expressed as Nuclear Content (NC), which is an abridged version of a CT formed in a medium, e.g., the expression of ideas through mark-making, art, and language. The environment takes on the role of mediating our ideas and starts to contain representations of real or invented phenomena. The cognitive load of thinking is partially offloaded onto the world, our cognition becomes distributed and embedded in the world. We enter the organizational zone of the creative process and manipulate the stuff of our environment through understanding the signs attached to them and by constructing further sings to place in the environment for others to find.

### Stage 3.4: The Mediating Environment

Representations are fully embedded in the environment. Exposure to Nuclear Content (communication) results in further CTs. However, CTs derived from NCs are not qualitatively the same as those derived from direct perceptual experience; e.g., the CT of a real horse is not the same as the CT of a drawing of a horse. Experience gained through NC results in *diminished* CTs. One does not have to have real experience of something to know something about it or be able to communicate that knowledge to someone else. While all semiosis takes place through the interpretation of representations of objects, it is important to remember that Peirce states that representations can be interpretants in their own right and vice versa. The actual object does not have to be present because semiosis is about using something to stand for something else.

### Stage 4: Molar Content

Direct authentic experiential knowledge coupled with inauthentic experiences of mediated NCs expands the cognitive type. Associative mapping takes place in relation to recognition. The process of semiosis is internal. Nuclear content and experiential content share some recognizable features and combine to form Augmented CTs. Conceptual blending occurs, domains of knowledge grow, and categorization starts. More and more knowledge of both real and mediated experience results in molar content. Exclusively real content might result in authentic/natural molar content (an unlikely possibility), or more likely exclusively mediated nuclear content will result in diminished molar content. Dictionary and encyclopedic knowledge is produced and deposited in the world. In terms of creatively interacting with media, we essentially reflect on and think about the content of this type of material rather than physically manipulate it.

## 9.5 Towards Understanding Interactive Media

Semiosic primitives, metaphor theory, and the motor theory of language all seem to suggest that we have an innate ability for thought that is not based on having a representational rational mind, but is based on our embodied perceptual interactions with the world that surrounds us. As such these ideas lend much weight to Gibson's vision of practiced knowing and Mearleau-Ponty's idea of the intentional arc.

If these theories are correct, then embodied cognition points towards a "reality" in which our cognitive abilities have been shaped by our interactions with the world around us over a long evolutionary period. Our ability to "know" is an effect caused by being directly coupled to the world around us. Fundamental human concepts, used everyday, such as up–down, front–back, etc. are purely spatial and possible only through our embodied relationship with our environment, from which they are derived. Thus, our higher cognitive rational thinking mechanism is a function of our existence in a "real" world. We think because we exist and we have existed in evolutionary terms since life emerged on this planet.

However, as our knowledge spills out of our minds and into the environment, as we use it to express ourselves, help us think, and communicate with one another, we are faced with the problem of having to live in a world saturated by media of various types, interactive and otherwise.

More and more we find that our everyday experiences are rarely of an authentic natural "real" kind. We encounter the varied entities of the world and gain most of our knowledge of the world through reflections and representations of it, i.e., the media, TV, films, books, newspapers, the Internet, VR, and mixed reality systems. We spend more time experiencing the world through these mediated means where our CTs are significantly made up of more mediated, or second-hand, representations rather than authentic personal ones. Thus, not only is our understanding of the world made up of socially expressed descriptions of it, but also our physical environment becomes more and more layered with representational material and the manifest expressions of our understanding. We live with, among and surrounded by, the physical manifestation of the complexes of our minds, the reflections of our experience of being in the world. Over generations, layer after layer of representations are placed in the world and we have to learn, know, and live with the residue of previous mediated ideas.

This postmodern condition moves towards the total simulation of reality, as proposed by Baudrillard (Baudrillard 1994). To paraphrase DeBord, our lives become more and more spectacularized (Debord 1994). Not only does semiosis take place in our personal mental interpretation of the play of signs laid before us, but the entire fabric of our environment becomes part of the semiotic game, intertextualy existing as referential manifestations of previous physical forms, whether in cinema, architecture, automotive design, or interactive technologies. Thus, all representational mediating artifacts can be considered as inauthentic.

If taken to its logical conclusion, this then renders all forms of communication from speech and writing to television and radio as resulting in inauthentic experiences. The nature of our being-thrown-into-a-designed-world then results not only in an inauthentic aspect of our reflective activities, but in problems with regard to creating an inauthentic aspect to our ready-to-hand mode of experience. One might argue that when using a hammer (incidentally, a designed object), which even if our reflections on it seem to disappear through our use of it, we cannot help but be having an inauthentic experience of hammering, because the hammer itself is not only mediating the act of hammering, but is, in itself, the result of a mediated process of design and manufacturing. Heidegger would probably argue that these concerns disappear through our use of the object, and that the very use of something results in a move towards authentic experience. However, this example serves to highlight a difficulty in theorizing in such a way about our designed world, particularly in light of the increasing layers of mediation that arise through the continued expansion of our reliance on digital technologies. What emerges from examining Heidegger's theories, among others, is a realization of the threshold between authentic and inauthentic experiences.

Essentially, this is exactly the same threshold that semioticians have been dealing with, in attempting to establish the limits of semiotic enquiry. For Heidegger, the threshold exists between tacit knowledge, which is embodied in a person (being) when they encounter the world as ready-to-hand, and knowledge about the world that is derived from reflection and thought. Only ready-to-hand experience of an untouched natural habitat can be said to be totally authentic whereas, in general, we tend to inhabit socio-culturally mediated inauthentic environments. For philosophers such as Kant, the problem was one of explaining how we move from sensations within the manifold of intuition to higher concepts through transcendental idealism. For semioticians, it is the problem of understanding the presemiotic conditions that make semiosis possible. Through the interdisciplinary examination of thought presented here, we have uncovered that several theories exist from various disciplines that explore the same territory of this threshold and explain it in complementary ways. For instance, several theories point to a distinction between authentic direct perception and inauthentic mediated perception. Because we must perceive before we conceive, we find that the body is at the root of our conceptual apparatus as well as being able to engage with the world without having to think about it.

Embedded as we are in a mediated world, we must not forget that the very bedrock that allows us to make sense of it is deeply entwined with our physical relationship to it. While our world becomes more and more inauthentic, we still make sense of it from an authentic grounding in the real, which, via our bodies, provides us with the primary schema that allow us to make sense of it. Without up and down, or on and under, where would we be? How would any of our most abstract theories make any sense to us?

As Arthur I. Miller points out in his book *Insights of Genius*, metaphorical imagery plays a significant part in the formulation of understandable scientific theory (Miller, 1996). If this metaphorical imagery is derived from our very embodied nature, then despite how creative and inventive our flights of fancy might be, they all must have their root in some element of our experiences of the physical relationship we have with the real world around us.

The explanatory power of the set of theories explored here, when brought to bear on understanding interactive media in particular, allows us to ask all sorts of questions about makeup, structure, and function, as well as our physical interactions with it, and what it means to anyone who might engage with it. In the next chapter we will take these ideas forward in order to explore how our new integrated perspective, in the form of our spectrum of embodied semiotics, can be applied to a number of interactive media forms in order to make sense of them.

# References

Allot, R. (1992). The Motor Theory of Language: Origin and Function. In: J. Wind, B. Chiarlli, B. Bichakjian and A. Nocentini (Eds.), *Language Origin: A Multidisciplinary Approach*. Kluwer Dordrecht, pp. 105–119.

Allot, R. (1994). Language and the Origin of Semiosis. In: W. Noth (Ed.), *Sign Evolution in Nature and Culture, Part III Glottogenesis: Phylogeny, Ontogeny, and Actogeny,*. Mouton de Gruyter, Berlin, pp. 255–268.

Baudrillard, J. (1994). *Simulacra and Simulation*. The University of Michigan Press, Michigan.

Brandt, P. A. (2000). The Architecture of Semantic Domains – A Grounding Hypothesis in Cognitive Semiotics. Retrieved 08/02/02, 2002, from http://www.hum.aau.dk/semiotics/docs/epub/arc/paab/SemD/SemanticDomains.html

Brier, S. (2001). Cybersemiotics and the Question of Informational and Semiotic Thresholds. Paper presented at The International Colloquium on the Semiotic Threshold form Nature to Culture, Kassel, Germany.

Clark, A. (1997). *Being There: Putting, Brain, Body and World Together Again*. The MIT Press, Cambridge, MA.

Debord, G. (1994). *The society of the Spectacle*. Zone Books, New York.

Deely, J. (1990). *Basics of Semiotics*. Indiana University Press, Bloomington.

Deely, J. (2001). Umwelts Semiootika osakonna kodulehekulg. *Semiotika 134*, special volume about Jakob von Uexkull (1/4), 125–135.

Eco, U. (1976). *A Theory of Semiotics*. Indiana University Press, Indiana.

Eco, U. (1999). Kant and the Platypus: Essays on Language and Cognition. Secker and Warburg, London.

Fauconier, G. and Turner, M. (1998). Conceptual Integration Networks. *Cognitive Science*, 22 (2), 133–187.

Imaz, M. and Benyon, D. (2007). *Designing with Blends: Conceptual Foundations of Human--Computer Interaction and Software Engineering*. The MIT Press, Cambridge, MA.

Imaz, M. and Benyon, D. (2007). Designing with Blends: Conceptual Foundations of Human-Computer Interaction and Software Engineering. The MIT Press, Cambridge, Massachusetts.

Lakoff, G. and Johnson, M. (1980). *Metaphors We Live By*. University of Chicago Press, Chicago.

Lakoff, G. and Johnson, M. (1999). *Philosophy of the Flesh*. Basic Books, New York.

Miller, A. I. (1996). Insights of Genius, Copernicus an imprint of Springer Verlag, New York.

O'Neill, S. J. (2005). *Exploring a Semiotics of New Media*. Napier University, Edinburgh.

O'Neill, S. J. (2006). Semiotics, Embodiment and Interactive Media. Paper presented at International Conference on Organizational Semiotics ICOS2006, University of Campinas, Brazil.

Sebeok, T. A. (1979). *The Sign and its Masters*. University of Texas Press, Austin.

Sharov, A. (2001). Umwelt-theory and Pragmatism. Semiotica, 134, p 211–228. de Gruyter, New York.

Ungerer, F., Schmid, H. (2006). An Introduction to Cognitive Linguistics, 2nd Rev Ed, Pearson Education Limited, London.

# Chapter 10
# Understanding Interactive Media

## 10.1  Interactive Media Design

The Interactive Media Design (IMD) course at the University of Dundee is the first
of its kind to be run at the undergraduate level in the United Kingdom. Started in
2002, it is jointly coordinated across the School of Computing and the School of
Design. The aim of the course is to deliver a genuinely interdisciplinary interactive
media design experience to the students in order to educate designers who are as
well versed in computer programming and HCI as they are in graphic design, physical prototyping, and interaction design.

Presented here are four projects that exemplify the kind of work that designers
of this caliber can produce. Needles to say, these projects encompass many of the
characteristics of interactive media that have been discussed throughout this book.
From remediating older media to enhance mental healthcare, to employing different convergent media elements in an antisocial behavior public awareness campaign, to exploring the relationship between audience as reader and user as author,
these projects are the standard bearers of the interaction designers cf tomorrow.

As such, they clearly show the wide range of media skills that interactive media
designers need to employ at the cutting edge of design. More importantly, they also
show how new designers can design for physical affordance as well as maximize
interpretative sense-making in interaction by considering where and where not to
cross the semiotic threshold without diminishing the rich experiences that interactive media can deliver.

It is by examining these types of projects, from the embodied/semiotic perspective outlined in this book, that we can see how an understanding of emergent interactive media design might develop.

## 10.2  Emotional Text

"Emotional Text" is an installation by designer Ross Cairns that aims to explore the
issue of "presence" in social networks that use interactive technologies to provide
a virtual social space for people to meet over the Internet. The aim of the project is

S.O'Neill, *Interactive Media: The Semiotics of Embodied Interaction*,
doi: 10.1007/978-1-84800-036-0, © Springer Science + Business Media, LLC 2008

to make apparent the differences between real-world social presence and virtual social presence mediated by new technologies (Fig. 10.1).

The central element of the project is an anonymous user who has the privilege of sending messages about his or her emotional well being, to a central message board that is present in a different location, via a mobile phone. The user never sees the displayed messages or knows where the message board is. All he or she knows is that someone out there is listening to/reading what he or she has to say. The message board, erected in a public space such as a corridor, meeting room, square, or other public thoroughfare, presents the messages from the user to passing members of the public, who constitute the audience for the work.

The installation was designed to probe the user's experience of being able to communicate to other parts of society anonymously, as well as the associations the passing public made with the user. In such a way, the installation attempts to transfer the concept of social "blogging" from virtual space to real space, subverting the practice of privately recording information to share among a few friends to publicly announcing it to groups of total strangers. In doing so, Cairns highlights that social presence is not just about what you say about yourself, or even how you say it. More often than not, it is about how your personality is embodied in the world, real or virtual.

In developing this piece, Cairns prototyped two different versions of the project and experimented with them to see which one worked better. For the first version, a screen was set up in a section of a university campus where students would meet up to study in their own time. The anonymous user was asked to text messages about his emotional wellbeing whenever he felt the urge to communicate to someone about how he was feeling. The messages were then relayed via a mobile network to a website that collated the information and then passed it to the application that Cairns had written to present them on the large screen. The screen permanently displayed the most recent text and updated every time a new message was sent.

The second version ran at the same time in a completely different location on the campus and used a motion-sensor-activated speaker, rather than a screen, to present

**Fig. 10.1** A visualization of emotional text in a public space

the same material. The speaker was placed inside the door of a study room at the end of a corridor and every time someone entered, the message sent by the user was spoken aloud by the text-to-speech software.

The words "I feel" were used as a precursor to any messages the user sent in order to constrain the context of the content to be published. This was done in order to stop the user from deviating from the purpose of the message board while maintaining some element of creativity in how to express oneself.

Both projects ran in tandem for two weeks, and Cairns interviewed the anonymous user and members of the audience to see how they both felt about how the installation worked and what their experience of using it had been (Fig. 10.2).

The screen-based version proved to be much more popular than the speaker-based version, as it presented the material in a way that seemed more appropriate for the surroundings. Audience members commented on how hearing the same message over and over again, in the speaker-based version, really intruded on their own space and quickly became annoying. Indeed, it proved to be too much of an intrusion even after the system was limited to speaking only after a new message had come in.

Comparing the two versions on this level is interesting because it reveals how the two different media forms make the messages from the user, and thus the user

| Anonymous user | "The constraints were quite frustrating sometimes because I don't think that they always gave you the scope to say what I maybe felt at the time. I had to reword things…But I think in some ways… that was probably necessary to have some kind of limit. Otherwise I could have maybe just gone on and on sometimes…I liked that fact that in a way it prompted me to text something, you know, text how I feel rather than send five texts a day it doesn't matter what they say or what they are about. I think that would have maybe been harder to do." |
| --- | --- |
| | "I think the aspect of knowing that someone is going to see it is quite a sort of a comforting thing or a rewarding thing." |
| Participant 1 | "Yeah, that's what I was saying, I could empathize with the person, maybe not necessarily in the sense that I'm feeling exactly the same thing right now, but its just like I know what it feels like. In the past I have been in that same situation" |
| Participant 2 | "A lot of the comments have been very general stuff that anyone would feel. But one in particular was very salient, the thing about feeling embarrassed using a cheque. It was a real kind of comment on the way I feel sometimes. I feel embarrassed using a cheque. It's like, 'yeah that's right on'. It's kind of a social comment as supposed to a personal comment." |

**Fig. 10.2** Table of participants' responses

himself, present to those in the audience. The speaker version needs to constantly repeat itself as people walk by, to keep the messages available to the audience so they do not miss them. The medium of sound is inherently temporal and therefore lasts as long as the duration of the speech act performed by the computer. This, of course, is annoying because a voice repeating itself over and over is inherently annoying regardless of whether it is human or computerized. Unfortunately, this version of the project either runs the risk of diminishing the presence of the user by limiting how often he speaks, or it gives the user persistent and irritating characteristics that the audience cannot bear to listen to. Either way, the potential for some kind of emotional bond to develop between audience and user is reduced.

In the screen-based version, the experiences of the audience are quite different. The messages become available to the audience as part of their spatial environment, and the invariance of the image announces the presence of the user in a persistent but quieter way. Of course, the message has to be read to be understood, but it is the particular characteristics of the medium that afford this possibility. Simply appealing to the eye rather than the ear in this case gives the message more impact because it is present for longer in the environment, maximizing the take-up of the information. It also does not intrude into the audience's personal space as much as the voice. It is less demanding and annoying by simply being around rather than talking all the time.

Clearly, this type of interactive media relies on the semiotics of language and visual grammar to get the message across. As such, this kind of interaction is firmly across the semiotic threshold positioned mainly within the reflective zone of interaction. Arguably, it is just another messaging system, where the technical challenge is simply to maximize the legibility of the visual and audio elements delivered to the audience.

However, this is not quite so. The really interesting thing about this installation is the way the audience reacted to the two different versions. For instance, the quiet visual messages garnered a much more favorable response as a stand-in for the anonymous user than the more human equivalent of the voice. Strange, you might think? Surely a voice is more human than letters on a screen?

Of course, this might have been due to the repetition of the voice or maybe its annoying computerized tone. More probably though, it was because the visual representation, while still conveying the same content, delivered it in a way that is much more like having a person in the room than hearing a disembodied computer voice. The simple persistence of the screen image is what gave the anonymous user a presence in the environment. The screen gave him a representation of his body more than the voice did and in doing so the persistence of this "body" reached more of the audience in a way that seemed more natural in their environment. Maybe this is simply because people are more comfortable with screens than they are with disembodied voices, but maybe it is because the persistence of the embodying screen gave a better form to the messages allowing the personality of the anonymous user to shine through.

In this instance then, the role of the body is played by the screen and the persistence of the words on the screen that embody the emotional content of how the anonymous user is feeling as he goes about his daily routine. The medium and the messages

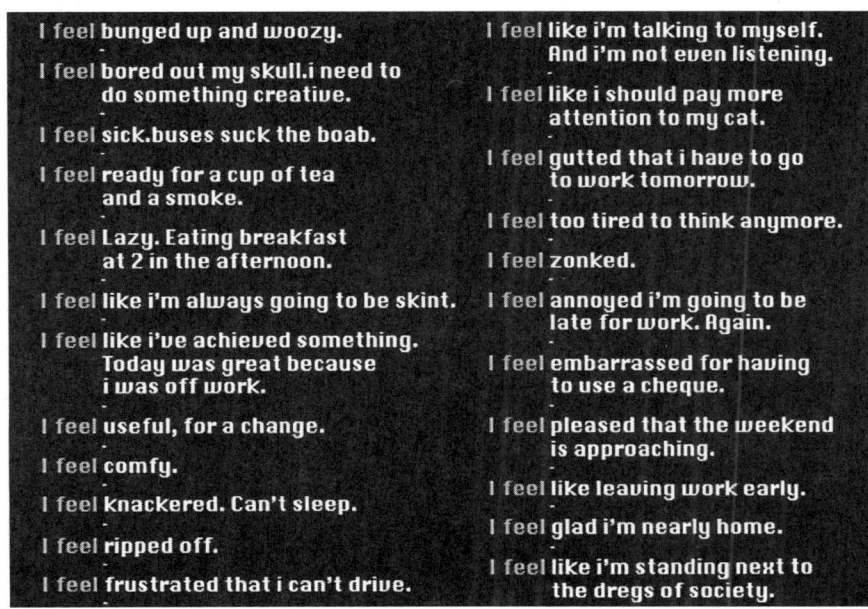

I feel bunged up and woozy.

I feel bored out my skull.i need to do something creative.

I feel sick.buses suck the boab.

I feel ready for a cup of tea and a smoke.

I feel Lazy. Eating breakfast at 2 in the afternoon.

I feel like i'm always going to be skint.

I feel like i've achieved something. Today was great because i was off work.

I feel useful, for a change.

I feel comfy.

I feel knackered. Can't sleep.

I feel ripped off.

I feel frustrated that i can't drive.

I feel like i'm talking to myself. And i'm not even listening.

I feel like i should pay more attention to my cat.

I feel gutted that i have to go to work tomorrow.

I feel too tired to think anymore.

I feel zonked.

I feel annoyed i'm going to be late for work. Again.

I feel embarrassed for having to use a cheque.

I feel pleased that the weekend is approaching.

I feel like leaving work early.

I feel glad i'm nearly home.

I feel like i'm standing next to the dregs of society.

**Fig. 10.3** Examples of the anonymous users' messages

it conveys come together to provide not just a window into the anonymous user's world, but also a physical presence that allows an emotional connection to be made between the user and the audience who are kept informed about how he feels.

In the final version of the installation, Cairns placed the same large screen in a similar public space at a gallery opening, along with the phone number for the audience to text to. Thus the audience also became the authors of the content. As a result, they began to communicate with one another via the public screen, further subverting the medium and using it for their own ends. Sometimes, these were genuine statements about how they felt, and others were humorous or witty responses to previous texts (Fig. 10.3). This turn in the project then removed the sense of a physical relationship with one particular person and transformed it into a form of social communication open to all. Interestingly, it was the fact that it retained a strong visual presence within the environment that allowed everyone to share in the fun and provoked a great deal of interaction.

## 10.3 Do Not Disturb

Like Cairns' work, Jenny Kelloe's project "Do Not Disturb" also tackles an interesting social issue through interactive media. Concentrating on nuisance noise as antisocial behavior, Kelloe's project aims to engage with this potentially thorny problem in a lighthearted and playful way, raising the profile of the issue by getting it out in the open. Of course, noisy nuisance neighbors can often be intimidating or belligerent, but Kelloe's project does not aim at solutions as such, rather it attempts to make it a talking point by bringing it to the wider community as a whole.

The project consists of three main parts: a special postage pack called a Noise Bomb, a speaking poster and a Web site that shows a map of the city reporting on the location of posters and Noise Bombs in use.

The Noise Bomb is presented as a pack for people who suffer from noisy neighbors and do not know how to approach the subject with them (Fig. 10.4). The pack allows the person suffering from the nuisance noise to record their neighbor being noisy, write some comments on the pack, and then post it through their neighbor's letterbox. Upon receiving the noise bomb, which may be configured to play continually, the noisy neighbor is confronted with his or her own noise as heard from the perspective of the sufferer. They can then read the comments as well as information about the "Do Not Disturb" campaign. This information directs them to the Web site, where they can see that the problems they are causing have been exposed to the public who come to the site. The noise bomb comes with a key code that allows the noisy neighbor to access the site and respond to the sufferer within the public domain. Using the pack will not necessarily resolve the situation but will make people aware that nuisance noise does affect people.

Alternatively, the "Noise Poster" allows a member of the public to record nuisance noise of any kind on their mobile phone and then send it to the poster (Fig. 10.5). The poster, suitably positioned in a public space, will then play the noise every time someone walks past it.

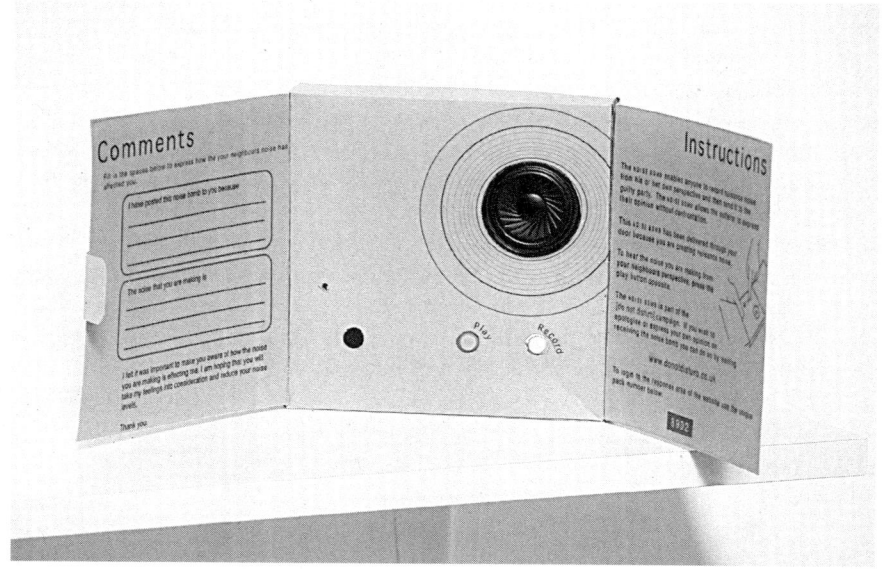

**Fig. 10.4** The Noise Bomb Pack

**Fig. 10.5** The Noise Poster

The idea behind the poster is to re-create the annoyance and irritation that derives from nuisance noise, thereby making the public aware of a problem that may not necessarily affect them specifically. Allowing the public to send nuisance noise that personally affects them means that the public can hear the problem for themselves. Kelloe suggests that this will have a greater impact than just telling people about the problem.

The poster consists of a large backing board, in the form of a "Do Not Disturb" sign, a motion sensor to trigger the sound, and a speaker. As someone walks past the speaker, it is activated and the poster begins to shout abuse at the passer by. Although the poster is demonstrating antisocial behavior, and is therefore technically a nuisance in itself, using this extreme method effectively makes people more aware of the issue.

Similar to the Noise Bomb, the poster is tied to the Web site in terms of its location. Information on the poster directs passers by to the Web site and allows them to comment on the noise played by the poster, thereby enabling a dialogue to develop around the issue in the wider public arena.

The Web site itself is the center of the campaign and brings together the Noise Poster and Noise Bomb pack. The Web site is the main place from which to obtain the Noise Bomb packs and posters as well as the place where the receivers of the packs can respond to comments. The Web site also has a map displaying the locations of the posters and a list of the nuisance noises the posters have received. People who have sent noises to the poster are also to write comments on the Web site explaining about how the noise affects them.

The idea of a Web site is to bring together through the poster and pack a community of people that is affected by nuisance noise where the members can discuss and share their experiences of using the pack and poster. In turn, this will help bring better awareness of nuisance noise to the wider community as a whole.

The interesting thing about this kind of interactive media is that it combines many different media elements together, not only in the different devices themselves but also across the campaign as a whole. We can see this in the way that the campaign has been branded as well as in the choices made about how users will interact with the component parts of the project. Moreover, people at the center of the campaign, i.e., the general public as audience, are also encouraged to be authors as well as readers of the information that surrounds the project. This puts the users at the center of the issue and in control of how the media are used to communicate this issue to each other.

For example, individuals are encouraged to use their own mobile phones as recording devices for part of the project. These recordings in turn are sent to the Web site and the individual posters located in the public domain. Like Cairns' work, this gives a certain public presence to an essentially private issue, but unlike Cairns' work, the aim is not to develop lasting emotional relationships with disembodied people, but to make the public aware of the irritating nature of nuisance noise. Here, the irritating aspect of the medium that Cairns found getting in the way of his project actually comes to the fore because it enhances the purpose of its use.

The same can be said of the Noise Bomb, too. By simply using the pack as a recording medium that mirrors the actual nuisance noise, neighbors are forced to confront their own antisocial habits. Interacting with this device then begins with a physical relationship from the perspective of the sufferer, where they must first understand how to make the recording and how it can be packaged to be posted. This is all reflective-zone activity, where the sufferer is reading the instructions and reflecting on how to use the noise bomb. The sufferer then moves to record with it, perhaps standing near the wall to get a good volume level and holding down the various record and play buttons to capture the noise and test the play back. This is all production-zone stuff, where the sufferer is making a recording of the nuisance noise. Similarly, packaging it and posting it through the letterbox is also production activity.

Once it is delivered, the neighbor has a different experience of the device. If it is making a noise, then the first experience is a "what is that?" type of experience, where the neighbor is trying to make sense of what is going on. Then there is a kind of physical relationship to the device as it is picked up and explored in order to make sense of it. This is all organizational-zone stuff that takes place near the embodied end of the continuum of interaction, where the users experience the device as unready-to-hand as they try to make sense of it. Once they encounter the comments and instructions, they are immediately shifted to the reflective mode of interaction where they learn more about the purpose of the device, their own role in the noise it is making, and what they can do about it.

The format of the pack in itself is particularly interesting, as it contains many different media elements. Like all the campaign parts, it is designed graphically to convey the branding of the campaign and to direct users and receivers alike to the Web site for more information. More interesting though, is the relationship between the instructions and the mechanics of speaker section. For instance, the flaps of the box both fold out revealing information on the inside with the central control panel and speaker in the middle. The comments section is on the left-hand (given) side of the box because they are required to contextualize the noise being played from the central panel. They are also the first things that the receivers should read about the noise, once they hear it. The instructions on how to get to the site follow on the right-hand side after the noise-emanating central panel.

By fixing the play button prior to posting, the box can be playing the noise as it enters the neighbor's house, sitting on their doorstep until they come and see what is happening. The form factor of the box is also integral to its success as a device. Of course, it must be small enough to fit through a letterbox and it must be robust enough to keep working after it has landed on the other side of the door. Kelloe has thought quite clearly here about the relationship between the sufferer and the neighbor as well as the way in which each individual will relate to the bomb and to each other through the device itself.

More than that though, Kelloe has imbued the bomb with the feeling of being a present. It is beautifully packaged and is the perfect size for holding in two hands as you read the information. This feeling of being given a present should not go unnoticed, as this goes some way to encouraging the neighbor to engage with the problem on a personal level. In being sent a present of a noise bomb, one is alerted to the fact that someone cares enough about the problem to give you a gift that explains how you can improve the quality of the environment you live in, for both parties. The noise itself provides a visceral experience of the problem, and the information on the pack provides the link to the understanding of the issue as well as a way into the debate surrounding nuisance noise. In such a way, Kelloe has brilliantly combined the physical elements of interaction in the poster and the Noise Bomb with the wider social issue. One is not distracted from the message sent in the pack or the poster by any complex form of interaction. One is simply forced to experience the noise in the first instance and then engage with the written information on the pack and on the Web site. The physical act comes first and the interpretation and reflection come later.

## 10.4   Kensho

Kensho is a self-help computer, developed by designer Ruben Villanueva Gill, as a tool primarily to help people suffering from moderate forms of anxiety, like Social Phobia or Generalized Anxiety Disorder (GAD). It is based on the practice of Cognitive Behavior Therapy (CBT) and is to be used as part of the therapy process alongside other elements and techniques. It has two primary functions: a diary section, which prompts the user to record day-to-day thoughts, and descriptions of relaxation techniques to help users at stressful times during the day.

Keeping a diary of thoughts, events, physical feelings, and emotional responses is central to CBT as a means of improving clients' self-awareness and challenging negative patterns of behavior. By linking the observation of their own thoughts and responses to certain exercises, Kensho aims to help users gain control of anxiety when it appears. Although CBT can be very successful without the help of computers, it can often be hard for people with anxiety to have the discipline to keep a detailed diary as required in CBT practice. By offering the user an adaptive interactive diary, linked to relaxation exercises, and a stress-relief bracelet, the whole activity becomes less of a chore and more of an enjoyable exercise in self-care.

For example, if users are anxious, and for some reason cannot or simply do not want to use Kensho to write about their thoughts at the time, they can squeeze the special bracelet to record the time and intensity of the distress they are feeling. This allows them some relief, as they know they can temporarily "park" their stressful feelings and carry on with what they are doing. This also alleviates guilt, as they know Kensho will not ignore the event, because whenever the bracelet is in close range to Kensho, the data it holds is transmitted to the main device. At a later time, when the users decide to use Kensho, it prompts them with the time(s) when the bracelet was squeezed, ensuring a more detailed record of events is recorded for the therapist. The prompts encourage the users to remember what happened and to make a diary entry of the thoughts or events that caused that particular episode of anxiety. Kensho then ranks these in order of frequency. Events that keep recurring stay near the top in order to alert the user to their prevalence as part of the habitual behavior they are trying to change. During therapy sessions the therapist and clients can download the data from Kensho to a PC. Using special software, this data can then be graphically represented in order to monitor progress and spot trends, which is particularly useful as the basis of therapy.

Kensho, with its bracelet and simple interface, is an attempt to make a device that is closer, more personal, and easy to use than conventional diaries. It uses a combination of readable text, and a pen interface to write and select objects on the screen. It is as simple to use as a paper notebook but has more functionality, as its internal ranking system makes the users realize what their thought habits are as soon as they have used it a few times.

Kensho takes the form of a portable device, similar in size to a Personal Digital Assistant (PDA) or a small tablet PC (Fig. 10.6). It has a simple touch-screen interface, and requires very little knowledge of how to use computers, as its dedicated

**Fig. 10.6** The Kensho prototype

operating system takes virtually no time to start up or load new information. Its shape and size are a compromise between reasonable portability and an easy-to-use readable touch screen. The on-screen buttons are big enough to be pressed with fingers and a pen-size stylus allows comfortable handling and fine handwriting.

Dedicated hardware and software mean no waiting for boot up or content update. Kensho turns on when you shake it and turns itself off after a short period of inactivity and once restarted it resumes at the same place you left off. This is as close to paper notebook immediacy as it gets.

If Kensho has not been used for a few days, it calls the user's attention by flashing its screen, vibrating, or producing some sound. Kensho produces sounds only if it is stationary and lying flat on a horizontal surface. If it is sitting vertically and/ or moving, it assumes it is being carried and it stays quiet. The interval of calls is automatically regulated by an adaptive schedule system that learns the user's most convenient times.

Kensho is designed with a specific purpose in mind, i.e., that of improving the self-help aspect of CBT. In essence then, the interesting thing about Kensho is that it is a remediation of a number of CBT practices, particularly the diary-keeping task, which is central to successful CBT. In Kensho, the focus is not on automating any part of the therapeutic process; it is only intended to be part of the wider context of therapy. However, in remediating the diary through interactive technology, the process is enhanced by the time-stamping feature of the bracelet and the ranking system of Kensho itself. These two features, in particular, address the endemic problem in CBT of developing detailed and correct diaries that reflect an accurate description of the client's feelings and anxieties. Gill has done an excellent job here of differentiating between these two particular activities even though they are part of the same process.

In particular, what Gill has done exceptionally well is to clearly delineate the relationship between Kensho and the client, in an embodied and locative sense, as well the kind of information that it needs to store about the user. For instance, the bracelet part of Kensho becomes the proxy by which Kensho is always involved in the daily activities of the client.

By recording only the time and the intensity of the squeeze, the client engages in a productive act, at the ready-to-hand end of the continuum of interaction, without having to engage with the bulky and cognitively demanding interface of Kensho itself. This ingenious approach to the problem allows the user to mark stressful times without having to note down details, while maintaining the connection to the therapeutic process by shifting the moment of reflection to a calmer, safer space where the client can think more deeply about the problem.

Kensho is also designed to behave as much like paper as possible. For instance, there are no buttons on the device, and to turn it on you just pick it up. Immediately you can write on the screen and it remembers which page you left it on the last time you were there. All this moves the cognitive load of operating an essentially symbolic representational device across the continuum of embodied interaction towards the ready-to-hand end. The reason it is so successful is that it lets users engage with the device as quickly as possible with the minimum of fuss. The physical acts of squeezing the bracelet and shaking Kensho afford easy access to the device that do not have to be thought about in great detail at the time. This leaves more headspace for the important part of reflecting on and noting down stressful feelings and anxious events. This, of course, is done at the interface and takes the normal form of text input, but again Kensho is designed to take in hand-written entries and requires no typing skill or technical capability to make it work.

Not only is Kensho beautifully crafted but it is also a very well thought-out piece of design that successfully establishes which aspects of interaction should be on the embodied side of the semiotic threshold and which elements are required to support deep reflection and interpretation.

## 10.5   Tactophonics

This project began life with a rather ambitious aim, i.e., to restore tactility and spontaneity to computer-based musical performances by redesigning not only the input device to the computer but also the act of performing with computers. Recognizing that the restrictive logical nature of the keyboard and mouse are designed for fast and efficient data entry rather than to facilitate real-time expression,

the designer of this project, Andrew Cook, sought to break this paradigm by introducing new ways to manipulate computational data while retaining the physical
relationship that musicians have with their instruments. The aim of tactophonics
then is to allow musicians to take advantage of the new possibilities for sound production offered by computers, but to do so in real time, spontaneously affording
them the opportunity to create viscerally rather than cerebrally.

"One struggles to express the paradox that is present in musical expression using
computers. While computers have opened up new possibilities in music, both soni-
cally and in terms of eliminating the physical limits of human players, they have
also reduced the modes in which we can interact to create sound. Something so
simple as a wood block certainly has limited parameters of sound, its timbre always
being that of a wood block, yet it seems there is an unlimited number of ways we
can physically express ourselves with it; to hit it hard, or hit it softly, or stroke it,
or throw it in the air and listen to it clatter back down, or rub it against a rough surface or hum into it are just a few in a universe of possibilities. Computers seem to
be the antithesis of this, offering potentially unlimited parameters to work within,
but only a tiny number of ways to express ourselves." (Cook, personal communication 2006)

Cook understands completely the nature of the very physical relationship that is
at the heart of any virtuoso performance using any traditional instrument. He also
understands that, as a result, remediating or simulating traditional instruments electronically or with computer software will not give us the same kind of experience
of resistance, tactility, subtlety, or timbre. For Cook, the physicality of our lives is
the overwhelming feature of how we engage with the world at large, and musical
instruments in particular. Despite the numerous opportunities that computers offer
us, they force us to relate to them in a restrictive, logical way that is at odds with
the creative process, particularly a musical one. As a result, Cook suggests that they
rob us of our own nature and limit the expressive possibilities of the musical
medium.

Arguing that new modes of expression should be sought rather than simply
attempting to simulate traditional expressive methods, Cook develops tactophonics
as a way to enhance musical performance through interactive media that subverts
existing computer music practices to reclaim the act of the performance for the
musician over and above the automation of the computer.

This particular perspective acknowledges that the act of performing is an important part of the mediatory process whereby the performer and the audience are
inseparably bound together through a mutually shared experience of sound as musical expression. It also acknowledges that the relationship between the physical
action of the performer and sonic result, witnessed by all, needs to be made more
explicit to allow performers to express themselves effectively, in order to communicate and build a rapport with the audience.

In order to make this possible through interactive media, Cook came up with the
ingenious solution of delivering the performative element through common everyday objects that could be linked to a computer system which could be set up to
manipulate the sound on the fly, rather than control its every parameter.

As a result, the tactile and physical elements of performance remain in the stuff of the world and the hands of the musician rather than ending up locked inside the formalization of programing languages and computational processing.

A tactophone then, is a device, essentially a contact microphone, that you can stick to your favorite object in order to capture the sounds it makes as it is physically manipulated or "played". These sounds are then fed into a computer in real time, which filters and processes them, depending on how the system has been set up before the performance begins. Of course, like most computational systems, the interface allows you to adjust the computational parameters on the fly, but the main performative interface revolves around manipulating the object itself in front of an audience. As a result, the problem of the physical and emotional connection between the performer instrument and audience is resolved, while harnessing computational power to produce interactive musical media (Fig. 10.7).

The elements of the computational interface consist of a number of graphical representations that signify different computational objects, which react to sonorous and percussive elements of the input from the tactophone, as well as the potential to increase and decrease the sensitivity of these objects or have them running in tandem. The elements of the physical interface that Cook employed in particular were a large tree branch that could be bent, bashed, dropped, stroked, etc., as well as a baseball bat coupled with an old television set that was smashed to smithereens in a one-off performance.

Clearly, Cook is deeply engaged with the issue of affordance and the nature of musical performance that relies on the perceptual processes rather than an intellectual

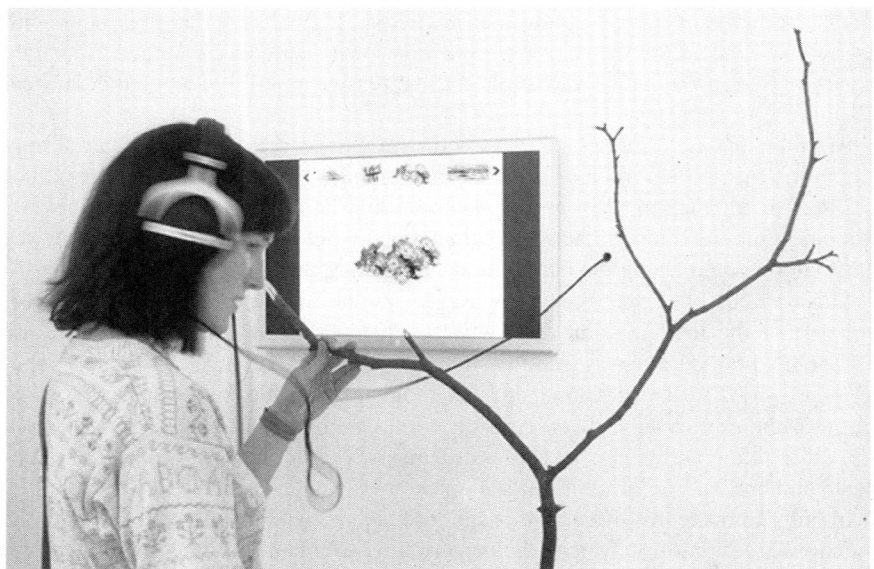

**Fig. 10.7** Playing the tactophone

formalization of its constituent parts. In order to make music in a performative way, one must be able to manipulate the medium in a sensitive and visceral way rather than in a logical compartmental way.

Of course, the computer music tools of today do the latter very well, and most recording studios revolve around computerized consoles and digital recording devices. However, this is not what Cook is after. Cook's tactophonic medium is about the direct relationship between a human being and the medium being manipulated. In this sense what Cook has attempted to do is to move all the logical and formal aspects of computer music to one side in order to rediscover what this relationship consists of. In doing so, he has discovered that it is about a kind of thoughtless interaction with the material of the medium, rather than a symbolic or representational one. It is therefore quite telling that cook should choose something as natural and as physical as a tree branch as the basis of his input device.

What this demonstrates is that the kind of interaction that Cook is after is clearly in the ready-to-hand/productive zone of interaction, rather than in the organizational or reflective zones that most modern computational music software inhabit. What Cook does here is to avoid falling into the same old trap of simply trying to simulate the process of making music in a symbolic way by returning to the body and its relationship to the environment. In doing so, he reforms the practice of making music with interactive media, from an essentially organizational set of activities to a more immediately productive one, in order to ensure that the relationship between the performer and the instrument retakes the centre stage.

# Chapter 11
# Concluding Thoughts

## 11.1   Signing Off

The kind of interactive media that we have just explored is what we will increasingly come across in our daily lives. As technology advances and changes the way in which we relate to our already media-rich environment, we are forced to re-evaluate not only the way in which we engage with the media itself, but also the way in which we theorize and think about it. This book is an attempt to do just that.

As we have seen, the idea of interactive media is a complex beast and the theories that surround it are even more so. Where technology continues to transform more of our existing media and interactive media become remediated, we find ourselves confronted with even more complexity. As a result, theories abound about technology and the way in which we use and interact with it. Some of these are political in nature, while others are philosophical, and some are even practical. What I have attempted here is simply to outline some of these different theories and explore the relationships between them in order to establish how best to use them as part of an overarching framework for understanding interactive media.

In the process, I have examined the meaning of the term 'medium' from the artistic perspective to that of the communication theorist. I have identified some of the fundamental characteristics of interactive media and their origins in other media forms, as well as outlining what Human Computer Interaction can tell us about interaction and the effects of technology on such media. I have taken detours into the vagaries of affordance, the philosophical perspective of phenomenology, the ins and outs of cognitive psychology and the interpretations of semiotic theory, in order to clarify what each of these perspectives can bring to the theoretical table. Having done all that, I have also pieced together the jigsaw puzzle that is an understanding of interactive media and I have explored this understanding in relation to some examples of recent cutting edge interaction design.

Whether this constitutes a complete understanding of all the issues that surround interactive media is still undecided, particularly as interactive media are always evolving and changing. Suffice it to say that if I have succeeded in establishing an understanding of interaction that is useful and broad enough to encompass the

S.O'Neill, *Interactive Media: The Semiotics of Embodied Interaction*,
doi: 10.1007/978-1-84800-036-0, © Springer Science + Business Media, LLC 2008

many emerging forms of media that our examples point toward, then I have at least established something.

With regard to who is winning the determinist debate between McLuhan and Williams, it is difficult to say which side we should come down on. Clearly interactive media have an effect on us and clearly they are changing the way we perform certain activities in our lives, but of course, we 'the people' are still in charge of what these media do and say about us, because more than ever it is the people who make them what they are. Maybe in the future this will change, maybe the robots will take over or maybe this debate will simply just continue.

# Index

Printed in the United States